JACK THE
REVEA

JACK THE RIPPER

JOHN WILDING

CONSTABLE · LONDON
IN ASSOCIATION WITH
VOLCANO BOOKS LTD

First published in Great Britain 1993
by Constable and Company Ltd
3 The Lanchesters
162 Fulham Palace Road, London W6 9ER
in association with Volcano Books Ltd
Copyright © 1993 John Wilding
The right of John Wilding to be
identified as the author of this work
has been asserted by him in accordance
with the Copyright, Designs and Patents Act 1988
ISBN 0 09 472950 6 (hardback)
ISBN 0 09 472960 3 (paperback)
Printed in Finland by WSOY

A CIP catalogue record for this book
is available from the British Library

FOR MY BROTHER AND SISTER-IN-LAW,
WILLIAM AND IRENE WILDING,

WITH LOVE AND THANKS FOR THEIR CONSTANT
SUPPORT.

Table of Contents

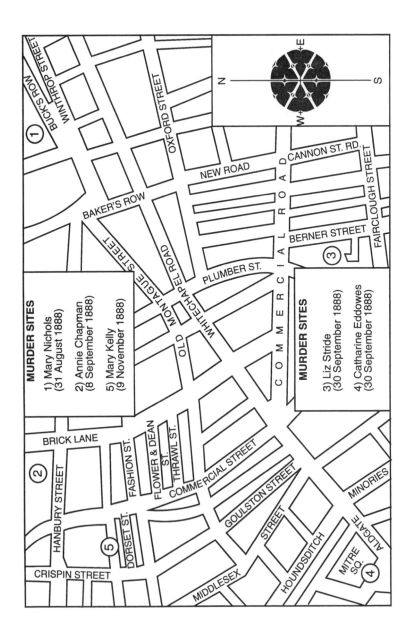

MURDER SITES

1) Mary Nichols
(31 August 1888)

2) Annie Chapman
(8 September 1888)

5) Mary Kelly
(9 November 1888)

MURDER SITES

3) Liz Stride
(30 September 1888)

4) Catharine Eddowes
(30 September 1888)

BUCK'S ROW

WINTHROP STREET

OXFORD STREET

NEW ROAD

CANNON ST. RD.

COMMERCIAL ROAD

BERNER STREET

FAIRCLOUGH STREET

BAKER'S ROW

FLEUR DE LIS STREET

OLD MONTAGUE ROAD

WHITECHAPEL ROAD

PLUMBER ST.

BRICK LANE

HANBURY STREET

FASHION ST.

FLOWER & DEAN ST.

THRAWL ST.

COMMERCIAL STREET

DORSET ST.

CRISPIN STREET

MIDDLESEX

GOULSTON STREET

STREET

HOUNDSDITCH

MINORIES

MITRE SQ.

ALDGATE

N E S W

Foreword

In a work such as this, there are, of course, many people to whom one owes a debt of gratitude. I would like to thank, with love, my two sisters, Veronica McDonnell and Joan Orsmond for their unflagging support. Many thanks are also due to my brother Donald for his line illustrations of the murder sites: these are meant only to serve as an outline for clarification.

My brother Harold and sister-in-law Peg have been unfailingly in the background, as have my nephews, David Orsmond and his wife Sophie, Benedict McDonnell and his wife Lynn, and my niece Louise Orsmond and her fiancé, Mark Young.

Batuk Gathani has helped, in no small measure, to launch this book, as has the distinguished writer of that excellent work *Tornado Down*, William Pearson. Roderick Brown, Sally Partington, and Robin Butler have also made valued suggestions for which I have been deeply grateful. Howard Chesner has dispensed legal advice – Graham Taylor continues to help, and my kind near-neighbours, Frank and Dorothy Oliver have been invaluable.

Special mention has to be made of my long-standing friends Hymie and Renee Udwin. Hymie has been tireless in his advice and patience. Another long-standing friend, Ron Moody also merits special thanks, as do Melorie Chilton and Elspeth Cochrane.

My many friends in the Royal Ballet have listened to my Ripper ramblings with great patience, and I must thank Stephen Jefferies, Keith Grey, Jacqui Tallis, Paul Benson, Robert Jude, Jonathan Payn and Juliet Darnley for paying heed without appearing to become too glassy-eyed. I would like to remember, with deep appreciation, the late Sir Kenneth MacMillan who took a great interest in my researches. I will greatly miss his wisdom.

My friend, Stuart Potterton has lent me valuable reading material on Jack the Ripper, and my neighbour, Peter Draper, has been endlessly helpful, as has the distinguished Australian psychiatrist, Dr Anthony Orsmond. My friend Robert Dyer displayed endless patience whilst helping me with word processing, and I am most grateful to him.

Henry Lee has faxed and received documents for me, and thanks are also due to John Hewett (who can deal with an ailing photocopier better than anyone I know), Neil Collier, Chris Simmonds, Andrew Mack, Bob and Chris Brown, and their charming children, Mark and Kate, Alan Pilkinton, Nigel Pearce, Darran Lane, Annis James, Tricia Larby, Charles Hart, John Healey (who has found so many valuable books for me), and to Pierre Spake at his Old Ephemera and Newspaper Shop – the 1888 cuttings which Pierre unearthed for me were of great assistance in my researches.

My long-standing and valued friend Kathleen MacCormack has been her usual charming and helpful self, and thanks are also due to Patricia Matthews and Daphne Stone, who found me so much interesting reading material. Thanks are also due to Richard Bennett of the Gravesend Framing Centre and Edward and Louis Matarrazzo of the Gravesend Tile Centre.

I would also like to thank the three Ripper experts with whom I have been in close touch, Paul Begg, Keith Skinner and Martin Howells. All three have been kind and helpful.

Permission to use copyright material has been granted by: Paul Begg and Robson Books (*Jack the Ripper: The Uncensored Facts*); Paul Begg, Martin Fido, Keith Skinner and Headline Books (*The Jack the Ripper A to Z*); Tom Cullen (*Autumn of Terror*); Melvyn Fairclough and Duckworth (*The Ripper and the Royals*); Martin Fido and Weidenfeld and Nicholson (*The Crimes and Detection of Jack the Ripper*); Martin Howells and Keith Skinner and Sidgwick and Jackson (*The Ripper Legacy – The Life and Death of Jack the Ripper*); Chambers Publishers for Stephen Knight (*Jack the Ripper – The Final Solution*); Donald Rumbelow and Virgin Publishing (*The Complete Jack the Ripper*).

I am grateful for permission to use short extracts from the above books. W.H. Allen, an imprint of Virgin Books, has generously given permission for use of photographic material from *The Mystery of Jack the Ripper* by Leonard Matters. Crown copyright material in the Public Record Office is reproduced by permission of the Controller of Her Majesty's Stationery Office. Files HO/144/221/A49301C8a, HO/144/220/A49301C, MEOP/3/140, MEOP/3/141. Special thanks to Anne Crawford for her help.

Chapter One

Background

London has always been a violent City, from the earliest recorded times, during the Roman occupation, up to the present day. A Roman historian, Cassius Dio, writing in the third century, relates details of Boudicca's attack on Londinium;

'As to the male prisoners, there was nothing of the most dreadful kind which was not inflicted on them. Of the women, they hung up the noblest and the most beautiful naked, cut off their breasts and sewed them to their mouths.'

Imported Roman cruelty, involving fights to the death between gladiators and slaves pitted in savage contests against wild animals, is well documented. That was the start of London's violent 2,000-year history, a history full of martyrdoms, murder and painful death. However, the invaders found the native Britons equally barbaric.

Sir William Wallace, who led Scottish resistance to the English king, Edward the First, was betrayed by a friend, Sir John Menteith. Wallace was captured and imprisoned in 1305. After abusive treatment from his gaolers he was dragged from The Tower by horses, hanged, and, whilst still alive, was disembowelled before being beheaded and quartered. His head was displayed on a pole on London Bridge.

Arbitrary beheading was commonplace throughout the Middle Ages. In 1431 an unnamed weaver from Abingdon who had threatened to 'make priests' heads as plentiful as sheeps' heads', lost his own head, which was displayed on a pike.

There were many other kinds of death. 'Smoothfield', then a large open plain to the north of Saint Paul's, which became 'Smithfield', present-day location of the famous meat market, was once the site of spectacular cruelty. Here, for several centuries throughout the Middle Ages, any person who had been convicted of the charge of poisoning was slowly boiled alive. The leader of the Peasants' Revolt, Wat Tyler, was torn to pieces at Smithfield in 1381, after brandishing a dagger before King Richard the Second. Protestant martyrs were bound in chains and burned to death at Smithfield in the sixteenth century.

Near present-day Marble Arch is the site of Tyburn, where the rage of King Henry the Eighth was vented on five monks who refused to acknowledge the King's supremacy over the English Church: they were hanged until they were semi-conscious, the rope was then cut, and the bodies were laid on a plank, where their stomachs were slit open and the entrails pulled out. Ten other monks who refused to sign the necessary declaration were chained up in Newgate Prison and allowed to starve to death.

Terrible though these events were, such barbaric tortures and cruelties are now largely forgotten, whilst a series of nineteenth-century murders committed by a man nicknamed Jack the Ripper has become the most famous in the history of crime.

The *Star* newspaper summed up public feeling about these murders in a famous article printed in September 1888:

'London lies today under the spell of a great terror. A nameless reprobate – half beast, half man – is at large. The ghoul-like creature who stalks through the streets of London, stalking down his victim like a Pawnee Indian, is simply drunk with blood, and he will have more.'

That prediction was to prove correct.

* * * * *

Londoners of the nineteenth century were used to reading and hearing about violence in their city. This violence was aggravated by the use of alcohol, which was plentiful and cheap. That great chronicler of London life, Henry Mayhew, in his famous 1885 publication *Mayhew's London* reported that:

'In a "good time" it is not unusual for a costermonger to spend 12 shillings out of every 20 shillings on beer and pleasure.'

Most public houses throughout London were open from before dawn until late at night, and they were well patronised at all times, which means alcohol must have played its part in the violence, thieving, and petty crime which were endemic in the poorest, most deprived and most notorious part of London, the East End. The area was a maze of badly lit, narrow streets, criss-crossed by unlit, foul smelling, litter strewn alleyways – passages which often led to dangerous cul-de-sacs. Criminal gangs regularly patrolled the East End streets, dodging police patrols wherever possible. These gangs often contained pimps who controlled local prostitutes, beating them up with impunity on the slightest pretext.

The prostitutes themselves frequently solicited in riverside public houses, plying sailors with gin. Once intoxicated, the seamen were then taken to dark lonely areas, where, instead of rendering a sexual service, the women would hit their clients with a stone, leaving them drunk, unconscious and robbed. Despite repeated warnings, sailors continually allowed themselves to be tricked.

Fights between rival gangs, neighbours, and, of course, husbands and wives continually disturbed the peace, and murder was reasonably commonplace. The list of East End homicides involving women in 1888 was long. To quote just two examples: a middle-aged prostitute, Emma Smith, was attacked in Whitechapel by a gang of young men. She was robbed, beaten and raped, and a member of the gang then forced a blunt instrument into her vagina, causing serious internal injuries; the unfortunate woman died in agony a few days later. Martha Tabram, a thirty-seven-year-old prostitute was discovered dead on an unlit Whitechapel staircase. She had been savagely and repeatedly stabbed.

With incidents such as these occurring on a regular basis, East Enders were not easily shocked. Yet Jack the Ripper's crimes caught the public imagination; local East End shock soon spread to the remainder of the capital, then the countryside at large, and finally world-wide.

These are the basic facts. In 1888, over a period of approximately ten weeks, between the hours of midnight and dawn, and only at weekends, a savage killer roamed the mean East End streets, where he met and subsequently murdered five prostitutes. Three of the victims were laid out on a public street, their stomachs ripped open and their vaginas slashed.

Policemen regularly patrolled the streets where Jack would kneel over his corpses, cutting into the flesh, then pushing his hands into the hot guts. Indeed, the East End was busy both day and night, but this did not seem to worry Jack: he appeared to carry out his work with impunity. After the fourth murder, *The Times* newspaper remarked on this fact:

'The assassin, if not suffering from insanity, appears to be free

3

from any fear of interruption while on his dreadful work.'

To add to the puzzle, Jack the Ripper's hunting ground was not large: the East End comprised Whitechapel, Spitalfields and several surrounding parishes – an area of only a few square miles. The district had once been fashionable. Nicholas Culpeper, the noted herbalist, had lived in Spitalfields in the seventeenth century, as had Lord Bolingbroke, the writer and MP. The area was then colonised by French Protestants who were forced to flee from their own country in the late seventeenth century for the following reason. An earlier French king, Henri IV, after abandoning his own Protestantism, nevertheless signed a decree known as the Edict of Nantes guaranteeing toleration for his Protestant subjects. This Edict was revoked by Louis XIV, causing great bloodshed. Large numbers of French settlers fled to London where they quickly established a silk trade around Spitalfields. When the French moved in, the East End was still a delightful country district, an oasis cut off from the hurly-burly of London life. John Stow, writing a century before their arrival, describes the silk-weavers' environment:

'On all sides without the houses of the suburb are the citizens' gardens and orchards, planted with trees. On the north side are pastures and plain meadows, with brooks running through them, turning water mills with a pleasant noise. Not far is a great forest, a well-wooded chase, having a good covert for harts, bucks, boars and wild bulls.'

As late as 1799, less than 90 years before the murders, Horwood's map shows a single road starting at Blue Anchor Lane, Bermondsey, and running eastwards. This road meandered through deserted countryside until it reached the East End villages.

Rapid industrialisation soon changed this charming landscape. The settlers' silk trade grew into a major industry, and, by 1832, 50,000 people were employed as weavers. Then mechanisation replaced the hand-worked looms and production was quickly transferred from workers' cottages to vast, soulless factories. These factories attracted large numbers of workers, especially immigrants, into the area – more workers than there were jobs. As a result, by 1888 the East End contained a collection of the poorest people in the world. Thieves, derelicts and prostitutes lived alongside hard-working, honest citizens: citizens who were held back by low wages and unreliable employment, and unable to rise above the barest level of subsistence. Houses were dirty and dilapidated, and had only the most basic facilities. Whilst some houses had a single cold water pipe in the back yard, other buildings had only a standby cold water pipe in the street.

Sewage was piped raw into the Thames causing a terrible stench along the entire stretch of the waterway. Even at Westminster the smell from the river was so appalling that windows had to be kept shut during debates in the House of Commons. If the open air was so polluted the atmosphere in the actual sewers must have been atrocious, yet, incredibly, some East Enders, nicknamed 'toshers', made a living from wandering around the sewerage system searching for lost treasure. That mine of information, Henry Mayhew, discusses toshers at some length:

'To enter the sewers and explore them to any considerable distance is considered, even by those acquainted with what is termed 'working the shores', an adventure of no small risk. The brickwork in many parts – especially in the old sewers – has become rotten through the continual action of putrefying matter and moisture, and parts have fallen down and choked up the passage with heaps of rubbish; over these obstructions, nevertheless, the sewer-hunters have to scramble in the best way they can.'

Mud-larks, men, women and children of all ages, would wade along the river banks in a slime composed of sewage mixed with mud, searching for small pieces of coal, chips of wood, old iron or copper nails. Mayhew vividly describes mud-larks:

'They may be seen of all ages, from mere childhood to positive decreptitude, crawling along the barges at the various wharfs along the river; it cannot be said that they are clad in rags, for they are scarcely half covered by the tattered indescribable things that serve them for clothing; their bodies are grimed with the foul soil of the river, and their torn garments stiffened up like boards with dirt of every possible description.

'Among the mud-larks may be seen many old women, and it is indeed pitiable to behold them, especially during the winter, bent nearly double with age and infirmity, paddling and groping among the wet mud . . .'

A glance at Mayhew's list of contents reveals the vast number of East Enders who eked out a living as street sellers – sellers of ham sandwiches, bread, hot peas, sherbet, elder wine, curds and whey, milk, boiled puddings and cough drops, to name but a few.

Some comparatively affluent workers with reasonably steady employment could afford to rent rooms on a semi-permanent basis. Their families often owned animals but there was no safe outside place in which to keep their livestock: the animals would have been stolen even from their own back yards. It was, therefore, not unusual to find whole families living with their goats, pigs and hens indoors. When the time came to eat the animals they would frequently be slaughtered on the streets, their blood mixing with urine in the gutters.

Many poorer families could not afford to rent decent rooms. They lived in semi-darkness, in deep cellars built under houses. The only entrance to and exit from these dungeons was a wooden trap door let into the pavement above, and if objects were placed on these traps, the family would be entombed until the obstacle was removed. As late as 1928, when the Thames burst its banks, 14 people were trapped in basement rooms and drowned. These underground cellars often doubled as both living and working quarters, the most usual employment being an amateur attempt at cobbling. An anonymous writer in 1878 graphically describes the condition of these 'cave dwellers'.

'To look down into one of these cellars at night-time and find father, mother, and the elder male and female branches of the family clustered in all their dirt and raggedness in the midst of the unsavoury heap of half-rotten leather, with wisps of wax-end to keep their hair from bobbing into their eyes as they hammer and stitch by the light of the tallow candle or paraffin lamp, is not a spectacle to make a man thrill with pride.

'They fetch their material from their employers in a great sack, and it consists of a pell-mell collection of "oddments" in the way of foot coverings, reeking of mould and mildew.

'In one place I found, besides the parents toiling at the heap of malodorous leather, four small children crouching, half naked and unclean, by the fire hearth, and looking exactly as one might expect children to look, who, all through the long winter, live in semi-darkness, and breathe air that would ultimately undermine the constitution of a horse or donkey, and who see no more of the living and moving world than the muddy boots of pedestrians hurrying to and fro above their ceiling.'

Old people with adult diseases bedded down with children suffering from childhood diseases, the bed being often no more than a heap of shavings, straw or filthy rags. Occasionally a dead body would remain in the living quarters for an extended period until arrangements for a burial could be completed.

Overcrowding was endemic in the East End. Many people found temporary shelter in houses which provided rooms for up to 60 lodgers. A 'deputy' would sit in a doorway hutch demanding money from clients as they entered. Terms were strictly payment in advance. One landlord complained that 'unscrupulous rival establishments' had reduced rents from the standard fourpence for lodgings to threepence, in order to attract more patrons. Even this cut-price lodging proved too expensive for many East Enders; large numbers of destitutes were forced to creep into graveyards to sleep among the tombstones, whilst many others slept in the parks. A garden alongside Christchurch Spitalfields became so famous for its congregation of patrons who suffered from ticks, fleas or skin diseases that it became known as 'Itchy Park'.

The anonymous 1878 writer records one member of the Victorian judiciary who had his own solution to the homeless problem. A petty East End offender, who had been brought before this judge, remarked, 'We've all got to live'. The judge offered his own opinion in reply. 'I really don't see why,' the learned gentleman said, 'but if that is the case, then it will be necessary to make persistent vagabondism a capital offence.'

The law itself was kinder – but not much. Policemen regularly harassed people sleeping in the open, and, in order to curb the large number of destitutes who drifted into Trafalgar Square, many East Enders amongst them (including Mary Nichols, the Ripper's first victim), Sir Charles Warren, the Metropolitan Police Commissioner, demanded, and received, new powers: he closed Trafalgar Square on various dates, an act which led to riots described in later chapters of this book.

Many landlords were quick to grasp the opportunities afforded them by the restriction on open-air sleeping. They placed rope

7

across their rooms and charged customers a few pence to lean against the webbing all night. This at least provided indoor shelter. Occasionally an establishment allowed its patrons to lie in rows on the floor, using their arms folded under their heads as a pillow.

Sick people were not allowed to remain in any lodging house for more than 24 hours. Whatever the illness the sufferer had to be moved away. A missionary was, on one occasion, summoned to treat a sick child in an East End lodging house. He discovered the six-year-old girl, near to death from scarlet fever, lying on the floor of a small room amongst 15 other lodgers: a mixture of old and young, males and females.

Included in the standard fourpenny rent might be the guarding of one's clothes by the deputy and the use of a communal kitchen. Here, 30 to 40 lodgers would share dirty utensils and cook together. A grate would extend five or six feet along a wall with half a dozen large frying pans on the coals. Lodgers would drop their pieces of raw food onto a chosen spot in a pan then pay close attention until the food was cooked. A custodian would stand guard, armed with a long iron spit, to help settle the many ownership arguments which broke out.

Yet these were the luckier ones – the ones who had shelter and food to eat. Many hungry, sick people had to make a choice between sleeping rough or trying to gain admittance to a workhouse, and Victorian workhouses were notorious for their harsh regimes. The writings of a Reverend Milman from the 1880s illustrate Victorian sentiments on this subject:

'The workhouse should be a place of hardship: of coarse fate: of degradation and humility, where we must learn to love our enemies and discover only our duty to God. The workhouse must be administered with the greatest severity and strictness, where you must avoid the sin of anger or malice. The workhouse must be as repulsive as it is consistent with humanity.'

Clearly the workhouse administrators agreed wholeheartedly with that dogma. Meals usually consisted of rock-hard bread, served with a bowl of watery gruel which often contained dead insects or the occasional drowned mouse. Inmates were told when to go to bed and when to rise – usually before dawn: their every movement was controlled.

To pay for this spartan food and shelter the inmates were expected to work – and work hard – at a variety of tasks. Even children as young as eight were made to work, often having to grind corn or bones until the dust settled as a paste on their sweaty faces. Grit or small pieces of bone frequently flew into the paupers' eyes causing serious damage.

Inmates were also expected to collect leftover meals from the various infirmaries. Such debris often included scraps from the infectious wards which had been sprinkled with disinfectant, but the tainted food was still frequently stolen for consumption or for sale. After the day's labours up to 20 inmates were expected to bath in the same water.

It was in these appalling conditions that Jack the Ripper hunted, and it was his crimes which focused the whole of London's attention onto the disgraceful living conditions of many East Enders. George Bernard Shaw, in his much-quoted letter, opined, after the Ripper murders had caused such an outcry:

'Whilst we conventional Social Democrats were wasting our time on education, agitation and organization, some independent genius has taken the matter in hand . . .'

Jack, that independent genius, began his work on 31 August 1888 when he found his first victim.

Chapter Two

Mary Nichols

The number of murders attributed to Jack the Ripper varies from four to around eleven, but most authorities on the crimes agree with Sir Melville Macnaghten. Macnaghten joined Scotland Yard as Assistant Chief Constable in 1889, approximately eight months after the Ripper crimes had finished, but he took an intense interest in the case, which he was able to examine in detail from a privileged position inside the police force. In private notes, Sir Melville wrote:

'The Whitechapel murderer had five victims, and five only.'

On this basis, Jack's first victim was Mary Nichols, a petite forty-two-year-old prostitute, who had a delicate bone structure and grey eyes. Five of her lower front teeth were missing, either lost in a vicious fight with another prostitute – such disputes were commonplace – or lost through poor dental care, another common defect in East End life. Yet despite the dental disfigurements and greying hair, a journalist who saw Mary after her death remarked that she looked much younger than her age.

Writing biographical material on the Ripper victims is difficult as only minimal information was ever recorded – after all, why would anyone have written about these women *before* their deaths? Even if a contemporary had noted the women's every move there would have been little to record; they led typical lives of unparalleled dreariness – lives ruled daily by two endlessly repeated questions:

1) Where do I get enough money to buy alcohol and food? (In that order.) Answer: from trying to sell my body.

2) Where can I sleep? Answer: in a doss-house if there are a few pennies left over at the end of the day.

Drink was more important than sleep, and it was cheap – a cup of coffee cost more than a nip of alcohol. A popular sign in public houses read: 'Drunk for a penny, dead-drunk for twopence. Clean straw free.' Gin ruled the murdered prostitutes' lives – and this was understandable. Enough drink could dull the pain of East End living, and no one could blame the women for wanting to do that.

Mary (nickname 'Polly'), was the wife of a printer, William Nichols, and the union had produced five children, three boys and two girls. This was not an especially large family in Victorian times, when provision had to be made for the high infant mortality rate: only about one third of all children born lived to the age of five. Life was, of course, especially hard for poor families with a high survival rate of offspring: children as young as seven often had to start work to help support the unit: half-starved, terrorised young boys forced to climb high, thickly-sooted chimneys, and child matchbox-makers spring instantly to mind. The day-to-day living conditions of the Nichols family is not known, but a great many poor families lived in one room, the whole unit usually sleeping in two beds. Charles Booth's written account of contemporary life (started in 1889, only one year after the Ripper murders had ended) records that the 'one room' system led to acts of gross indecency and incest. In the 1880s Marchant Williams, Inspector of London Schools, visited an East End lodging house and asked the female tenant, 'How many in the family?' 'Eleven.' 'How many beds?' 'Two.'

In 1881 the Nichols' marriage failed, and William blamed the break-up on his wife's heavy drinking. There is no doubt that Mary was a typical alcoholic, a lady who would sell her body and soul for a drink. Mary's family claimed that the parting was caused by William's affair with another woman – the midwife who attended the birth of the Nichols' fourth child, which, if true, seems singularly callous. Whatever the truth, William certainly felt himself the aggrieved party, while Mary appears to have had no compunction about leaving her family behind – the power of mother-love was easily defeated by the might of alcohol. Only the eldest boy left home with his mother; William therefore cared for the other four children. He even provided maintenance of five shillings a week for his wife, but when he discovered that she had turned to prostitution in order to fund her alcoholism, the maintenance was stopped. Mary, supported by local parishes, hounded William through the courts to try and regain support, but once William proved to the judiciary's satisfaction that he was caring for the children, Mary lost her case.

After leaving the home that she had shared with her husband, Mary and her eldest son moved in with her father, Edward Walker, a blacksmith, who lived in Walworth, South East London. As might have been expected, her drinking habits soon caused friction, and after rows and arguments, Mary moved lodgings once more, this time leaving her eldest son to stay with his grandfather.

Once she was free from all family restraints (children and husband) Mary embarked upon the itinerant lifestyle which was eventually to lead to her death. She moved between various workhouses, and, on occasions, required unspecified medical attention in various infirmaries – perhaps for sexual ailments (a common East End complaint. Children as young as nine would frequently require treatment for venereal diseases.) Occasionally Mary slept rough on the streets, which cannot have been much worse than living in the workhouse.

To be a penniless, middle-aged prostitute with faded charms and an incessant craving for drink (and with few means of satisfying that craving) must have been a torment. Mary's life, however, was not without opportunities.

Between April and July 1888 she was employed as a maid by a respectable couple, Mr and Mrs Cowdry, who lived south of the Thames at Rosehill Road, Wandsworth. The Cowdrys were an upright, religious, teetotal couple; it is easy to imagine the family bible and religious pamphlets in their neat parlour. Could they not have recognised that Mary would not be a suitable addition to their home? Perhaps in engaging her they were indulging in good work, attempting to save Mary's soul, a fashionable Victorian pastime. If so, they did not succeed. The couple foolishly trusted their new maid to the extent of leaving her in charge of their home from time to time. In a letter to her father dated April 17, Mary wrote:

'. . . you will be glad to know that I am settled in my new place, and going all right up to now. My people went out yesterday, and have not returned, so I am left in charge. It is a grand place inside, with trees and gardens back and front. All has been newly done up. They are teetotallers, and religious, so I ought to get on. They are very nice people and I have not much to do. I hope you are alright and the boy has work. So goodbye for the present – From yours truly, Polly. Answer soon please and let me know how you are.'

It is difficult to understand Mary's statement, 'They are teeto-tallers and religious, so I ought to get on.' Was that Mary's attempt at ironic humour? Edward was never to hear from his daughter again.

One would have imagined that after a hard life in workhouses and on the streets Mary would have clung tenaciously to her new and easy life-style, living in a 'grand place' with food and lodgings provided and not much work to do. The fact is that she betrayed the Cowdrys' trust and stole clothing valued at £3.10s, a considerable sum in those days. That act of dishonesty led Mary back to the East End and eventually cost her her life.

After absconding from the Cowdrys' house Mary stayed for a couple of nights at the Gray's Inn Temporary Workhouse, then she moved to Thrawl Street where she shared a room with three other women before she moved once more, this time to Flower and Dean Street. That was her last known address. On 31 August 1888, the final night of her life, Mary was seen wandering around the Whitechapel area, clattering along on the cobblestones, wearing a pair of men's boots. She roamed the grim streets until, in the early hours of the morning, she tried to find lodgings back at Thrawl Street, only a block away from Flower and Dean Street, but she could not meet the rigid requirements of the East End doss-houses – pay first or no bed. Mary, later described as 'slightly tipsy', was turned away from the Thrawl Street doss-house because she was penniless, not because she was drunk, but first she uttered the now famous words, 'I'll soon get my doss money. See what a jolly bonnet I've got now.' Such optimism was misplaced, because Mary was soon to meet Jack the Ripper.

From around 1.30 a.m. Mary wandered the streets of Whitechapel, no doubt exhausted, but, apparently, not without trade. This penniless down-and-out could have had no inkling that from that night on, hundreds of researchers, for over a century, would probe her every move. The last reported sighting of her was made by a prostitute friend, Ellen Holland. The two women met on the corner of Whitechapel High Street at 2.30 a.m: the exact time had been set by the striking of a church clock. A melodramatic scene is conjured up by the picture of two penniless prostitutes standing together in a dangerous East End street, touting for clients, not knowing that Jack the Ripper was on the prowl, whilst a church clock solemnly chimed away the hours. They were to be the last hours in Mary Nichols's life.

Ellen Holland described her friend as 'very drunk'. As Mary had been reported penniless and only 'slightly tipsy' a few hours earlier she must have found several clients but spent the money on gin. In various unlit corners Mary would have offered herself, standing up, her dress raised high to expose her 'surprisingly clean thighs' (a doctor's comment after he had examined her body in the mortuary). On the night of her murder Mary confessed to Ellen Holland that she had: 'had her doss-house money three times'. Unfortunately, on each occasion, the craving for alcohol had proved too strong. Then Mary, another glass of gin on her mind, met her last client: the bargaining with Jack the Ripper completed, the prostitute would have led her killer to a dark place.

Although no one can be certain, strong medical evidence suggests that Jack stood before several of his victims; he would have grabbed Mary's throat – probably as her hands were holding up the voluminous Victorian outfit. Jack then choked his victim into unconsciousness, and, as the body sank down, he slashed viciously at the throat with a sharp knife, before kneeling over the dead woman to complete his work. That scenario has been a general consensus.

The facts concerning the finding of Mary's body have been told and retold many times.

Buck's Row was a typical, dirty, cobbled East End thoroughfare, running from Brady Street through to Baker's Row, and lit by a single gas lamp. Warehouses on one side faced shabby terraced houses on the other side. A stable yard gateway was placed between the houses and a school.

On Friday morning, 31 August 1888, around 3.15 a.m. no less than three policemen, each on his own business, passed along Buck's Row within a short space of time. All was peaceful. Half an hour later, Charles Cross was walking along Buck's Row on his way to work. Halfway along the street he saw a bundle lying near the stableyard gates which he thought looked like a tarpaulin. Being a carter, he thought a serviceable tarpaulin could be put to

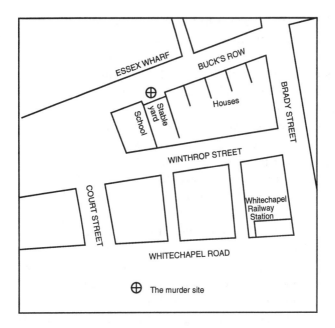

good use. Cross moved over to the bundle, and, after a quick examination, found not a piece of canvas but a woman collapsed onto the pavement.

Robert Paul, also a carter, was also on his way to work at Smithfield Market. He was startled when a figure rose from the shadows in Buck's Row and asked him to come over and look at a body. After a brief examination the two men, unable to see properly in the dark, could not decide whether the woman was hurt, drunk, raped or dead. It was not, of course, uncommon to find alcoholics lying around the streets of London, and 'drunk' would probably have been the men's first assumption. Then Cross decided that as the woman's hands were cold and limp she was dead, but Paul thought he detected a faint heartbeat, which indicated to him that she was alive. These two strangers, meeting together down a narrow dark lane in the middle of the night before debating over the state of a dead woman's health, could not have known that they were setting the groundwork for one of the world's greatest murder mysteries.

As both men were on their way to work and did not want to be late (that could have meant dismissal) they went in search of a policeman without further examination of their find.

Shortly after the men had hurried away, Police Constable John Neil walked along Buck's Row on his return beat. The bundle also caught his attention – it had not been there on his last patrol of the street half an hour earlier. The policeman was able to bring some light to bear and his bull's-eye lantern now revealed clearly that the woman was dead: her throat had been slashed. Mary Nichols, Jack's first victim, had been discovered.

PC Neil hailed a colleague who went to find a doctor, and whilst waiting for medical assistance Neil made his own examination. Mary's hands may have been cold but other parts of her body were still warm. Her left arm was outstretched, her hand touching the stable yard gate. A Dr Llewellyn arrived quickly but under such difficult conditions, with the corpse lying in darkness sprawled out on the pavement, he could make no more than a cursory examination – sufficient only to pronounce the woman dead. An ambulance was called – this would have been little more than a cart – and the body was taken to a shed (which served as a mortuary) at the rear of the Old Montague Street Workhouse Infirmary.

Police Inspector John Spratling, who went to Buck's Row after the body had been removed, then went on to the mortuary to compile notes for the coroner. It was whilst making a description of the body that Spratling lifted the skirt and discovered a series of terrible mutilations. The stomach had been stabbed and slashed deeply in several places, allowing the intestines to protrude, and the vagina had also been savagely cut.

Dr Llewellyn, who had meanwhile returned home, was quickly called back, but by the time he reached the mortuary, several elderly attendants had undressed and washed the corpse.

Inspector Spratling recorded details of the body's mortuary examination:

'. . . her throat had been cut from left to right, two distinct cuts being on the left side. The windpipe, gullet and spinal cord having been cut through, a bruise apparently of a thumb being on the right lower jaw, also one on the left cheek. The abdomen had been cut open from centre of bottom of ribs on right side, under pelvis to left of stomach: there the wound was jagged. The omentum or coating of the stomach was also cut in several places, and two small stabs to private parts appeared done with a strong bladed knife . . .'

An identification of the body was now required, but enquiries were hampered by the East Enders' natural prejudice towards the police force. 'Don't get involved', was an even stronger creed in Victorian times than it is now. Nevertheless, various people in the neighbourhood did wander into the mortuary to view the corpse – many would have made the visit out of curiosity – but no one could identify the dead woman.

Mary's entire worldly goods comprised the clothes in which she was dressed: a brown ulster; a brown linsey frock; various underclothes; a black straw bonnet; and a pair of men's boots cut on the uppers. It was the underwear which revealed the secret of Mary's identity. A 'Lambeth Workhouse' mark led the authorities to William Nichols, who went to the mortuary on 1 September.

The drama of identifying Mary's corpse was compounded by William meeting with his eldest son (Edward John) for the first time since the lad had left home with his mother. Edward Walker, Mary's father, also attended the grim affair, but it was William who formally identified the body. Bitterness towards his dead wife can be plainly recognised in William's comments as he viewed the corpse: 'I forgive you, as you are, for what you have been to me.' Mary's father was less forgiving. On viewing his daughter's body, it is reported that he said, 'I knew she'd come to a bad end.'

The inquest on Mary was held almost directly after the body had been formally identified. The affair was presided over by Coroner Wynne Baxter, who appeared brightly dressed in check trousers and a white waitcoast, this dashing ensemble topped off by a scarlet-coloured scarf – an outfit more suitable for the races than a murder inquest. Baxter appeared to be enjoying his authority as he threw his weight around and snappishly criticised the police for failing to find the mutilations before the corpse was undressed at the mortuary, conveniently ignoring the difficulties accompanying the finding of the body. Baxter also criticised the police for allowing the body to be washed before Dr Llewellyn could examine it. This caused a row, as one of the elderly paupers, James Hatfield, who had assisted in washing the corpse, denied that the police had instructed that the body should not be touched, while the police said the opposite; this contretemps was closed without any satisfactory outcome. The coroner then presided over a rigorous examination of the case.

Residents of the cottages adjoining the murder site were questioned. A Mrs Emma Green, who lived in the house next door to the stable yard, had been sleeping in a front room, which she shared with her daughter. This front room almost overlooked the murder site. Habitually a light sleeper, Mrs Green slept fitfully on the night Mary was killed, but she had heard no noise.

The manager of Essex Wharf, Walter Purkiss, and his wife had spent the night in a bedroom directly opposite the murder site; they had not been disturbed. Such mystifying silence and such eerie invisibility naturally added to the atmosphere of terror which had sprung up. Jack's spell was already beginning to work.

Despite a thorough examination by Coroner Baxter no significant clues as to the murderer's identity emerged, but Baxter was in no hurry to close the case. The inquest was adjourned several times, but before a final verdict could be recorded ('Wilful murder by person or persons unknown') Jack the Ripper, on the night of 8 September, sensationally and successfully stalked a second victim, Annie Chapman.

Chapter Three

Annie Chapman

Annie Chapman was a short, beefy woman aged forty-five. Rumour (possibly encouraged by Annie herself in an attempt to enhance her miserable social standing) encouraged the community to believe that her husband had been a vet. In fact, John Chapman was a coachman to a farm bailiff in Windsor; very little else is known about him.

The couple had wed in 1869. There were several versions as to the cause of the Chapmans' marriage breakdown in 1882. There was a rumour that John had lost a previous job as a gentleman's valet due to his wife's dishonesty. If this were true it could certainly have soured the relationship, but there is no proof to confirm the story. Inspector Frederick George Abberline, whilst investigating the murder, reported that husband and wife had separated because of Annie's drinking habits, but John died in 1886 from cirrhosis of the liver, which would infer that *he* was the heavy drinker. Moreover, friends of Annie insisted that she drank only modestly, although she was 'prone to get drunk on a Saturday'. This is not the behaviour of a chronic alcoholic.

Annie's immorality was also blamed as the cause of the marital break-up, but an examination of the facts would seem to refute this rumour. Once alone, Annie had tried pathetically hard to earn an upright living by selling crochet work, matches and flowers, presumably without any great success. John Chapman had acted decently and made Annie an allowance of ten shillings a week up to the time of his death, which does not indicate any deep-seated animosity. After that, Annie, a middle-aged widow, would have been in the same position as many other Victorian women, with no money and no possessions. Soliciting arose from absolute necessity not from choice. With no state benefits prostitution was often the only way to earn the money needed to provide food or to help raise children left pauperised by the death or desertion of the father.

Annie, a middle-aged, unattractive woman, destitute and ill, had no family from whom she could seek help. Although there were three children from the marriage one daughter had died, the second daughter was reputed to be living in France in an unnamed institution and one son was said to have been placed in a home for cripples.

There are records of at least one brother and sister. Shortly before her death, Annie mentioned her intention of trying to borrow boots from her sister so that she could go hop-picking. Clearly this scheme did not materialise. Her brother, Fountain (sometimes written as 'Fontain') Smith attended both the inquest and the funeral. Fountain testified that he had seen Annie shortly before her death and he had given her two shillings. Clearly her family could provide only limited and infrequent help.

A week before her death, Annie had been involved in a fight with another prostitute, Eliza Cooper, who testified:

'On the previous Saturday, she [Annie Chapman] brought Mr Stanley into the house where I lodged in Dorset Street, and coming into the kitchen, asked the people to give her some soap. They told her to ask 'Liza' – meaning me. She came to me and I opened the locker and gave her some. She gave it to Stanley who went outside and washed himself in the lavatory. When she came back I asked for the soap, but she did not return it. She said, 'I will see you by-and-by.' Mr Stanley gave her two shillings and paid for her bed for two nights. I saw no more of her that night. On the following Tuesday I saw her in the kitchen of the lodging house. I said, 'Perhaps you will return my soap?' She threw a halfpenny on the table and said, 'Go and get a halfpenny worth of soap.' We got quarrelling over this piece of soap, and we went out to the Ringers public-house and continued the quarrel. She slapped my face and said, 'Think yourself lucky I don't do more.' I struck her in the left eye I believe and then in the chest. I afterwards saw that the blow I gave her had marked her face.'

Annie received severe bruising, which must have been especially painful for a woman in such a poor state of health. At the time of the fight Annie was suffering from two potentially fatal illnesses: a chronic disease of the brain and another affecting her lungs. If she had not been murdered, a rapid death from natural causes would have been likely, probably before the end of 1888. On the night of her murder Annie had been to an infirmary. This, presumably, would have been the outpatients' department at St Bartholomew's Hospital near Newgate Street, East London, which was within walking distance of her usual lodgings. St Bartholomew's was renowned for its free treatment of the poor. In 1868 a spokesman announced, 'This hospital received, upon petition, cases of all kind, free of fees; and accidents or cases of urgent disease, without letter, at the surgery, at any hour of the day or night'. This benefit was frequently abused by rich patients queuing for the free treatment. One freeloader was told, 'Madam, this is a charity for the destitute, not for ladies in rich silk dresses. Order your carriage and get out.' There would have been no such trouble for Annie. She was given liniment for her bruises and pills to treat the more serious conditions.

On the eve of her murder Annie had been drinking in a public house. She returned, some time after midnight, to her usual lodgings in Dorset Street: here the deputy, Timothy Donovan, found Annie in the kitchen eating a baked potato. Her box of pills had broken, and she had placed the tablets in a torn envelope which was crested 'Sussex Regiment'. When asked to pay for her bed Annie replied that she did not have the money, adding, 'I am weak and ill, and have been in the infirmary'. Donovan callously observed that she could afford food and her breath smelt of drink. He wanted his money, and, in keeping with the inflexible East End rule of payment in advance, Annie was asked to leave the doss-house.

She protested that apart from the potato she had had no food all day. Annie's protestation that she felt very unwell must have been an understatement: a middle-aged woman suffering from severe lung and brain diseases, her body badly bruised, and with very little food over an extended period (an inquest report mentioned malnutrition) would have been feeling extremely unwell. But even so, Annie was forced to leave the doss-house around 2.00 a.m. and search for clients willing to pay eight or nine pence (if she was lucky) for her sexual favours. As we know from Eliza Cooper's inquest evidence, a gentleman friend, Edward Stanley, occasionally gave Annie money. At least this truly sad woman had some warmth and affection in the last few months of her life.

Unfortunately her friend was not around on the night of 8 September.

After being turned out of the doss-house Annie accepted her misfortune stoically, and, like Mary Nichols, she seems to have been full of optimism: she asked for her bed to be kept, promising to be back soon. John Evans, a night watchman, saw Annie leaving Dorset Street at approximately 2.00 a.m. as she prepared to tramp the dark, dangerous streets, looking for trade to provide at least fourpence for her night's lodgings. This would have been no easy task as she was not an alluring woman, with her moon face, bulbous nose and double chins, her dumpy body wrapped in layers of clothing to keep out the cold, and unsteady on her feet due to illness. When Annie took her last walk the streets would have been taken over by late-night workers hurrying to their jobs or by prostitutes and thieves, the latter dodging policemen with their heavy 'persuaders' hanging from leather belts. Did the vicious murder of Mary Nichols only a week earlier prey on Annie's mind? We will never know, but we do know that within four hours of being turned away from the doss-house, Annie was destined to meet Jack the Ripper and her death.

Hanbury Street was approximately ten minutes' walk from Buck's Row. It was another typical East End street, dirty and lined with neglected, over-populated houses. A door between 27 and 29 Hanbury Street led, by way of a twenty-foot passageway (which contained stairs leading to the rooms) to a swing door and two stone steps. These steps gave access to a small, enclosed back yard. The fact that this yard was in constant use at all hours of the day and night by the 16 or 17 tenants (accounts vary) squeezed into 29 Hanbury Street did not prevent prostitutes from taking their clients into the yard from time to time. And although on 8 September, the house was packed with tenants both asleep and awake, crammed between the thin wooden partitions, no one was disturbed by unusual sounds during the night.

Amelia Richardson rented two floors at 29 Hanbury Street, where she sublet part of her premises. At 4.45 a.m. before dawn had broken, Mrs Richardson's son John went into the yard at the rear of the house with two tasks in mind. He needed to check that the cellar entrance was secure and he needed to attend to his boots which were hurting him. After checking the premises and finding everything in order, he sat on the rear steps and trimmed some leather from his shoe before leaving the yard. Nothing was amiss.

At some point during the next hour the unfortunate Annie, tired and ill, led Jack the Ripper down the long, dark and no doubt smelly passageway into the yard. Had they conversed, apart from settling terms? What had Jack said to gain Annie's confidence? How and where had they met?

Conflicting reports of Annie's last hours on earth make the facts difficult to assess. At 5.30 a.m. on the Saturday morning a Mrs Elizabeth Long, one of a large band of labourers setting out before dawn, was walking along Hanbury Street on her way to work. Once again the chiming of a church clock confirmed the time. Mrs Long saw a couple standing together outside 29 Hanbury Street – a man whose face she could not see and a woman whom she later identified as Annie Chapman. As Mrs Long passed the couple, she heard the man ask, 'Will you?' to which the woman replied, 'Yes'.

However, fifteen minutes earlier, at 5.15 a.m. a carpenter, Albert Cadosch, went into the yard at 27 Hanbury Street, and heard sounds from the adjoining yard at number 29: a noise which might have been the crash of a body falling against the fence. If that sound was indeed that of Annie's death fall then Mrs Long's testimony was incorrect.

At 6.00 a.m. – after dawn had broken – John Davis, an elderly resident of the over-crowded Hanbury Street slum-house, went into the yard and found the butchered remains of Annie Chapman lying in a pool of blood, head between the stone steps and a bloodstained fence. (See drawing on page 24: the body has been placed below steps for pictorial clarity.) The usual Ripper myths accompany the finding of the body. One report had Davis hysterically rushing into the street, yelling, 'Murder', a cry which was heard by Detective Inspector Joseph Chandler, whose involvement is outlined below. A second version had Mr Davis running along to the Commercial Road Police Station to report his find, ignoring the fact that he was an elderly, stooped man. In fact, Davis was too terrified to examine the body. After a quick glance he ran into the street and summoned help from two passers-by. They examined the remains of Annie Chapman then hurried to Commercial Street Police Station, where Inspector

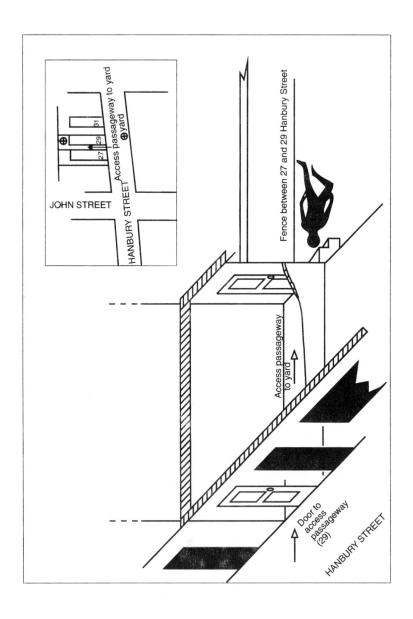

Chandler was on duty. Chandler's official statement records the scene:

> 'I at once proceeded to number 29 Hanbury Street, and in the back yard found a woman lying on her back, left arm resting on left breast, legs drawn up, abducted, small intestines and lap of the abdomen lying on right side above right shoulder, attached by a cord with the rest of the intestines inside the body; two flaps of skin from the lower part of the abdomen lying in a large quantity of blood about the left shoulder; throat cut deeply from left and back in a jagged manner right around the throat.'

News of the murder quickly circulated and a crowd of curious onlookers gathered. Once this mob had been cleared away by the police entrepreneurial neighbours charged customers a few pence to survey the scene from windows overlooking the murder site.

Dr Bagster Phillips was called to examine the body officially: he arrived on the scene at 6.30 a.m. and quickly declared that Annie had been dead for around two hours, which would have set the murder at 4.30 a.m. thus contradicting the statements of both Mrs Long and Albert Cadosch. After his medical examination Dr Phillips then turned detective. He examined the area around the body and discovered that Annie's pocket had been slashed open: the contents – a piece of muslin, a comb, and several brightly polished coins – had been laid out neatly at her feet. This action gives a glimpse into the murderer's mind and may even give us a clue as to his identity.

From Dr Phillips's report, we discover that Jack had stood in front of his victim and strangled her. Newly-raised bruises, mixed with contusions from the fight, were discernible on Annie's face. Her tongue was swollen and protruding from the teeth and her face was livid – further signs of strangulation. After her death Jack appeared to attempt complete decapitation, and almost succeeded. Annie's stomach was slashed open, after which her intestines were lifted on to the shoulder, which means Jack must have scooped the guts from Annie's belly with his hands. The vagina was slashed open and the uterus cut out. Jack took this part of the body away with him.

Once again the murderer had carried out his crime with people, both awake and asleep, in the surrounding houses –

possible witnesses who had heard no cry, no scuffle, no noise, apart from Mr Cadosch and his brief, 'sound of falling against the fence'.

There was some excitement when a leather apron was found partly submerged in a dish of water in the yard. After Nichols's murder an Inspector Frederick George Abberline wrote a report which mentioned that several prostitutes had revealed their terror of a man known as 'Leather Apron'. He had been demanding money from the women, ill-using them and threatening to rip them open with a knife. The press quickly latched on to this new story and on 5 September the *Star* featured an article on 'Leather Apron'. It was widely assumed that he was the killer and a detailed description of this suspect was soon in circulation. 'Leather Apron' was described as short, thick-necked, with small closely-set glistening eyes and a leering expression, a description straight out of a pantomime. Given this widespread belief, it is not surprising that finding a leather apron in the yard at Hanbury Street seemed to be a major clue, and perhaps the authorities were disappointed when Amelia Richardson revealed that the apron belonged to her son. She had recently washed it, leaving it on the fence to drain. The second inquest on a Ripper victim was again presided over by Wynne Baxter, who was now firmly into his stride, and who seemed to delight in his authority. He cross-examined Dr Phillips relentlessly, but the doctor appeared curiously reluctant to state the full facts, and made a strange statement – a statement which, as we shall see, would be echoed at a later Ripper murder inquest: 'I feel that in giving these details to the public, you are thwarting the ends of justice.' It is difficult to understand what injuries a doctor thought he should conceal, and Phillips was under a legal obligation to disclose all medical information in his possession. The purpose of an inquest is to record and preserve all relevant facts in regard to the death.

In his summing up, Baxter launched into grand melodrama: '. . . with Judas-like approaches, the wretch must then have seized the deceased. He pressed her throat, and whilst thus preventing the slightest cry, at the same time produced insensibility and suffocation. There is no evidence of any struggle. The clothes were not torn. Even in these preliminaries, the wretch seems to have known how to carry out efficiently his nefarious work. The deceased was then lowered to the ground and laid on her back; and although in doing so may have fallen against the fence, this movement was probably effected with care. Her throat was then cut in two places with savage determination, and the injuries to the abdomen commenced. All was done with cool impudence and reckless daring; but perhaps nothing is more noticeable than the emptying of her pockets and the arrangement of their contents with business-like precision, in order, near her feet. The murder seems, like the Buck's Row case, to have been carried out without a cry. Sixteen people were in the house. The partitions of the different rooms are of wood. Davies was not asleep after 3.00 a.m. except for three-quarters of an hour or less, between 5.00 and 5.45 a.m.; Mrs Richardson only just after 3.00 a.m. and heard no noise during the night. Mrs Hardman who occupies the front ground-floor room, did not waken until the noise succeeding the finding of the body had commenced, and none of the occupants of the house by which the yard is surrounded heard anything suspicious . . .'

Baxter made his final summing up of the case (possibly to everyone's relief, given his verbosity) on 26 September. Annie had, by this time, already been buried. The verdict was predictable: 'Wilful murder against some person or persons unknown.'

Chapter Four

Panic and Investigation

The murder of Mary Nichols caused great alarm in the East End, and considerable press comment throughout the land. Why, in those violent times, when it was fairly routine for women to be attacked, beaten and all too frequently murdered, did Nichols's death create such an impact? Firstly, in many minds, the murder was mistakenly linked to an earlier killing of a prostitute, Martha Tabram, who had been found stabbed to death in Spitalfields on 6 August. This attack had caused little press comment, but Nichols's murder only three weeks later presaged a possible pattern; this became a reality once Jack entered the picture. Perhaps the catalyst which propelled Nichols's murder into such widespread public prominence was the fact that she was left sprawled on a London pavement, her dress raised high, with no effort made to hide intimate parts of her body. In prudish Victorian times, when the glimpse of an ankle was considered improper, the intimate exposure of Nichols's body may well have been as shocking as the murder, and it may have been this aspect which caught the public's imagination. The murder of Chapman and Nichols established the feared pattern and created widespread panic. One mutilated, partly eviscerated body laid out on a London street was bad enough, but a second disembowelled woman lying in a public place broke open the floodgates of fear.

The newspapers thundered their opinions. The *Daily Telegraph*, which was not known to be sympathetic to 'wanton women,' used Chapman's nickname 'Dark Annie' in an editorial. But although it described her as a 'forlorn, despised citizeness of London', the editorial continued on a more humane note:

'Dark Annie's dreadful end has compelled a hundred thousand Londoners to reflect what it must be like to have no home at all except the common kitchen of a low lodging house, to sit there, sick and weak and bruised and wretched, for lack of fourpence with which to pay the right of a "doss": . . . "Dark

Annie" will effect in one way what fifty Secretaries of State could never accomplish.'

A September issue of *The Times* thundered:

'. . . nothing in fact or fiction equals these outrages at once in their horrible nature and in the effect which they have produced upon the popular imagination.'

Punch blamed the murders on advertising for the popular Victorian melodramas of the day:

'Is it not within the bounds of probability that to the highly-coloured pictorial advertisements to be seen on almost all the hoardings in London, vividly representing sensational scenes of murder, exhibited as "the great attractions" of certain dramas, the public may be to a certain extent indebted for the horrible crimes in Whitechapel?'

Possible suspects were arrested and questioned daily. Tens of thousands of leaflets were printed and distributed and countless newspaper editorials were written. Contemporary papers report details of numerous arrests – Edward Stanley, Chapman's friend, was taken in for questioning – but no charges were laid against any of the suspects. This vigorous activity did not prevent criticism from being levelled at the police from all directions – including criticism from Buckingham Palace. (After the fifth Ripper killing, Queen Victoria, who took a keen interest in the Ripper crimes, wrote personally to the then Prime Minister, Lord Salisbury, enquiring about the murder investigations.) Things were not proceeding well. Despite the large number of men being arrested and closely questioned, there were no results. The police grew more and more desperate in their attempts to solve the case. A man was even taken into custody for investigation because he had 'grinned' at a lady whilst walking over Westminster Bridge. The Ripper, however, remained at large.

Due to the continuing popular rumour, arrests of men who wore leather aprons became commonplace. This was quickly followed by arrests of men who carried Gladstone bags, as speculation that the murderer carried a similar kind of case had become intense. Meanwhile the police force had other problems: those in charge of the investigations were not entirely in harmony. Sir Charles Warren, the Metropolitan Police Commissioner, was not on good terms with the acting Commissioner for the City of

London Police, Major Henry Smith. In addition, relations were strained between the Assistant Metropolitan Police Commissioner James Monroe and the Home Secretary, Henry Matthews, and neither of these men were on friendly terms with Sir Charles Warren.

The press praised or criticised all the above men in varying degrees, adding to the simmering cauldron of bad humour. The *East London Observer* noted on 22 September 1888:

'We have had enough of Mr Home Secretary Matthews, who knows nothing, has heard nothing and does not intend to do anything . . .'

The popular press levelled endless criticism at Sir Charles Warren. The *Star* wrote in September:

'We can talk of larger reforms when we do away with the centralised, non-efficient military system which Sir Charles Warren has brought to perfection'.

On 22 September the *East London Observer* opined: 'It is clear that the Detective Department at Scotland Yard is in an utterly hopeless and worthless condition.' Yet another newspaper commented 'If sheer fright grows into crazed fury, we shall hold Mr Matthews and Sir Charles Warren responsible'. Public feeling was becoming inflamed.

More criticism came crashing down on Warren and Matthews because the Government did not offer a reward for the capture of the murderer. The Home Office put forward their point of view on this subject: 'Rewards for the discovery of criminals were discontinued some years ago, because the experience showed that such offers of reward tended to produce more harm than good.' There was clearly a fear that offering a reward in the East End would result in a deluge of false or fabricated evidence being offered.

'The excitement in Spitalfields is now rendering the people almost frantic,' one reporter wrote. He was not exaggerating.

In October 1888 *The Times* published an editorial outlining a previous homicide investigation when bloodhounds had been used to track down a murderer. This suggestion evoked a flood of correspondence on the merits and otherwise of *The Times*'s advice.

In desperation, the police force heeded the suggestion; they decided to call dogs into action. On 9 and 10 October trials were conducted in two London parks. On the second outing Sir Charles Warren even allowed himself to become human bait in order to test the dogs' powers. Although the trials in the parks were successful, it soon became apparent that the animals could not follow a scent in an area so densely populated as the East End and the dogs' services were not retained. Sir Charles then became the object of ridicule, as rumour spread that the dogs had lost themselves and Warren's men had had to go out searching for them.

A trio of insane medical students were the next serious subjects to be sought. Two were traced and intensive enquiries were made concerning the third student, who was reported to have gone abroad. That particular investigation, in line with all previous investigation, was eventually abandoned. Despite exhaustive searching, probing and questioning the police appeared to be no closer to finding the killer than they were at the start of their enquiries.

* * * * *

So who was 'Jack the Ripper'? That is a question which people have been asking for well over a century. *The Jack the Ripper A to Z*, published in 1991, written by three leading Ripper experts, Paul Begg, Martin Fido and Keith Skinner, contains a list of around 150 suspects. I feel confident that that list could be considerably reduced if the class structure to which Jack belonged could be established. Was he from the lower classes, who, in the main, populated the East End? Or did he have an upper-class background?

Firstly we will examine several popular suspects from the working classes to see whether eliminations can be made there.

The 'leather apron' rumour caused suspicion to fall on a shoemaker, John Pizer, a Polish Jew whose unfortunate appearance (black hair almost covered his face) reinforced public prejudice. The shoemaker was known to have used violence towards several prostitutes, as Inspector Joseph Helson made clear in a police report on 7 September.

A search was made for Pizer (who was probably tipped off that he might be under suspicion): he had wisely taken precautions and had stayed indoors in his stepmother's house in Mulberry Street where he was eventually arrested. Pizer could prove his whereabouts on the 30/31 August the night of Nichols's murder. He had questioned a policeman in Seven Sisters Road about a large fire in the London Docks which was visible for many miles around. And he had lodged in a Holloway Road doss-house for the remainder of the night. The deputy of this doss-house and the policeman confirmed these details. Pizer's friends and relatives swore that he had not left the house on the days before or after Chapman's murder. Once these enquiries were completed the police were satisfied that Pizer was innocent, but he could not be immediately released from custody for his own safety. The panic and fury which the first two Ripper killings had unleashed continued to rise daily, fuelled by wild rumours and an endless barrage of sensational press stories, not all of them true.

Despite irrefutable evidence of Pizer's innocence, he was still summoned to Annie Chapman's inquest for questioning. This appearance led to his innocence being publicly acknowledged.

After this court appearance and his total exoneration, Pizer successfully sued several newspapers which had stated that he was definitely the Whitechapel murderer. The sums awarded to him are not known, but no doubt the money would have supplied him with leather for some years to come.

A second popularly accepted suspect from the working classes was also a Polish Jew, Aaron Kosminski, who worked, when he worked, as a hairdresser. The case for Kosminski as the legendary killer has been thoroughly discussed by Paul Begg in his book *Jack the Ripper: The Uncensored Facts*. An American television programme, chaired by Sir Peter Ustinov and broadcast in 1988, decided that Kosminski was the most likely Jack the Ripper candidate, as did an English television programme, *Crime Monthly*, broadcast in the London area in 1990.

Kosminski was known to harbour a hatred of women, and appeared to have homicidal tendencies; it was reported to the police that he had once used a knife to threaten the life of his sister. Kosminski was first named as a suspect by Sir Melville Macnaghten in notes which he wrote in 1894.

According to Sir Melville, Kosminski lived in 'the very heart of the district where the murders were committed'. He appeared to have a supportive family, who, it was suspected, would cover up for their brother in regard to bloodstained clothing and any other evidence which might prove incriminating.

Macnaghten's notes state that Kosminski was committed to Mile End Old Town Workhouse Infirmary and then Colney Hatch Insane Asylum in 1890. Workhouse records confirm that admittance: entries in the workhouse's infirmary register state that Kosminski had been insane for two years. Records of the man's personal habits state that he would only eat food he himself found in the gutters, and that he refused to wash or bathe. 'No one ever saw the murderer', Macnaghten's notes claim. However, an equally senior Scotland Yard officer, Sir Robert Anderson, who was in charge of the Ripper murders from October 1888 states, '. . . the only person [unnamed] who ever had a good view of the murderer, unhesitatingly identified the suspect [Kosminski] the instant he was confronted with him . . .' Clearly one of these two high-ranking officers was wrong.

* * * * *

I now wish to argue against the allegations that Kosminski, Pizer or any other member of the lower classes was Jack the Ripper. Take Kosminski: his house was only a few minutes walk from Flower and Dean Street and Thrawl Street, and he was known to roam the area which contained the lodging-houses used by the murdered prostitutes, which means he must have been known to the victims. Now although the prostitutes were not fussy over their clientele, they would only have gone with a man who was likely to pay. Furthermore, Mary Nichols went into a lonely, dark street with her killer and Annie Chapman went through a long, dark, narrow passageway into a small yard with the same man. Neither of the women would have accepted a local lunatic as a client. It has been pointed out to me that (as recorded above) Kosminski was only taken for treatment for his mental condition in July 1890, almost two years after the murders ended: but, as we have seen, the Mile End Workhouse Infirmary declared that Kosminski had been insane for two years, which means he must have been adjudged insane *well before* the Ripper murders started. And, of course, such people usually display signs of impending madness over a period of time, not overnight. Kosminski, who clearly was very odd, was also a noted woman-hater. As he lived near to the murdered prostitutes' usual lodging houses, they must have known these facts, and would not have been willing to go into dark, lonely places with him. It is just possible that Kosminski might have used a knife to force the women to go with him, but the silence of the murders tends to rule this out. The women would have made some kind of a fuss – spoken protests or a scuffle – even if they did not yell out. They would have been on their guard against trouble, and the evidence points towards a surprise attack. The last murder, allegedly of Mary Kelly, took place in a room, as we shall see later in this book. It would certainly have been possible to refuse to take a lunatic vagrant home. Mary Kelly was an intelligent woman. If threatened she would have led the tramp to a place where help was available – possibly from the local policeman on his beat or from a friend – and not into her own lodgings.

* * * * *

In refuting the theory that Jack the Ripper was a member of the working classes, we must consider another element – literacy. A message linked to the Ripper was chalked on a wall in the East End, and various letters were sent to the police. These will be discussed in later chapters of this book: they are mentioned here because if we can accept that even one of these communications was genuine, then we must also accept, even from the little we know about the characters of Pizer and Kosminski, that the case against these prime suspects from the working classes is seriously weakened. It is clear from Mary Nichols's letter that not all East Enders were illiterate – although many of them were – but it is highly unlikely that a character such as Kosminski (a much-favoured suspect amongst some Ripper experts) or even the less-favoured Pizer would write taunting letters to the newspapers and the police, or chalk a message on a wall. Mentally unbalanced people frequently put pen to paper, but it seems out of character for a disturbed lunatic or a violent shoemaker in Victorian times to write letters. Morever, we must remember that Nichols only wrote her letter when she was living in a middle-class home with pen and paper readily to hand. Many working class East Enders carried their few belongings around with them. Pen and ink would have been low on the list of priorities and not an accepted part of life as they are today.

There are other arguments against Jack being a shambling local lunatic. For a start, the murderer must have been plausible, as he was clearly able to gain the confidence of his victims. There is also circumstantial evidence which suggests that Jack, in contrast to most of the working class suspects, was not a local man. The yard in which Annie Chapman met her end was well-known to locals as a place where a woman might risk a quick servicing of her client, the partners pressed together and standing up in the dark; if they were caught together there was no great harm done. However, to commit murder in such a place would have been decidedly risky. The yard at 29 Hanbury Street was well known as a busy place, especially around dawn, the time when Annie was most probably murdered. The residents of the doss-house used this yard for storage and work purposes; they also used it for relieving themselves, and might appear at any time of the night. Anyone entering the yard through the swing door at the end of the passage and down the steps could easily have had their only means of escape cut off. It is highly unlikely that a local man, with murder on his mind, would have taken Annie to a place from which a hasty exit might prove so difficult.

Other clues indicate the class of the killer. The contents of Annie Chapman's pocket, arranged at her feet, included a few coins. No East End working-class man would have left money behind, no matter how small the amount. Every farthing counted around Whitechapel. In addition, the murders (the two already studied and the three which were to follow) were all committed on a weekend, which would point towards a professional class. Blue collar workers, if they were in employment, worked long hours at least six days a week. It is, of course, possible that they still had the energy to prowl the streets most of the night committing foul murder instead of resting, but in that case, why did they not release their fury on any other day of the week? Lunatics and itinerants roamed free at all hours and there is also no reason why they should have restricted any murderous activity only to the weekends. Common sense dictates that the killer was probably free only from Friday night to Monday, and this might indicate a man who lived away from the East End; a man who was only able to travel at restricted times.

Further circumstantial evidence indicates that the killer did not belong to the working classes. Given the terrible injuries inflicted on Mary Nichols and Annie Chapman, the murderer would clearly have been bloodstained when he left the scene of the crime.

The East End contained many slaughterhouses and these were open at night, but workers wore coats and protective clothing, if only to save on laundry bills: and there would have been water for the men to wash their hands after handling carcasses. Abattoir workers would not have walked the streets soaked in blood (especially not with the heightened police activity) as the murderer must have done. Jack had to wash the blood away somewhere; but houses were crowded and private washing facilities almost non-existent. This is a further sign that the killer had private facilities denied to most East Enders. Jack might, of course, have carried a spare cloak to cover any soiling, but his hands would certainly have been heavily stained, which would have smeared even replacement garments, and, in any case, a spare cloak would have been another pointer towards affluence. Poor people owned only one set of working clothes and one set of Sunday best, which was frequently pawned. Jack would have needed several pairs of trousers and overcoats with private laundry facilities for cleaning those garments – a further sign of affluence. Given the above collected observations I contend that there is considerable circumstantial evidence against Jack having been a member of the working classes. But is there any case to indicate that he might have belonged to high society? Let us leave that question until we have examined the other Ripper killings.

Chapter Five

The Double Killing

Three weeks passed after the discovery of Annie Chapman's body in Hanbury Street with no further murders in the area to arouse intense excitment.

Three weeks in the East End environment, where every hour was a struggle to survive, sharpened the mind in favour of the present and blunted the power of the past. If Jack's killings had finished in Hanbury Street his deeds would probably have quickly faded into the mists of time – two unpleasant murders in a violent area made unremarkable by the passing decades. But on 30 September 1888 a double murder took place, carried out in the open on the streets of London, within the space of around 45 minutes, the murder sites within approximately half a mile of each other. This unique savagery immortalised Jack, creating a legend, and giving rise to a puzzle which has tantalised millions of people for more than a century: who was the Ripper?

* * * * *

The situation of Liz Stride, who, at the time of her death, was a forty-two-year-old East End prostitute, appears to differ from that of the Ripper's first two victims.

On the eve of her murder Liz had worked as a cleaning woman in Flower and Dean Street earning sixpence for her work. She was not so tragic a figure as Nichols or Chapman: she was better looking and probably in better general health, although she had received treatment for bronchitis and there had been problems with venereal disease in the past. But, on the night of her death, in contrast to the earlier victims, she was not turned away from lodgings in the small hours, forcing her to tout for clients in order to earn money for a night's lodgings. Liz appears to have been a genuine free spirit, restless at being in one place for too long and unwilling, or unable, to sustain a steady relationship over an extended period. Accurate details of Liz's former life and upbringing were difficult to distil into a clear picture, as she was in the habit of embroidering her past with fantasies and lies.

Nonetheless, we know that Jack's third murder victim was born in Torslanda, Sweden, the daughter of a farmer. She had one sister and two brothers. Liz left home in 1860 aged sixteen, presumably a few years after she left school – her restless spirit clearly dates from early in life. After settling in Gothenburg she worked as a domestic servant, but by 1865 the Swedish police had registered her – now in her early twenties – as a prostitute. Liz had been 'on the game' for almost half of her life.

Although a foreigner she apparently spoke perfect English, and she was also reputed to speak Yiddish fluently, accomplishments which would indicate intelligence.

It is not known why Stride decided to leave Sweden and move to Britain, which she did in 1866. Perhaps the death of her parents and the fact that she had given birth to a still-born baby drove her away from home. Or maybe her wanderlust had already taken hold. Once in London the Swede reputedly settled into a mansion in Hyde Park, a highly respectable area, where she became a 'gentleman's domestic servant'.

In 1869 she married a carpenter, John Stride (Annie Chapman had been married in the same year) but, following the depressing pattern of the Ripper's other victims, at some point in time this union broke down; by 1877 Liz's fortunes had reached a low ebb and she was living in an East End workhouse.

Acquaintances spoke well of Liz (nicknamed 'Long Liz'), describing her as 'good hearted'; 'pleasant'; 'clean' and so on. Having arrived in the East End she always declared that she had been widowed and had lost her children in a shipping accident. In 1878 the steamer *Princess Alice*, had struck the *Bywell Castle* in the Thames near Woolwich; the *Alice* had sunk with great loss of life. A News Agency report on 8 October 1888 printed a story that an Elizabeth Stride had indeed identified her husband and two children amongst the dead lying in Woolwich Dockyard, but the *Princess Alice* passenger and crew lists did not register the name of Stride. Liz's story of the loss of her family, and of her own escape climbing onto the funnel of the stricken ship, appears to have been a romantic fiction. The prosaic truth was that her husband, John Stride, died of heart failure in 1884, in an East London workhouse.

Liz's downfall appears to stem from character defects. If her husband did not abandon her, and, so far as one can speculate, John Stride appears to have been a decent man, then Liz must have abandoned him, presumably leaving her children (variously numbered from two to nine) and a reasonably secure domestic life for the uncertainties of the street. No doubt the widely-spread East End disease of alcoholism played its part in this choice of action.

Liz was frequently arrested for being drunk and disorderly. Once in the dock she was reputed to have given dramatic performances, blaming her symptoms on illness and not alcohol. Stride's second nickname was 'Epileptic Liz' and, as I can find no trace of that illness in her medical history, I must assume that the soubriquet referred to her famous performances in the court room. This heavy drinking free spirit begins to emerge as a distinct individual.

After the death of her husband Liz settled down with another partner, Michael Kidney, but even in this relationship the urge to roam made her disappear from time to time. Kidney, an apparently brutal, heavy drinking dockyard labourer whom Liz accused of assault, made an inquest statement which helps to illuminate Stride's life-style:

'. . . she was subject to going away whenever she thought she would. During the three years I've known her, she has been away from me altogether about five months. I've cautioned her the same as I would a wife. It was drink that made her go. But she always came back again. I don't believe she left me on Tuesday to take up with any other man. I think she liked me better than any other man . . .'

This last statement may well have been more than supposition. Although Liz charged Kidney with assault, she failed to appear in court for the prosecution, and the charges were dropped.

* * * * *

On the eve of her murder, 30 September, Liz left Flower and Dean Street mid-evening, presumably in order to enjoy herself drinking in pubs and searching for clients to refill her coffers and provide more gin. She was seen soliciting in the Whitechapel area by a number of witnesses, but, as usual, there is conflicting evidence about these sightings. The *Evening News*, 1 October 1888 recorded an interview with a Mr Best and a Mr Gardner. These gentlemen claimed that when they had entered an East End public house, *The Bricklayers Arms*, at 11.00 p.m on the night of the murder, Liz and a respectably dressed man had been leaving. They were hugging and kissing. The man was 5ft 5ins in height, clean-shaven, apart from a black moustache, wearing a black billycock hat and dressed in a morning suit and coat. Forty-five minutes later, a William Marshall claimed to have seen Stride with a man in Berner Street: both were travelling in the direction of Dutfield's Yard, a premises situated off Berner Street.

The *Evening News* tracked down an elderly greengrocer, Matthew Packer, whose shop was situated at 4 Berner Street. On 4 October the newspaper published Packer's statement. He claimed that he had sold grapes to a man and a woman (whom he subsequently identified as Stride) on the night of the murder. Packer also claimed that no detective or policeman had visited him to find out whether he had seen anything suspicious on the night in question. There are many conflicting reports around Packer's testimony, and he appeared to change the time of his transaction according to his audience, which tends to make his evidence unreliable. The main interest in the man lies in the fact that Sir Charles Warren interviewed him personally, a fact established by Stephen Knight, who found Warren's handwritten notes in police files: why should such a highly-placed police officer interview such a minor, innocent witness? Warren, in his spidery handwriting, indicates, in marginalia, that the CID wanted the times which Packer had given in many of his statements altered from 11.45 p.m. to 11.00 p.m.. For what reason would the CID wish to tamper with a witness's evidence? There is no conclusive proof that the man whom Packer saw with Stride was her murderer – it could well have been an innocent client, so why was the CID so interested? Clearly something very odd was going on behind the police scenes.

Mrs Fanny Mortimer, who lived at 36 Berner Street, only a few doors away from *The International Workingmen's Educational Club* at number 40, told reporters that she had been standing outside her door on the night of the murder to listen to the community signing from the men's club. Again, there are various differences in the reported timings of Mrs Mortimer's nocturnal vigil, timings which range from 12.30 a.m. to 1.00 a.m. The

Evening News, 1 October 1888 reported that Mrs Mortimer, '. . . heard the measured heavy tread of a policeman passing the house on his beat.' Paul Begg records that only one policeman, PC William Smith, is known to have passed along Berner Street within that time limit. Smith plodded his beat at 12.30 a.m. Mrs Mortimer said that whilst she was standing at her door she had seen only one man in Berner Street. He was traced and found to be Leon Goldstein, an innocent pedestrian who had passed by Mrs Mortimer around 12.50/55 a.m.. But as we shall see, if the lady had been outside her door from 12.30 a.m. she could not have failed to notice two other men, Morris Eagle and Joseph Lave.

A Charles Letchford, who lived at 39 Berner Street, told the *Manchester Guardian* that his sister had been outside her door for about ten minutes, from 12.50 a.m.; it is a reasonable assumption that Mrs Mortimer was the sister referred to. This later timing would fit in with the following evidence, which places Mrs Mortimer outside her door from around 12.45 to 12.55 a.m. Letchford's timing might well have been incorrect by a few minutes. The lady is said to have returned inside her house about five minutes before the man who discovered the body, Louis Diemschutz, passed by in his horse and cart. Diemschutz passed by at almost exactly 1.00 a.m.

The most illuminating evidence of Stride's last night on earth was given to Chief Inspector Donald Swanson by a Hungarian immigrant, Israel Schwartz. Schwartz claimed that at 12.45 a.m. he had turned into Berner Street from the Commercial Road, and, Swanson recorded:

'. . . having got as far as the gateway where the murder was committed, he saw a man stop and speak to a woman who was standing in the gateway. The man tried to pull the woman into the street, but he turned her round and threw her down on the footway and the woman screamed three times, but not very loudly. On crossing to the opposite side of the street, he saw a second man standing lighting his pipe. The man who threw the woman down called out, apparently to the man on the opposite side of the road, 'Lipski' and then Schwartz walked away, but finding that he was followed by the second man, he ran so far as the railway arch, but the man did not follow so far . . .'

As Schwartz described an event which took place only 15

minutes or so before Liz's death, he almost certainly saw her being attacked prior to the murder.

The police refused to give out Schwartz's name and address, but he was tracked down by the *Star*, which printed a long interview:

'Information which may be important was given to the Leman Street police yesterday by an Hungarian concerning this murder. This foreigner was well-dressed, and had the appearance of being in the theatrical line. He could not speak a word of English, but came to the police station accompanied by a friend, who acted as an interpreter . . . As he turned the corner from Commerical Road he noticed some distance in front of him a man walking as if partially intoxicated. He walked on behind him, and presently he noticed a woman standing in the entrance to the alleyway where the body was found. The half-tipsy man halted and spoke to her. The Hungarian saw him put a hand on her shoulder and push her back into the passage, but feeling rather timid of getting mixed up in quarrels, he crossed to the other side of the street. Before he had gone many yards, however, he heard the sound of a quarrel, and turned back to learn what was the matter, but just as he stepped from the kerb a second man came out of the doorway of the public house a few doors off, and shouting out some sort of warning to the man who was with the woman, rushed forward as if to attack the intruder. The Hungarian states positively that he saw a knife in the second man's hand, but he waited to see no more. He fled incontinently to his new lodgings . . .'

This story clearly differs in several respects from the one which Schwartz had given to the police a few days earlier. There are several possibilities for these changes. The interpreter might have been adding his own embellishments, but this is unlikely. The detail about a man rushing from a local public house brandishing a knife was also unlikely given the current climate of distrust – a Jew named only as Jacobs became a suspect merely because he wore a leather apron. He was continually attacked in the street, and frequently had to run for his life. In September 1888 the *Daily News* reported that doctors were kept busy on cases of serious assault which arose directly, and indirectly out of the mere discussion of the Ripper murders. In these circumstances only a lunatic would dare openly to carry a knife. Furthermore, what reason would a man have for attacking a fellow found arguing with a prostitute? This second story seems to reflect dramatisation by a news reporter in order to titillate his readers and increase circulation. Clearly the press has not changed a great deal.

The discovery of Liz's body was made by Louis Diemschutz, an entrepreneurial Victorian who managed *The International Workingmen's Educational Club*. This was a locally unpopular establishment which served as a meeting place for anarchists and intellectuals; the club appears to have been run mainly by Louis's wife whilst he peddled cheap jewellery from a market stall.

Between 40 and 42 Berner Street, a gateway approximately twelve feet wide led into a small yard, Dutfield's Yard, reached along two blind walls which formed a long alleyway between the Berner Street houses and the club.

It was 1.00 a.m. when Louis turned his horse between the Berner Street gates into the 20 foot long, unlit passageway leading

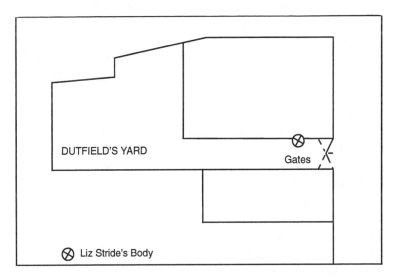

to Dutfield's Yard. The horse, as it was nosed through the gates, suddenly shied and refused to go any further. Singing could still be heard in the club as Louis urged his horse on without success. He then poked to the right of the pony's head with his whip, and discovered a bundle lying on the ground. A quick examination in the darkness showed that the bundle was an inert woman lying near to the wall. Unable to see in the darkness Louis struck a match which didn't help much. He hurried into the club and collected a lamp and several companions. They all hurried back to the gates.

Light revealed a woman lying on her back, face towards the wall, feet towards the street. Her left arm was extended and her hand still clutched a packet of cachous. These scented sweets would have been used to hide the smell of alcohol on her breath. Liz had clearly aimed to present a pleasant package to her clients, a package which included a corsage of fresh flowers pinned to her coat. Her right hand was folded over the stomach and her throat was deeply cut. When Louis and his colleagues examined the body with the aid of a light, the throat was still oozing blood, indicating that the entry of the horse might have disturbed the Ripper. It has always been thought possible that whilst Louis was initially examining the bundle in the darkness, Jack, having been alarmed by hearing the approach of the cart, had slipped behind the gates where he remained in hiding only a few yards away.

A large crowd quickly collected at the murder scene, forcing the police to close off the yard, which was then thoroughly searched, but without result. The club members were all detained and questioned, again without result. In the meantime, every available policeman in the area was being drafted towards Berner Street, a fact which did not seem to bother Jack. He walked through the East End, past any alerted policemen, in search of a new victim, and no one saw him apart from a prostitute, Catharine Eddowes, and she would not be giving evidence. The Ripper was her last encounter.

* * * * *

The inquest on Liz Stride opened on 1 October, the day after her murder, and the coroner was once again the indefatigable Wynne Baxter. Identification of the dead woman provided an immediate stumblng block and farce quickly entered the proceedings. The police testified that the body was that of an habitual drunk who gave the name of Annie Fitzgerald each time she was arrested. Then a Mrs Mary Malcolm came forward and testified under oath that the body was that of her sister, Elizabeth Watts. Mrs Malcolm bore a strong facial resemblance to the dead woman so her testimony was given serious consideration. The lady then launched into a tirade of abuse against her 'dead' sister, accusing her of gross immorality. A great deal of the inquest's time was taken up by the task of positive identification. Even Michael Kidney, the dead woman's lover for three years, could only state what he knew about Liz, and, as she frequently lied, it was difficult to disprove Mrs Malcolm's assertions, until the 'dead' sister arrived at the inquest and refuted the calumnies which had caused her great distress. Mrs Malcolm was not available for further comment.

The inquest was finally wound up on 24 October when PC Walter Stride identified the dead woman as the wife of his deceased uncle, John Stride. At least Liz had been truthful about her name.

* * * * *

We now arrive at yet another fascinating Ripper puzzle, one which, surprisingly, has been ignored by other writers on the crimes.

Let us examine the comings and goings around Dutfield's Yard half an hour before Liz Stride's murder. It was clearly a busy place, with endless activity going on, especially from the men's club – not a spot which any sensible man would select for murder. These statements are taken from witnesses at Stride's inquest:

12.30 approx. William West, a printer, was in Dutfield's Yard and noticed that the gates at the end of the passageway were open. He saw nothing unusual.

12.35 approx. Morris Eagle went along the passageway from Berner Street into Dutfield's Yard. He saw nothing unusual.

12.45 approx. Joseph Lave went along the passage. As it was so dark, he had to grope along the right hand wall and would have fallen over any body had it been there.

12.45 approx. The most likely time at which Mrs Mortimer stood outside her front door, staying there until approximately 12.55 a.m.

There is a general consensus that Israel Schwartz did see Liz Stride being attacked prior to her murder at around 12.45 a.m.. We must assume that Mrs Mortimer and Joseph Lave narrowly missed being present at the attack. But this timing provides a further mystery. If Stride was attacked at 12.45, why did her murder take place almost fifteen minutes later? Her throat was still pouring blood when Diemschutz and his companions examined the body, which means Stride was killed only minutes before she was found; Diemschutz was certain of the time as he had checked with a clock shortly before arriving at Dutfield's Yard. What happened to Stride in the fifteen minutes between her attack and her murder? Mrs Mortimer, standing a few yards away, saw nothing suspicious happening in the street. This is a problem which will be discussed in a later chapter.

* * * * *

At the time of her death Catharine Eddowes was a forty-six-year-old prostitute. She was born 14 April 1842 in Wolverhampton, the daughter of a metal worker. There are confusing reports about her early upbringing and education and it is impossible to sort out fact from fiction. In 1864 Catharine, a young woman, started living with Thomas Conway, an older man; newspapers reported that he was an army pensioner. The couple moved to London. It is impossible to say whether they ever married, but Conway was the father of her three children, a daughter and two sons. By 1880 the relationship had broken down. Their daughter, Annie, blamed the split on her mother's excessive drinking, but Eddowes's sister claimed that Conway's violence made Catharine leave him. If Conway had been a pensioner in 1864 (assuming that he had not been invalided out of the armed forces early), then he must have been an old man sixteen years later. Catharine, a much younger person with a fiery temper, would surely have been able to defend herself, so I tend to believe the daughter's version of the marriage breakdown.

Catharine's common-law husband was John Kelly. The couple had met one year after she parted from her first husband, if that was indeed a legal union: since then Catharine and John had lived together in apparent harmony and happiness for seven years.

Although Catharine is usually described as a prostitute, John Kelly and a lodging-house keeper both stated that she did not 'walk the streets'. However, her ever-present difficulty was to find enough money for a drink, and alcoholics, when desperate, will perform any service. She had a reputation as a scrounger and even her own daughter is reputed to have moved to an undisclosed address to avoid her mother's cadging ways. Thomas Conway was lucky – he had enlisted in the army under the name of Thomas Quinn: an army pension was paid to him under that name, so Catharine couldn't make a claim on it.

During September 1888 John Kelly and Eddowes travelled to Maidstone in Kent to earn money hop-picking – a traditional combined working/holiday much favoured by East Enders. Their hop-picking efforts did not appear to meet with success and the couple returned to London penniless. There are persistent reports that Catharine returned to the capital in order to claim reward money which had been offered to anyone able to name Jack the Ripper. 'I think I know who it is,' Catharine is reputed to have said to the superintendent of the Shoe Lane Workhouse where she was well-known, and where she went for a bed for the night after returning from the hop fields. When she was warned not to say such things in case she should become the Ripper's next victim, Catharine replied, 'Oh no fear of that.' She was wrong. On 29 September the impecunious couple pawned John Kelly's boots; he is said to have stood bare-foot on the pavement whilst Catharine arranged the transaction. The half a crown obtained in the morning from the pawnbroker, a not inconsiderable sum in late Victorian times, lasted only until early afternoon.

Penniless again, Catharine left her partner in Houndsditch, a road built over the site of the Roman moat which used to surround London in ancient times. The name is said to have originated from the number of dead dogs which were thrown into the water by the Romans. Houndsditch ran between Bishopsgate and Aldgate High Street, two places which were associated with Catharine's last night on earth. She left John Kelly at 2.00 p.m., saying she would go to Bermondsey to try and borrow money from her daughter Annie and would be back no later than 4.00 p.m.. This statement was puzzling as (to repeat) the daughter had moved away from Bermondsey to try and dodge her mother's unwelcome cadging and Catharine must have known this fact. Why then did she lie to John?

Ignoring her promise to return within two hours she went on a massive drinking spree, we do not know where, and this creates yet another puzzle. Given the fact that Catharine was penniless (and sober according to John Kelly at the inquest) in the early afternoon, and that she did not manage to borrow money from her daughter – she could not even find her daughter – it is difficult to know from whom Catharine obtained money to spend on drink, if not from clients in return for sexual favours. But where did she find these clients? She was not seen soliciting. The other prostitutes had all been seen with men, even in the middle of the night; Catharine's work would have taken place in the middle of the day in an area where she was well known. And, as it was still light, she could not take clients to dark corners in remote alleyways. She would have needed a place to use for her sexual encounters, but, at this point in time, Catharine did not even have a regular doss-house to go to. And even if she had, these places were so crowded that someone would have seen her with her pick-ups, and given the publicity surrounding the case, these sightings would have been reported. So where did Catharine go?

At 8.30 p.m. she was found in Aldgate High Street hopelessly drunk. Although it is not a hard and fast rule, most heavy drinkers need large amounts of alcohol to intoxicate them completely. Catharine had clearly imbibed – and spent – heavily. There is no satisfactory answer as to where she got the money to buy alcohol and where she went.

As Catharine was obviously intoxicated and disorderly (she was unable to stand upright), two constables took her into custody and she was locked in a cell at Bishopsgate Police Station. Around 1.00 a.m. – precisely the time Liz Stride was being attacked a quarter of a mile away – a constable looked into Catharine's cell and decided that she had sobered up sufficiently to be discharged. Before being released, Catharine's name had been registered as 'Mary Ann Kelly', a soubriquet she used from time to time. Many of the prostitutes used false names when they were arrested, in order to give the police a difficult time. Intriguingly, the alleged fifth and final victim of Jack the Ripper was also named Mary Kelly.

* * * * *

Mitre Square was one of the more respectable areas of the East End, near to the City border. The square had three entrances, which made it a busy place, especially on a Saturday: in Victorian times, Saturday night was an even more traditional day for fun after the week's labours than it is at present.

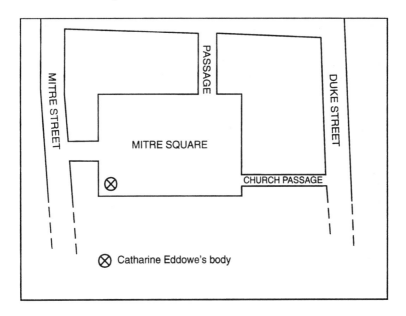

At 1.30 a.m., PC Watkins trudged his usual beat through Mitre Square. All was quiet.

At 1.35 a.m. three men, Joseph Lawende, Joseph Levy and Harry Harris, testified that they had passed Church Passage, which leads into Mitre Square. (See map.) Here, at the Duke Street end of the passage, they saw a man and a woman talking. They could not see the woman's face; however, Lawende later identified the woman as Eddowes by the clothes she had been wearing. ('I noticed she had a black jacket and black bonnet. I have seen the articles at the Police Station, and I recognise them as the sort of dress worn by that woman.') Recognising black clothing worn in a dark place on a dark night does not seem to me to be particularly convincing identification.

About 1.38 a.m. PC James Harvey went along Church Passage as far as the entrance to Mitre Square. Harvey testified that he had been at the end of Church Passage around that time but he saw no one and heard no cry or noise. At 1.45 a.m. when Constable Watkin's beat returned him to Mitre Square (that is about six or seven minutes after PC Harvey stood looking out into the Square), he discovered the body of Catharine Eddowes in deep shadow, lying on the pavement outside an empty house. She had been appallingly mutilated, with slashes cut into her cheeks, part of her nose sliced off and cuts made across her eyelids. By her side lay an old mustard tin box, containing pawn tickets.

To repeat the police time-table:

1.30 a.m. Watkins passes the murder site in Mitre Square.

1.38/9 a.m. Harvey stands at Church Passage entrance to Mitre Square.

1.45 a.m. Watkins returns to Mitre Square. Discovers Eddowe's body.

This gave the Ripper six or seven minutes to murder and carry out complicated mutilations on his victim. Watkins ran to Kearley and Tonge's warehouse in Mitre Square and roused the watchman, George Morris, a former policeman. Morris later testified that although he had had the warehouse door ajar, he had heard no cries or suspicious sounds in Mitre Square. PC Harvey, who, as we know, was near the murder scene, was summoned; he alerted a comrade who hurried to fetch a doctor; Dr George Sequeira was called to the body. He merely declared Catharine dead, which was obvious, and the City Police Surgeon, Dr Frederick Brown was sent for. Dr Brown's examination revealed the full extent of Catharine's injuries. Besides the facial mutilations her throat had been slashed, almost from ear to ear. (Her right ear lobe fell off when the body was undressed in the mortuary.) Catharine's stomach had been exposed and cut open, then the intestines were pulled out and slung over the right shoulder. A piece of intestine had been cut away and dropped underneath the left arm. One kidney and the uterus had been removed and were missing. Jack had also cut through the anal artery releasing feculent matter which possibly smeared him. This clumsiness was a main consideration in convincing the experts, including Dr Sequira and eventually Dr Brown that the killer had no surgical skill.

Jack's unprecedented night of terror, during which he had succeeded in ripping himself into everlasting fame, was over. But worse things were to come.

Chapter Six

Prelude to the Fifth Murder

Despite a massive police investigation the murders were baffling, the stealth and cunning of the invisible killer terrifying. Myths began to be born: Jack the Ripper was a vampire; he was an agent of the devil; he was a trained wild animal. Major puzzles arose, puzzles which were hard to solve.

The Ripper murdered Stride in Berner Street at one o'clock in the morning then set off in the direction of Bishopsgate and Mitre Square. Going directly to the Square on foot would have taken about ten minutes, but somewhere along the route Jack met Catharine Eddowes whom he must have engaged in conversation. They then went to Mitre Square together. We must remember that Dr Frederick Brown's post-mortem report on the mutilated body describes Eddowes's right kidney as, '. . . pale, bloodless, with slight congestion of the base . . .' – signs of Bright's disease, so Catharine was a sick woman. Typical symptoms of Bright's Disease include hypertension and loss of energy. It was a cold night, she was middle aged, and she had just slept off a massive drinking spree in an uncomfortable police cell. Given the above factors, Catharine cannot have been feeling too sprightly. Any journey on foot would be slow, yet we know this murder was committed within 40 minutes of Eddowes's release from custody.

Once in Mitre Square, in between PC Watkin's regular 15 minute patrol, Jack, with meticulous timing, murdered his victim, slashed her face, nicked her lower eyelids as though creating the face of a clown, and then carried out time-consuming surgery on his victim. He cut away a large piece of the intestine and placed it alongside the body. The uterus and a kidney were removed; although the kidney is buried deep in the body, and is not easy to find, Jack completed his work in seven to eight minutes at the most.

Having finished his butchery, Jack, no doubt bloodstained, and with human organs in his pocket or in a bag, escaped through an area where the police had already been alerted by the earlier killing. He must have walked past late-night revellers, yet no one, police or public, caught a glimpse of him.

Other puzzles began to emerge. Catharine's last recorded words to the policeman on duty were, 'I'll get a damn fine hiding when I get home.' She clearly remembered that she had promised to meet John Kelly eleven hours earlier, which predisposes rational thinking, although the remark had most likely been made in jest. A Frederick Wilkinson testified at the inquest that Eddowes and Kelly were '. . . always on very good terms'. They quarrelled occasionally, Wilkinson conceded, but '. . . not violently.' Eddowes, as we have seen, was not well, and, on the night in question, she would have been suffering from a hangover following her extreme intoxication of a few hours earlier. Close friends would have us believe that she was not a promiscuous woman, and the night of 30 September was cold and wet. Women had been warned to stay off the East End streets after sunset – and following the horrific murders not many warnings were needed. So why, when this set of circumstances should have sent her scurrying towards safety, did Catharine, once released from Bishopsgate Police Station, head off in a different direction from John Kelly's lodgings? After the day's lively experiences, the logical thing to do would be to head straight towards her partner. Better a possible quarrel with her lover than a meeting with Jack.

* * * * *

Londoners, their blood already chilled by the murders, now had to endure a series of frightening letters – and a message chalked on a wall at Goulston Street.

The Goulston Street beat was trodden by Police Constable Alfred Long. At approximately 2.15 a.m. on the night of the double murder, the constable passed Wentworth Model Dwellings, tenement buildings in Goulston Street; nothing out of the ordinary caught his attention. Retreading his beat at approximately 3. 00 a.m., PC Long noticed a piece of bloodstained apron near the base of common stairs leading to apartments 108/119 of the model dwellings. Later tests proved the fragment had been cut from Catharine Eddowes's apron. Jack had passed along Goulston

Street, and thrown away his memento.

Written in chalk on the wall above the apron, were the words 'The Juwes are the men that will not be blamed for nothing.' Was Jack anti-Semitic, trying to put the blame for his terrible deeds onto the Jewish race, in order to start riots?

That, apparently, was the belief of Sir Charles Warren. On hearing of the graffiti, Sir Charles immediately headed to the East End, and personally washed the message from the wall. The Commissioner was backed in his actions by Superintendent Thomas Arnold, who wrote in his Home Office report:

'Knowing in consequence of suspicion having fallen upon a Jew named John Pizer, alias "Leather Apron", having committed a murder in Hanbury Street a short time previously, a strong feeling existed against Jews generally . . .'

A relevant personal letter from Sir Charles Warren proves of great interest.

'. . . The most pressing question at that moment was some writing on the wall in Goulston Street evidently written with the intention of inflaming the public mind against the Jews, and which Mr Arnold with a view to prevent serious disorder proposed to obliterate . . .

'I considered it desirable that I should decide this matter myself . . .

'I accordingly went down to Goulston Street at once before going to the scene of the murder: it was just getting light, the public would be in the streets in a few minutes, in a neighbourhood very much crowded on Sunday mornings by Jewish vendors and Christian purchasers from all parts of London.

'There were several Police around the spot when I arrived, both Metropolitan and City.

'The writing was on the jamb of the open archway or doorway visible to anyone in the street, and could not be covered up without the danger of the covering being torn off at once.

'A discussion took place whether the writing could be left covered up or otherwise or whether any portion of it could be left for an hour until it could be photographed: but after taking into consideration the excited state of the population in London generally at the time, the strong feelings which existed against the Jews, and the fact that in a short time there would be a large concourse of the people in the streets, and having before me the Report that if it was left there the house was likely to be wrecked (in which from my observation I entirely concurred), I considered it desirable to obliterate the writing at once, having taken a copy of which I enclose a duplicate . . .'

Those sentiments appear to be clear enough, although surely, with a police guard, any covering would *not* have been torn down until photographers arrived.

There has been much discussion in regard to the authenticity and the meaning of this chalked message, but, to date, no satisfactory explanation on either count has been reached by any researcher.

* * * * *

A flood of obscene letters now began to arrive at newspaper offices, police stations and the Central News Agency. Amongst these letters was one which instantly wiped away the killer's nickname of 'Leather Apron' and replaced it with one of the world's most famous soubriquets. The letter, written in red ink, and dated 25 September 1888, stated:

'Dear Boss,

'I keep on hearing the police have caught me but they wont fix me just yet. I have laughed when they look so clever and talk about being on the right track. That joke about Leather Apron gave me real fits. I am down on whores and I shant quit ripping them till I do get buckled.

'Grand work the last one was. I gave the lady no time to squeal. How can they catch me now. I love my work and want to start again. You will soon hear of me with my funny little games. I saved some of the proper red stuff in a ginger beer bottle over the last job to write with, but it went thick like glue, and I cant use it. Red ink is fit enough I hope ha. ha. The next job I do I shall clip the ladys ears off and send to the police officers just for jolly wouldnt you. Keep this letter back till I do a bit more work, then give it out straight. My knife's so nice and sharp I want to get to work right away if I get a chance. Good luck. Yours truly,

Jack the Ripper'

A postscript read: 'Don't mind me giving my trade name.' Then at right angles underneath the main text was written: 'wasnt good enough to post this before I got all the red ink off my hands curse it. No luck yet. They say I'm a doctor now ha ha.' After the double murder a postcard, postmarked 1 October, was received with the same 'trade name':

'I was not codding dear old boss when I gave you the tip, you'll hear about saucy Jackys work tomorrow double event this time number one squealed a bit couldnt finish straight off. had not time to get ears for police thanks for keeping last letter back till I got to work again, Jack the Ripper.'

A flood of imitative material (around 1,000 letters weekly), much of it from cranks, poured into police stations and newspaper offices. These missives, combined with the general ambience of butchery and blood which surrounded the unsolved crimes, and the publicity of the Jack the Ripper letters, sent a tidal wave of terror across the whole of London. Music halls emptied overnight, locksmiths sold out of their wares, and one old lady died of terror, the evening paper which recorded Jack's latest deeds clutched in her hands.

One of the few interesting letters from the flood of material sent to the newspapers was recorded by J. Hall Richardson in his book *From The City To Fleet Street*.

'Liverpool, 29th inst. Beware, I shall be at work on 1st and 2nd Inst. in Minories at twelve midnight, and I give the authorities a good chance but there is never a policeman near when I am at work. Yours

Jack the Ripper.'

This letter was posted in Liverpool and is now unfortunately missing. The interesting fact is that the 'Dear Boss' letter, with the new soubriquet 'Jack the Ripper' was not published in the papers until 1 October 1888, so how did the writer of the 'Minories' letter know about the name on 29 September? And, as the authors of the *A to Z* so rightly ask, what did the writer mean by stating in a letter dated 29 September that he would be at work on 1st and 2nd inst. [meaning 'of the same month'.] It does not make sense to send a letter stating that you will be committing an outrage four weeks after a given date has passed. At present there is no explanation for this strange conundrum.

As the weeks rolled by, the popular press continued to fan the fires of hysteria. The *East London Advertiser* opined:

'It is so impossible to account, on any ordinary hypothesis, for these revolting acts of blood that the mind turns as it were instinctively to some theory of occult force, and the myths of the Dark Ages arise before the imagination.'

In early September, a Vigilance Committee had been formed, under the presidency of a George Lusk. He was a prominent local businessman. Lusk, and other members of his committee, were no doubt concerned by the murders, but they must also have been concerned about the dramatic drop in trade brought about by Jack's activities.

On 16 October 1888 Mr Lusk received, through the post, a small cardboard box wrapped in brown paper. The box contained part of a kidney, initially assumed to be that of an animal. But on examination, the kidney was discovered to be part of a human body. Dr Frederick Brown, the doctor who had carried out the autopsy on Catharine Eddowes, had declared that her remaining kidney had showed signs of Bright's Disease. (To repeat: 'Pale, bloodless, with a slight congestion at the base of the pyramid.') The kidney which had been sent through the post did indeed show signs of Bright's Disease. And the organ Lusk received was attached to one inch of renal tissue, which would have left two inches of gut remaining in Catharine's body. Two inches of renal tissue did remain in Catharine's body. There is a strong assembly of informed opinion which believes that the kidney was indeed from Catharine – a genuine gift from Jack the Ripper, along with a letter from the murderer. This letter read:

'From hell. Mr Lusk.

Sor,

I send you half the kidne I took from one woman prasarved it for you tother piece I fried and ate it was very nise I may send you the bloody knif that took it out if you only wate a while longer

      signed   Catch me when

                          you can

                                Mishter Lusk.'

London's panic continued to grow.

Suggestions on how to catch the murderer began to pour into Scotland Yard. One bright spark opined that the next woman approached by Jack should surreptitiously stick a piece of paper on the fiend's back, thus marking him out for the police. No brave lady volunteered to stroll along the dark alleys, sticky paper in her hands, waiting to be approached by the monster.

Further discrepancies arose. When Major Henry Smith, the acting Commissioner for the City of London Police, was told about the Goulston Street graffiti, he rushed to the area, although Goulston Street was just outside the City boundaries, and therefore within the jurisdiction of the Metropolitan Commissioner, Sir Charles Warren.

The writing had been erased by the time Smith arrived on the scene. The Major, undaunted, went sleuthing around the East End. In a public sink in Dorset Street, he found blood-tinged water still running down the drain. The Major always believed that he was within minutes of catching Jack the Ripper, ignoring the fact that the bloody piece of apron had been dropped at least an hour earlier. Jack was hardly likely to have been wandering around the area, hands dripping with blood, dodging the increasing police activity. But who had been washing blood from their hands in a public sink in the early hours of the morning? We shall return to this subject later in the text.

Despite a massive police presence in the East End, and the arrest and questioning of hundreds of men, the Ripper remained at large. The public waited in abject terror, and, on the night of 9 November 1888 Jack murdered again. It was to be his most savage and revolting attack.

Chapter Seven

Mary Kelly

Commercial Street in 1888 was exactly what its name implies, a crowded, busy street choked with market stalls, shops, pavement vendors and horse-drawn traffic.

A public house, *The Britannia*, whose main frontage was on Commercial Street, curved into Dorset Street, which was a notoriously dangerous area, its dozens of cheap lodging houses frequented by a wide variety of the lower social mixes, including violent criminals. Any policeman foolish enough to follow a suspect into Dorset Street was likely to be set upon, and his life might be in danger.

There was an arched passageway between 26 and 27 Dorset Street which led to Miller's Court, a cul-de-sac of six houses, three on either side. A rear room at 26 Dorset Street had been partitioned off, and an entrance (designated number 13, the unlucky number) had been constructed in Miller's Court, the door to this separation being immediately behind the arched passageway. 13 Miller's Court was rented by Mary Kelly, a young, attractive, blonde, blue-eyed prostitute. She paid her rent weekly, and thus had no need to search out a doss-house each night.

Mary was born in Ireland, into a large family. The Kellys were apparently affluent and middle-class. They moved to Wales when Mary was a youngster, and she is said to have spoken fluent Welsh.

In a Press Association report, a Mrs Carthy, a former landlady of Mary's, described her as academically bright and artistically talented from a family of good standing. Joe Barnett, Mary's last lover, confirmed that account. Maybe this is all true – very few solid facts are available about Mary's early life, but she certainly appears to have had the positive forces of confidence and enterprise which a comfortable upbringing tends to imbue.

When Kelly was sixteen, she married a man named Davies – we do not know his first name – who was killed in a mine explosion several years later. After this tragedy his young widow moved to Cardiff, where she began to work as a prostitute. Such an early fall from grace would point towards a typically youthful rebellion against family life; an extravagant use, and need of, money; or simply a powerful sexual drive which required constant fulfilment. Such an early marriage might point towards the latter.

In 1884 Mary moved from Cardiff to London, a move which is easy to comprehend. London, with its enlarged opportunities, its reputation of glamour and of streets paved with gold, would have been an understandable magnet for an attractive, ambitious girl with loose morals, such as Mary. It is, therefore, a major mystery as to how a moderately well-bred young lady ended up living and working in the East End of London. Whitechapel (and its surrounding districts) was an area where, in the main, drab, sad, middle-aged women tended to ply their trade. But an attractive and fully-fledged prostitute – and Mary had been that for some years – could have made a substantial living, and led a more comfortable lifestyle, in the salubrious surroundings of the West End of London, an area in which Mary is said initially to have worked.

According to Joe Barnett (her last lover), once in London, Mary was introduced to a rich man who took her on trips to France. This life of luxury had reputedly been arranged by a West End madame. So why, after only approximately 18 months of high living, did an engaging young woman end up amongst the unfortunate dregs of society? Did alcohol addiction aid Mary's rapid descent from West to East?

* * * * *

After reaching the nadir of the East End, Mary lived with several men. First there was an unnamed builder, then a man known only as Morganstone (possibly Morgan Stone), and then a tradesman, Joseph Fleming. In 1887 Kelly met Joe Barnett, and there was obviously an instant mutual attraction, since, within days, after one more meeting, they had formed an alliance and started living together, a state of affairs which continued for eighteen months. They initially lodged together at various addresses including Brick Lane, one of the toughest parts of East London, before moving to the now famous, ill-fated lodgings in Miller's Court, the address at which the fifth Ripper murder was destined to take place.

Barnett, who was aged around thirty, was, so far as one can glean, a decent, hard working fellow, but nonetheless a man certainly at the reverse end of the social scale from the admirer who used to pay for Mary's trips to France. But Barnett's probable decency has not stopped him from becoming a recent 'Ripper' suspect, on the flimsy grounds that by murdering prostitutes and causing a panic, he would keep his lover off the streets.

If this had been Barnett's strategy it clearly failed.

Mary was reported as being on the streets up to a few hours before the Ripper visited her room. And if the violent murders had continued they would have been more likely to drive Mary back into a bordello, which, for obvious reasons, was safer. Alternatively, any continuing violence might have made her leave the country. It was reported in the newspapers that Mary spoke of leaving London several times during the Ripper murders.

Part of the case against Barnett is that he was jealous of Mary's associations with other men. A Miller's Court neighbour, Julia Venturney, said that Barnett did not care for Kelly being on the streets. This has been turned into something sinister by certain theorists, but might not his objections have been due to concern for his lover's safety once the Ripper murders had started? The fact is that Barnett was not in the least bit possessive. He had met Mary whilst she was soliciting, so he knew what she was up to; and he was the person who told the inquest about his girlfriend's string of former lovers. Barnett alleged that one of these men continued to call on Mary. He was clearly not jealous, which entirely removes the basis of Barnett's indictment as the murderer. And, of course, had Barnett been the murderer, there would have been no cover-up by the authorities: more of that later.

The couple lived together in apparent harmony, although, at Mary's inquest, Barnett admitted that they did have rows which 'were soon over'. In November 1888 they had a violent argument in which a window pane got broken. From Mary's perceived character it is not unreasonable to suspect that it was her quick temper which led to the violent incident.

Joe was variously a dockside labourer and a market porter, but he became unemployed in the mid-1880s, which was not uncommon for Victorian workers without the protection of strong, influential unions or the enforcement of employment laws.

This must have been a difficult time for the unemployed Barnett. Life with Mary had grown tempestuous, and at some point, following the usual pattern of the Ripper victims, the relationship broke up. Two theories account for this parting. One story asserts that Mary, due to the loss of Barnett's wages, had returned to soliciting, and that the return to her old ways caused the rift. There is, however, no firm evidence that Mary ever broke away from her chosen profession in the first place.

A second, more interesting view of Joe's departure, asserts that he left Mary because she insisted on having other prostitutes (note the plural) in to live with them during the last few weeks they were together. This act led to charges against Mary of lesbianism, a not uncommon leaning in street women. Joe refused to share the single Miller's Court room, not to mention the one bed, with a second female, and so the couple split up.

This episode I find distinctly strange. There is no evidence of strong emotional ties between Mary and women until a few weeks before the end of the Ripper murders. After eighteen months of close association with her lover, Mary must have known that Barnett would not tolerate other women living with them. So quite clearly she knew that her actions would drive him away. Mary appears to have been trying to get Joe to leave their lodgings. Why? This is a question which will be discussed in a later chapter.

On the Wednesday, two days before her death, Mary bought a candle from her landlord's shop in Dorset Street. This was found in her room, half burnt, after the murder. Later on that same day she was sighted by Thomas Bowyer (an employee of her landlord) accompanied by a man in his late twenties; this man had a 'dark moustache and very peculiar eyes' and 'was very smartly dressed' said Mr Bowyer. The man was never identified.

Paul Begg, a leading Ripper expert who has written extensively on the crimes, remarked to me, with reference to this sighting: 'There is no reason why Mary should not have consorted with upper class men, but to find one of them visiting her in such an area as Miller's Court is very strange indeed.' Precisely. Well dressed people visited the East End frequently, but they would have kept to certain areas. Few would have been foolish enough to visit such a violent area as Dorset Street, even during daylight hours, so who was this man? And was he conducting only a sexual arrangement with Mary? On Friday, the eve of Kelly's death, Joe Barnett visited Miller's Court, where he found Mary entertaining a female whom he did not know. Later investigations proved the woman to have been Lizzie Albrook, a friend, and, as she was apparently unknown to Barnett, only a recent neighbour of Mary's.

Shortly after 8.00 p.m. Barnett left Kelly and returned to his new lodgings, where he played cards until after midnight before going to bed.

One testimony of Mary's movements on the night of her murder is important, but full of inconsistencies: George Hutchinson, a typical, unemployed, impecunious East Ender, who claimed to know Mary well, stated that he met her in Commercial Street at 2.00 a.m. on the night of her death. She asked to borrow sixpence, but he did not have any money. Mary moved off towards Thrawl Street, which Hutchinson had just passed on his way to lodgings in Commercial Street. George presumably turned around and watched Mary, although why, after a short conversation with a prostitute in the early hours, he should turn and wait and watch the lady walk away, when the night was cold and wet, and he was hurrying home, is puzzling. But there are many puzzles in Mr Hutchinson's testimony.

As Mary reached Thrawl Street, a man coming in the opposite direction stopped and spoke to her. After a short conversation the couple moved towards him, and passed by, and Hutchinson 'stooped down' in order to see the man closely. He described Mary's companion in minute detail:

'. . . age about 34 or 35, height 5 foot 6 inches, complexion pale. Dark eyes and dark lashes. Slight moustache curled up each end and hair dark. Very surly looking. Dress, long dark coat, collar and cuffs trimmed with astrakhan and a dark jacket under, light waistcoat, dark trousers, dark felt hat turned down in the middle, button boots and gaiters with white buttons, wore a very thick gold chain, white linen collar, black tie with horseshoe pin, respectable appearance, walked very sharp, Jewish appearance. Can be identified.'

For a one second glance under the brim of a hat, in a badly lit street, on a rainy night, this is a miraculously detailed description.

How, in such poor conditions, with the man's head bent, could Hutchinson notice 'dark lashes'?

The couple went into Dorset Street, and Hutchinson, in the early hours of the morning, presumably tired, in cold, wet weather, turned away from his own lodgings and followed the couple. This seems irrational behaviour. If he had hoped for Mary's favours for himself, he would, presumably, have fallen into step and moved off with her after their earlier conversation. But it was not until she had been taken up by another man that he turned and followed her.

Hutchinson then watched the couple standing outside Miller's Court for about three minutes, after which they both went into the Court. Hutchinson subsequently stood in bad weather for three quarters of an hour watching for the man's reappearance. Around 3.00 a.m., his patience exhausted, the spy gave up and returned home. If he had been concerned about Mary taking up with a stranger in the wake of the Ripper murders, Hutchinson now took no steps towards her safety. No police were called, but then why should they be? There was nothing suspicious about a prostitute entertaining a client all night, and the customer appeared eminently respectable, so Hutchinson's watch was purposeless if concern for Kelly was to be a motive.

Hutchinson's statement was not made to the police until 6.00 p.m. on the 12 November. This was the most perverse timing, as Mary's inquest was held on that exact date, and the proceedings had been concluded by 6.00 p.m. This meant that Hutchinson's evidence could not be closely questioned or examined further in court. Why did he (seemingly deliberately) wait until the inquest was over before coming forward? Could the extraordinary story be a fabrication which Hutchinson was encouraged to relate? And if so, who encouraged him? Why should anyone wish to spread such lies?

* * * * *

Apart from Hutchinson, several other people provided information about the period between 2.30 and 4.00 a.m., the hour in which Mary was thought to have been murdered, although there is no certainty about this estimate.

Mary Ann Cox, a resident of Miller's Court, returned home around midnight, and passed Mary Kelly (who was bareheaded and drunk) in the company of a shabbily-dressed man aged around mid-30s. As she passed the couple, Mrs Cox heard Kelly say, 'I am going to sing.' She then began to do so. Mrs Cox, a prostitute, quickly returned to soliciting, and Kelly was still singing as Cox left the court. After half an hour, another neighbour, Catherine Picket, became irritated by the noise, but her husband prevented her from going to protest. Kelly was still singing when Mrs Cox once more returned home, around 1.00 a.m.

Further conflicting evidence in this bizarre case then arose. Mrs Cox tried her luck on the streets once more and finally returned home at 3.00 a.m., later declaring that there was now no noise or sound from Mary's room: the remainder of the night was quiet. However, Mrs Elizabeth Prater, who lodged in a room directly above Kelly's, heard a cry of 'Oh murder' around 4.00 a.m. This cry was confirmed by another neighbour, Sarah Lewis, but as such cries were commonplace in the area both women ignored the call. They were wrong to do so: on this occasion, a murder was indeed being committed.

* * * * *

John McCarthy, from whose shop Mary had bought a candle two days before her death, was also her landlord. And Mary, amazingly, given the 'no credit' policy of the East End, had been allowed to run up arrears of 35 shillings on the rent of Miller's Court, a very large sum in 1888. Other less-favoured tenants had been turned out of doss-houses in the middle of the night because they could not produce fourpence. Indeed, Kelly and Barnett had been turned out of other lodgings because they could not pay the rent.

An immediate surmise of payment by sexual favours from Mary to her landlord might solve the problem, but it was Mrs McCarthy who usually dealt with the rents – presumably whilst her husband ran the shop: and Mrs McCarthy was a stickler for prompt payment, which makes Mary's arrears all the more puzzling.

Mid-morning on 9 November, McCarthy sent his employee, Thomas Bowyer, around to Miller's Court to ask Kelly for her rent. Just where the man thought Mary might have been able to obtain such a large sum of money as 35 shillings overnight (after all, he had seen her two days previously at the most) is not known. And why he should choose the very morning of Mary's death to try and collect his rent which was three months overdue is a further mystery.

Bowyer called around at 13 Miller's Court but his knock went unanswered. After trying, without success, to peer through the keyhole, and finding the door locked, he reached through the broken window pane, pulled back a flimsy curtain, and peered into the room. A mass of raw flesh lay on the bed surrounded by pools of blood on the floor. The corpse's stomach had been gutted, her intestines ripped out: her liver, breasts and various cuts of flesh lay near to, or under the body.

Bowyer, terrified, ran back and returned with Mr McCarthy, whose comments were recorded in *The Times*:

'The sight we saw . . . looked more like the work of a devil than a man. I had heard a great deal about the Whitechapel murders, but I do declare to God I never expected to see such a sight as this. The whole scene is more than I can describe.'

After the discovery of the body chaotic scenes occurred around Miller's Court and it is difficult to sort out fact from fiction and truth from rumour. Inspector Walter Beck was the first officer to be summoned to the scene as he was the senior officer on duty at the Commerical Road Station. (Several other policemen claimed that they were the first to be called.)

Reporters and crowds began to gather around Miller's Court, so Beck cordoned off the area and refused to answer any questions or to allow anyone to enter the murder site. This included the police surgeon, Dr Bagster Phillips; once again he was called out to a Ripper murder. He peered at the cadaver through the broken window and declared that all life was extinct, a statement which, as the corpse was literally hacked to pieces, any man, doctor or not, would have been able to make. Then, according to the reliable Paul Begg, Dr Phillips advised that no one should be allowed to enter the murder site until bloodhounds had been called in. The fact that a medical man was allowed to pontificate on police matters would indicate considerable indecisiveness on the part of Inspector Beck.

Policemen were posted outside the door of the murder room where they waited until 1.30 p.m. whilst a decision on calling in the dogs was sought from the Commissioner, Sir Charles Warren.

Even official photographers had to poke their cameras through the broken window and do their best under these unsatisfactory working conditions. Finally, having wasted the entire morning, with any possible clues which the murderer might have left growing colder by the minute, it was announced, with the most extraordinary timing, that Sir Charles Warren had resigned: as for the question of the bloodhounds – no dogs were available even if they had been needed, and if they *had* been available and *had* been needed they would not have been useful. No dog could have detected a single particular scent from the blood-drenched murder site. Farce had taken over the proceedings.

The authorities finally ordered McCarthy to break down the door of his premises. Why this action was thought necessary must be added to the lengthening list of mysteries in this case. The key to the door had been missing for some time, and Joe and Mary, to gain access to their premises, used to reach through the broken window pane and pull back a spring lock. Why were the police not able to follow the same routine?

A book, *The Ripper and The Royals* by Melvyn Fairclough, published in 1991, was based on the files of Joseph Sickert. Mr Sickert has claimed that he has extensive documents relating to the Ripper affair. Stephen Knight's work, which will be discussed later, was based on original material from Mr Sickert. In *The Ripper and The Royals*, it was claimed that the murderer, during his work on Kelly's body, had placed a heavy object behind the door. (Other researchers have also reported a heavy object placed behind the door, but I can find no trace of this in any official report of the affair.) This means that Jack, after his butchery, must have opened and crawled through the broken window. A heavy object behind the door might explain why the police ordered the door to be broken down instead of reaching in and working the spring lock. However, if Jack really did escape by climbing through the window, then he took a ridiculous risk. A blood-soaked figure, crawling out of a window in the middle of the night, with prostitutes continually on the prowl and with the local populace on the look-out for sinister activities would surely have invited discovery. On the other hand, a man leaving the door of a known prostitute's room would have caused little attention, so why did Jack, with all his cunning, not merely remove the heavy object when he wanted to escape? And if a heavy object had been placed before the door, why did the police not imitate the Ripper and climb in through the window? Smashing down the door might well have destroyed valuable clues. Further, there is an allegation that the room was entered a few hours after the murder – which would indicate no obstruction. One more Ripper mystery.

As the above shows, the initial investigation into Mary Kelly's murder involved a series of appalling errors on the part of the police. Dr Phillips presumably returned home after his brief adjudication, as a full on-site report on Kelly's body was produced by Dr Thomas Bond, once the authorities had given their belated permission for entry to the murder site. Dr Bond's report was highly detailed. His strange use of capital letters is reproduced in the extract below: was this a sign of mental strain showing in his handwriting? Dr Bond later committed suicide. His report from Miller's Court and his post mortem examination, stated:

'The body was lying naked in the middle of the bed, the shoulders flat, but the axis of the body inclined to the left side of the bed. The head was turned on the left cheek. The left arm was close to the body with the forearm flexed at right angles and lying across the abdomen. The right arm was slightly abducted from the body and rested on the mattress, the elbow bent and the forearm supine with the fingers clenched. The legs were wide apart, the left thigh at right angles to the trunk and the right forming an obtuse angle with the pubes.

'The whole of the surface of the abdomen and thighs was removed and the abdominal cavity emptied of its viscera. The breasts were cut off, the arms mutilated by several jagged wounds, and the face hacked beyond recognition of the features. The tissues of the neck were severed all round down to the bone.

'The viscera were found in various parts viz: the uterus and Kidneys with one breast under the head, the other breast by the Rt. foot, the Liver between the feet, the intestines by the right side and the spleen by the left side of the body. The flaps removed from the abdomen and thighs were on a table.

'The bed clothing at the right corner was saturated with blood, and on the floor beneath was a pool of blood covering about two feet square. The wall by the right side of the bed and in a line with the neck was marked by blood which had struck it in a number of separate splashes.

Post-mortem examination:

'The face was gashed in all directions the nose, cheeks, eyebrows and ears being partly removed. The lips were blanched and cut by several incisions running obliquely down to the chin. There were also numerous cuts extending irregularly across all the features.

'The neck was cut through the skin and other tissues right down to the vertebrae the 5th and 6th being deeply notched. The skin cuts in the front of the neck showed distinct ecchymosis. The air passage was cut at the lower part of the larynx through the cricoid cartilage.

'Both breasts were removed by more or less circular incisions, the muscles down to the ribs being attached to the breasts. The intercostal between the 4th 5th and 6th ribs were cut through, and the contents of the thorax visible through the openings.

'The skin and tissues of the abdomen from the costal arch to the pubes were removed in three large flaps. The right thigh was denuded in front to the bone, the flap of skin, including the external organs of generation and part of the right buttock. The left thigh was stripped of skin, fascia and muscles as far as the knee.

'The left calf showed a long gash through skin and tissues to the deep muscles and reaching from the knee to 5 ins above the ankle.

'Both arms and forearms had extensive and jagged wounds. The right thumb showed a small superficial incision about 1 ins long, with extravasation of blood in the skin and there were several abrasions on the back of the hand moreover, showing the same condition.

'On opening the thorax it was found that the right lung was minimally adherent by old firm adhesions. The lower part of the lung was broken and torn away.

'The left lung was intact: it was adherent at the apex and there were a few adhesions over the side. In the substances of the lung were several nodules of consolidation.

'The Pericardium was open below and the Heart absent. In

the abdominal cavity was some partly digested food of fish and potatoes, and similar food was found in the remains of the stomach attached to the intestines.'

The inflicting of such mutilations must have taken some considerable time, but again, no one heard or saw anything in the least bit suspicious. Once more the Ripper appeared to have melted away into thin air. In the grate there were signs that a fierce fire had been blazing, hot enough to melt the spout-solder of a kettle. Burnt clothing, including the brim of a woman's bonnet, was found in the grate. A passer-by would only have had to see the reflection of the flames on the curtain and reach through the broken window to witness the Ripper at work. No one did so. The murderer's extraordinary run of luck had continued.

As would be expected, the dramatic events in Miller's Court produced a flood of anecdotal evidence about Mary Kelly. People who knew her rushed to the press with quotes. Tom Cullen relates in his book, *Autumn of Terror*, that Kelly's nickname was 'Black Mary', and if this did not perversely allude to her conspicuously fair colouring then it must have referred to her character. John McCarthy, her landlord, said that she was very noisy when she had taken drink, but otherwise she was a quiet woman. This statement was confirmed by Elizabeth Phoenix who knew Mary from a past lodging house. She declared that Kelly was quarrelsome and abusive when drunk but very pleasant when sober. Mary's quick temper can be further confirmed by reiterating the violent argument with Joe Barnett – violent enough to break a window in their Miller's Court lodgings.

Tom Cullen, whilst writing his aforementioned book, *Autumn of Terror*, talked to a retired market porter, Dennis Barrett, who claimed that as a young man he had known Mary Kelly. Mr Barrett's description of the lady would, without doubt, have earned her the nickname Black Mary. He stated that if any woman tried to intrude on Kelly's territory then the woman would be violently attacked and stood the risk of having her hair pulled out in handfuls.

Tom Cullen was writing some thirty years ago, and he was enterprising enough to track down people who had been alive at the time of the Ripper murders. This research has provided some fascinating information.

'Black Mary was no stranger to the Britannia. Many was the time she had rushed into this pub after rolling some drunken sailor, to swop shawls with one of the whores there. Thus disguised, she would take to the streets again, knowing that the police would be looking for her under a different disguise,' Mr Cullen writes. The writer of *Tornado Down*, William Pearson, assures me that it was common practise for prostitutes to change both clothing and names to outwit the police.

Presumably Mary, if she were not just dodging the police but dodging danger, would have been devious enough to make this change-over of clothing appear to be done as a favour ('Try on my shawl, it really goes with that dress,' or some such excuse). She would not have disclosed the real reason for her generosity.

At Kelly's inquest, Joe Barnett revealed that Mary had once lived and worked in the notorious Ratcliffe Highway area near to the East End Docks. Ratcliffe had once been renowned for its collection of shops which housed wild beasts; sailors would visit the place to barter their pets and animals which they had brought from far-away places. In 1811 London had been struck dumb with terror by a series of murders which took place in this dangerous area. Mr Marr, a shopkeeper, and his wife were found savagely murdered at 29 Ratcliffe Highway. A shop-boy and a baby in its cradle were also found dead in other parts of the dwelling. Twelve days after this bloodbath, the landlord of a public house in Old Gravel Lane, Ratcliffe was found savagely beaten to death along with his wife and a female servant. These violent affairs faded from memory, perhaps because the murderer, a sailor named Williams, was caught.

It was in the Ratcliffe area that sailors were most likely to be lured into a dark place and robbed, so Mary, whilst she was living around there, might well have joined in the local sport by violently accosting her clients.

So, reading between the lines of various reports on the lady, Mary appears to have been somewhat of a Jekyll and Hyde character.

The usual pattern of searching, arresting, questioning and releasing followed by more of the same was carried out by the police after Kelly's murder. At one point Joe Barnett was arrested. He was questioned closely and his clothing was carefully examined, but Barnett had an alibi. He had been with company, playing cards all evening at his new lodgings on the night that Mary had been murdered. The police checked this out, and were eventually convinced that Barnett was not guilty of his lover's murder.

It quickly became clear that once again Jack had evaded capture.

Chapter Eight

Cover-Up?

We must now re-address the question, 'Was Jack the Ripper a man from the upper classes of Victorian society?' There is a long-standing belief, which has reached the status of a minor myth, that certain highly placed members of the Victorian Police Force had undisclosed information regarding the Ripper killings and the murderer's identity. Is it conceivable that members of Scotland Yard's hierarchy might have joined forces to organise a cover-up, and if so, why?

The obvious answer to that question is that the Victorian Establishment, for reasons of its own, wished to protect a member of the upper classes. Obviously this would have to be a man of great importance. I believe this general assumption to be correct, and I am not alone in such a belief; it is a suspicion which stretches back to the beginning of the affair. In November 1888 the *Star* wrote :

'We have heard the wildest stories . . . it is believed by people who pass among their neighbours as sensible folk that the Government do not want the murderer to be convicted, that they are interested in concealing his identity . . .'

Paul Begg, in his book *Jack the Ripper: The Uncensored Facts* wrote: 'Beyond question, there was something very strange going on after the murders of Elizabeth Stride and Catharine Eddowes. On 1 October, the *Evening News* reported: 'The police are extraordinarily reticent with reference to the Mitre Square tragedy.' The *Yorkshire Post* on the same date reported: 'The police apparently have strict orders to close all channels of information to the press.' Even the *New York Times* on 1 October was moved to complain of the police that, 'they devote their entire energies to preventing the press from getting at the facts. They deny reporters a sight of the scene or bodies, and give them no information whatever.'

After such criticism, there was a complete reversal of this

stance by the police. The *Manchester Guardian* reported on 2 October:

'The barrier of reticence which has been set up on all occasions when the representatives of the newspaper press have been brought into contact with the police authorities for the purpose of obtaining information for the use of the public has been suddenly withdrawn, and instead of the customary stereotyped negatives and disclaimers of the officials, there has ensued a marked disposition to afford all necessary facilities for the publication of details and increased courtesy towards the members of the press concerned.'

To repeat Mr Begg's words: 'Beyond question there was something very strange going on after the murders of Elizabeth Stride and Catharine Eddowes.'

My only query about this statement would be to question whether a cover-up started earlier than the third and fourth murders.

My late friend Stephen Knight also firmly believed in a cover-up. In his celebrated book *Jack the Ripper: The Final Solution*, published in 1976, Knight cites the authorities' conduct as being suspicious as early as the Chapman inquest. There is no doubt that the conduct of the police surgeon Dr Bagster Phillips, when called to give evidence, was evasive. He clearly did not wish to reveal pertinent facts about Chapman's injuries. The coroner Wynne Baxter was moved to say:

'Dr Phillips, whatever may be your opinion and objections, it appears to me necessary that all the evidence that you ascertained from the postmortem examination should be on the records of the court for various reasons which I need not enumerate. However painful it may be, it is necessary in the interests of justice.'

Yet by the the time of the third Ripper victim's inquest (Liz Stride) on 3 October, Baxter, who was again presiding, appears to have been much more lax. As we have seen, on 30 November 1888 Chief Inspector Swanson took evidence from the immigrant, Israel Schwartz. Let us repeat this man's evidence, as it is so important. Schwartz claimed that at 12.45 a.m. he had turned into Berner Street from the Commercial Road, and, Swanson recorded:

'. . . having got as far as the gateway where the murder was committed, he saw a man stop and speak to a woman who was standing in the gateway. The man tried to pull the woman into the street, but he turned her round and threw her down on the footway and the woman screamed three times, but not very loudly. On crossing to the opposite side of the street, he saw a second man lighting his pipe. The man who threw the woman down called out, apparently to the man on the opposite side of the road, 'Lipski', and then Schwartz walked away, but finding that he was followed by the second man, he ran so far as the railway arch, but the man did not follow so far . . .'

This statement was in the hands of the police during the extended inquest on Liz Stride, but at no time was Schwartz called on to give evidence. Now Schwartz was the only person in the land who possibly saw the Ripper about to begin work: he was the only person who could possibly identify the infamous murderer, a murderer who was being desperately hunted by every policeman in London. This makes the man's evidence absolutely vital, yet, astoundingly, let me repeat, *Schwartz was not called to give that evidence in court*. There could be no clearer sign of a cover-up by the authorities.

Matthew Packer, who claimed to have sold grapes to a man in the company of Stride shortly before her murder was not called upon to give evidence in court either, yet the police considered him important enough to be interviewed personally by Sir Charles Warren.

Mrs Mortimer's evidence, even if evaluated negatively (that she did not see anything out of the ordinary), might have been useful, but she too was not called upon to give evidence. And this limiting of justice occurred at an inquest presided over by Wynne Baxter. It is difficult to believe that Mr Baxter was not at least informed about Israel Schwartz, so why did this normally inquisitive man, a stickler for correct procedures, not insist that such an important witness be summoned to appear? We shall never know whether or not Baxter was involved in a plot, but, quite clearly, a cover-up of some sort, by unknown persons, for unknown reasons, was in place during the Ripper murder investigations.

Other writers have voiced that concern. Martin Howells and Keith Skinner in *The Ripper Legacy*, published in 1987, wrote:

'Edwin Thomas Woodhall, writing in the mid-1930s admits when talking of his own particular search for Jack the Ripper that his main difficulty had been the minimal assistance from those concerned with the crimes.'

Woodhall was not writing without considerable experience. He was, at various times, a member of the CID, the Special Branch and The Secret Service. These appointments should have given him unique access to restricted information.

Stephen Knight further cites the Coroner's conduct during the inquest into Mary Kelly's death as evidence of something highly suspicious. It certainly was. Indeed, Roderick MacDonald's conduct at this fifth inquiry was so peculiar several newspapers of the day made their own comments. Immediately after the abrupt termination of proceedings, the *Daily Telegraph* wrote:

'Much surprise is expressed that the inquest should have been closed before an opportunity was given to the relatives of the deceased to identify the body. As they are believed to reside in Ireland, there was some delay to be expected in finding them. It is in the power of the Attorney general to apply to the High Court of Justice to hold a new inquest, if he is satisfied that there has been rejection of evidence, irregularity of proceedings, or insufficiency of inquiry . . .'

The inquest into Kelly's death is so esssential in piecing together the truth about the Ripper murders that we need to examine it in great detail.

This controversial affair was conducted by Coroner Roderick MacDonald, a distinguished former police surgeon. As such, he had given evidence at many proceedings similar to the Kelly inquest, and must, therefore, have known the court procedure better than most other members of the judiciary. Yet the Coroner did not enquire whether any parts of the body were missing. There was no attempt to discover the extent of the body's injuries, and no attempt to discover any details of the weapon which was used to kill Mary.

King Edward The First, who reigned from 1272 to 1307, was a renowned law-maker, although he did not care to be personally held in check by his kingdom's legal system. It was Edward who first established the office of Justice of the Peace and, as Tom Cullen rightly points out, it was during Edward's reign that laws were enacted which made it mandatory to note, in cases of death, all injuries to the body, the depth and extent of all wounds and the weapon which caused the injuries. MacDonald failed in all these requirements, and, by neglecting to uncover such basic and important details, he broke the law of the land. Mary Kelly's inquest opened with the now famous argument between MacDonald and an unnamed, independently-minded juror who voiced a strong opinion:

Juror.   I do not see why we should have the inquest thrown on our shoulders, when the murder did not happen in our district, but in Whitechapel.

Hammond.   (Coroner's officer) It did not happen in Whitechapel.

MacDonald. Do you think that we do not know what we are doing here? The jury are summoned in the ordinary way, and they have no business to object. If they persist in their objection I shall know how to deal with them. Does any Juror persist in objecting?

Juror.   We are summoned for the Shoreditch District. This affair happened in Spitalfields.

Coroner.   It happened within my district.

Second Juror. This is not my district. I come from Whitechapel and Mr. Baxter is my coroner.

MacDonald. I am not going to discuss the subject with the jurymen at all. If any juryman says he distinctly objects, let him say so. I may tell the jurymen that jurisdiction lies where the body lies, not where it was found.

There is conflicting evidence over MacDonald's assertion that he had every right to preside over the inquest. The affair appears to have been an administrative nightmare, difficult to understand even today. Stephen Knight asserted that the authorities were wrong. He saw this contretemps as an attempt by the authorities to take the case away from that meticulous searcher after the truth Coroner Wynne Baxter, but, as we have already seen, Mr Baxter appears to have slackened his enquiries by the time of the third inquest.

So what is the truth in this complicated legal matter? In *The Jack the Ripper A to Z* Paul Begg and his associates Martin Fido and Keith Skinner all appear to have cleared up the puzzle in their usual efficient manner. The *A to Z* claims that the affair may have been an administrative anomaly. The juror was correct in thinking that the murder site in Spitalfields was normally under the jurisdiction of Whitechapel, but, apparently, this jurisdiction did not include coroners' inquests, which came under the jurisdiction of Northeastern Middlesex: this would mean that MacDonald was rightfully holding the inquest, unless the Shoreditch authorities had refused to pay the mortuary expenses for Mary Kelly, who died outside their jurisdiction. Such legalities are difficult to understand, even when read over several times, so these complex arguments would have been even more difficult for Victorian working men to understand. Why, therefore, did MacDonald not try to explain to the jurors, as simply as possible, the legal arguments, instead of snapping at them?

The affair obviously rattled the coroner, because once the spat was over he returned to the subject, castigating the newspapers for making such a fuss over the inquest's change of venue, and adding that Kelly's body was, without doubt, within his jurisdiction, and there the matter would end. Quite a storm in a teacup.

Whatever the legality of MacDonald's appointment, there is a marvellous arrogance inherent in the Coroner's language. 'The jury are summoned in the ordinary way, and they *have no business to object.*' Why not? MacDonald then threatens the jury. 'If they persist in their objection, I shall know how to deal with them.' How? 'I am not going to discuss the subject with the jurymen at all.' Why not?

If we continue to examine this strange and significant inquest in more detail other puzzling aspects emerge.

Inspector Abberline led the jury to the mortuary where Mary's mutilated body lay. Apart from her slashed, unrecognisable face, she was covered by a dirty sheet which was not removed for the jury to see her wounds. That restricted viewing could only have proved that there was a faceless corpse lying in the mortuary and nothing else. The jury were next shown the murder site, which might have been of some importance in their deliberations, although, due to the police bungling after the discovery of the body, some clues may well have been destroyed. After this tour the jury returned to the town hall to hear evidence.

Joe Barnett, as we have seen, discussed his relationship with

Mary. There was one pertinent question directed at Barnett. The Coroner asked whether there was anyone of whom Mary had been especially afraid. Barnett replied yes: he had read her everything about the Ripper murders, although he added there was no particular individual whom Mary feared.

If we think this statement through logically, it testified that Mary Kelly (and presumably all the other prostitutes in the area) was terrified of meeting Jack. Yet on the night of her death Kelly fearlessly walked the streets in the early hours, picking up men with impunity before taking them back to her lonely room. Why was she not afraid any more?

The inquest then heard an electrifying piece of evidence, which, in itself, should have heralded a lengthy, more probing investigation. A Mrs Caroline Maxwell, who lived in Dorset Street stated, under oath, that she had seen Kelly standing at the entrance to Miller's Court *at eight o'clock on the morning following Mary's supposed murder.* Medical evidence proved Kelly must have been dead for at least four hours prior to this supposed sighting.

Coroner. Did you speak to her?

Maxwell. Yes. It was unusual to see her up at that hour. I spoke across the street. 'What, Mary, brings you up so early?' She said, 'Oh Carrie, I do feel so bad.'

Coroner. And yet you say you had only spoken to her twice previously? You knew her name and she knew yours?

Maxwell. Oh yes, by being about in the lodging-house.

Coroner. What did she say?

Maxwell. She said, 'I've had a glass of beer, and I've brought it up again.' I imagine she had been in the Britannia beer shop on the corner. I left her saying that I could pity her feelings.

Coroner. Then what did you do?

Maxwell. I went to Bishopsgate to get my husband's breakfast.

Coroner. Did you see Kelly again?

Maxwell. Yes. When I returned I saw her outside the Britannia public house talking to a man.

Coroner. This would be about what time?

Maxwell. It was about a quarter to nine.

Mrs Maxwell maintained that she had been going to a shop in Bishopsgate which she did not use a great deal, and that made her certain of the time and date of her conversation with Mary. The shop later confirmed Mrs Maxwell's visit.

In November, *The Times* reported that a tailor, Maurice Lewis, a resident of Dorset Street, also claimed that he had seen Kelly briefly leave her room around eight o'clock on the morning after her supposed death. Mr Lewis maintained that later on that same day, at around ten o'clock in the morning, he had seen Kelly drinking in a local public house. *The Times* also reported that a young, unnamed lady claimed to the police that she had seen Mary Kelly alive and well around 8.oo and 8.30 a.m. after her 'murder'.

MacDonald most probably did not know of the other two supposed sightings of Mary after the time of her presumed death, but he nonetheless peremptorily dismissed Mrs Maxwell's assertions, and, after a day's hearing, to everyone's astonishment, closed the case.

'There is other evidence which I do not propose to call, for if we at once make public every fact brought forward in connection with this terrible murder the ends of justice might be retarded,' opined MacDonald.

As Tom Cullen asks in his book *Autumn of Terror* 'What did he mean by this extraordinary statement? . . . what were the police trying to hide?' What indeed?

MacDonald, after brazenly breaking the law by not establishing the full facts concerning Kelly's injuries and the weapon used to inflict them, then closed the inquest with indecent haste and with, to repeat the *Daily Telegraph*'s words 'undoubted insufficiency of evidence'. As a final insult, he failed (as *The Jack the Ripper A to Z* records) to complete or sign the certificate of findings to which the jurors' signatures had been appended. Did MacDonald, at the last moment, draw back from adding something so concrete and important as a signature to a document which recorded his bizarre and unlawful handling of the case? There is an inherent reluctance in human beings to sign a false declaration – men have faced death rather than do so in the past. Did MacDonald have that same instinctive misgiving? Certainly the omission of a signature on so valuable a document, recording a case of such wide interest, is highly unusual.

It was in this air of rushed incompetence and illegality that

Mary Kelly's inquest was closed. The mutilated corpse was buried with considerable ceremony at St Patrick's Catholic Cemetery in Leytonstone. The funeral was attended by many of the residents of Miller's Court, and Joe Barnett was there, no doubt replete with memories.

One question which I find puzzling, and which, to the best of my knowledge, has never before been fully considered by any Ripper writer, concerns Mary Kelly's relatives.

In a November 1888 interview with a newspaper, Kelly's landlord, John McCarthy, revealed that Mary received correspondence from Ireland, letters which he understood were from Mary's mother.

Joe Barnett told Inspector Abberline that Mary had a brother, Henry, who served in the Scots Guards; he added that Henry had visited Mary. Now Kelly and Barnett had only been living together for eighteen months, which means that Mary, and at least one or two members of her family, were in touch almost to the end of her life. Considering that Mary was part of a large clan, and considering the world-wide publicity given to the case, it is strange in the extreme that not one of her relatives came forward, either after her death or after her funeral. No member of the family could be contacted despite a search. What had happened to the relatives? Why did they disappear without trace? Mary was reputed to have six or seven brothers and a sister. Surely one of them should have turned up to mourn their close relative? Not one of them did so. Why?

The authorities complacently accepted the rushed, one-day inquest into Kelly's complicated last night on earth, although, as the *Daily Telegraph* had pointed out, it was possible to recall witnesses and hold a new inquest. Mrs Maxwell's extraordinary testimony, now backed by two independent witnesses (that Mary Kelly was seen alive after she had been declared dead) should by itself have merited a new hearing. And clearly George Hutchinson's evidence, which was considered in an earlier chapter, should have added further argument for a re-opening of the case. If this had been done, Hutchinson's evidence could have been examined under oath and under cross-examination. Hutchinson could have been asked why he had waited until the inquest was closed before revealing what could have been crucial information about the murderer and so on. There is a list of perplexing issues upon which Mr Hutchinson could, and should, have been asked to shed light. Let us examine some of them.

Everyone in the East End knew that a reward had been offered for the arrest of Jack. George alleged that he had taken a close look at a likely suspect, so why did the impecunious Mr Hutchinson not rush forward with his detailed evidence, in the hope that this would result in the man's capture, thus winning himself a fortune of £1,200 (in today's money around £54,000) plus a life's pension? Hutchinson inexplicably kept the possibly vital information to himself until the inquest was closed, ignoring the fact that every day's delay made the arrest of his suspect more and more difficult, and so his reward more and more unlikely.

In his evidence George described a very rational conversation between himself and Kelly on the night of her death; when they met at 2.00 a.m. in Commercial Street, Mary is said to have asked for the loan of money. This statement also raises questions. A witness, Mary Ann Cox, testified that she had seen Kelly in Dorset Street at about a quarter to midnight with a man:

'. . . as they were going into her room, I said goodnight Mary Jane. She was very drunk and could scarcely answer me, but said goodnight. The man was carrying a quart of beer. I shortly afterwards heard her singing. I went out shortly after twelve and returned about one o'clock, and she was still singing in her room. I went out again shortly after one . . .'

So we have testimony that Mary was 'very drunk' at midnight, and barely capable of speech. She was with a man carrying a quart of beer, which, presumably they drank until at least 1.00 a.m., by which time Mary must have been paralytic. Yet an hour later she was reported by Hutchinson as apparently sober, holding a rational conversation, asking for money. Clearly one statement is wrong. Which one? And if Kelly was merely pretending to be drunk, what was the purpose of such an act? Several other questions arise from this episode. If Mary had had a client less than an hour earlier, what had she done with the payment for services from this man? And if, as seems apparent, Mary had had a full ration of drink and sex for the night, why did she risk her life roaming the dangerous streets in the early hours of the morning, looking for more of the same? Especially given her

81

particular fear of the serial killer, which Joe Barnett had outlined.
The Jack the Ripper A to Z states:
'Conspiracy theorists have alleged that Hutchinson was deliberately excluded from Dr MacDonald's very abrupt inquest. It
has been speculated that Hutchinson's very detailed description
is too elaborate to be accurate.'
I heartily concur with this solid conspiracy reasoning. There is
a strange air of 'staginess' around Mary's last supposed night on
earth. It was as though a charade was being played out for public
consumption. Was it reasonable for a prostitute to take a man
home at midnight, then proceed to sing to him loudly for around
an hour? A chap who had sex on his mind might sit and listen to
a few stray bars, but it is difficult to imagine him sitting patiently
through 60 minutes of solid serenade. Having had her fill of both
beer and sex, why did Mary go out on to the dangerous streets
once more? What did she do with the money which she must have
received from her last client? Why did she ask George Hutchinson
for sixpence in the middle of the night? The whole scenario is
extremely odd.

Let us return to our original query – to what social class did
Jack the Ripper belong? Points arguing against the killer belonging
to the working classes have already been enumerated. As we have
seen, there is considerable evidence pointing towards a cover-up
of the crimes by the authorities, and clearly such an action would
only be conducted for someone of very great importance; this
would indicate that Jack did indeed belong to the highest class in
the land. The question we must now ask is – who could that
person be?

Chapter Nine

Royal Involvement?

There has, for several decades at least, been a popular and well-discussed theory which maintains that a member of the British Royal Family was directly involved in the Ripper murders. I firmly believe, and will prove, that the Ripper affair did indeed have a royal link, although direct involvement is absurd, and possibly a member of the Royal Family was not aware of what was being done in his name. Perverting the course of justice was common practice in Victorian times. Certainly in the 1880s the law sometimes turned a blind eye, within limits, if prosecution would damage members of the aristocracy.

Clear evidence of the Victorian police force perverting the course of justice can be found during the early 1890s. The police raided a homosexual club in Cleveland Street and discovered Queen Victoria's grandson, Prince Albert Victor (nicknamed Eddy), on the premises. Although several members of the aristocracy were, on this occasion, arrested, there was no mention of the Prince's involvement in official reports of the affair.

Could the blatant suppression of facts during the Ripper investigations, and the equally blatant perversion of the course of justice, again mean that the highest in the land were being protected? Certainly Eddy had that rank. He was the eldest son of the Prince of Wales, later King Edward the Seventh, and, as such, he was directly in line to succeed to the throne of Great Britain.

Eddy, as we shall see in detail in Chapter Twelve, has been mentioned as a Ripper suspect in the past. This allegation has been taken up by several distinguished writers.

Yet Eddy does not fit a psychological portrait of the murderer. Jack's crimes displayed a towering confidence, and, it must be said, courage and fearlessness in his defiance of the London Police Force and the watchful citizens of the East End. In their execution and positioning the murders undeniably showed great daring, although less daring than was initially thought, as we shall see.

Eddy was, by all accounts a shy, diffident young man who suffered from an inherited partial deafness. It is highly unlikely that a man with hearing difficulties would crouch over dead bodies on a public pavement committing outrages with a knife, when his sole defence against detection would be the ability to perceive the sound of approaching danger. Even if Eddy were accompanied by conspirators, whispered not shouted warnings would be essential. And, of course, as a future heir to the throne, Eddy's activities and whereabouts would always be carefully monitored by the Palace, although judging by the peculiar places in which he was occasionally found, Eddy must have used diversionary tactics. To put Palace officials off the scent he may well have gone around to an approved friend's house then disappeared to lower venues through a back entrance, but this can only have been an occasional ploy.

To untangle the complicated threads of the Ripper crimes it will also be necessary to understand fully the forces which moulded the character of Eddy's father, The Prince of Wales (nicknamed 'Bertie'). The officials surrounding Bertie knew his every move until he was married, with a home, staff and children of his own: not until then did Bertie enjoy any real freedom. Whilst in his late teens studying at Cambridge University, Bertie found this unremitting surveillance too much to bear and one evening he sneaked out of his lodgings and took a train to London. When he arrived in the capital city officials were waiting for him at the station. Presumably Eddy's movements, whilst he was still unmarried and dependent on his parents, would have been just as tightly controlled. As we have stated, Eddy might occasionally have been able to sneak away for a night on the tiles, but it is absurd to think that the young Royal could wander around the violent East End in the middle of the night, even with companions. Officials based at the Palace, an establishment ruled with a rod of iron by Queen Victoria, did not allow such liberties.

There is no known link between Eddy and London's low life, or between Eddy and female prostitutes. From the information available Eddy was a gentle, charming boy, needing affection, who did not display any signs of the violent temper which characterised his father's youth.

However, the above words, 'female', 'low life', and 'prostitute', immediately bring Eddy's father to mind. Bertie's outrageous exploits, both as Prince of Wales and later as King Edward the Seventh, at every level of society and amongst women in particular, are now legendary.

* * * * *

Seeds for the Ripper murders were sown decades before the murders occurred. Surprisingly, it was the behaviour of the future King Edward the Seventh which reached out and destroyed the lives of at least five penniless East End prostitutes.

In order for the Prince of Wales's actions to be fully understood – and this is vitally important to the Ripper story – we must consider in detail the formative influences which moulded the future King's character. We must understand why he turned into an irredeemable Victorian rake.

Queen Victoria's first son was born on 9 November 1841 at Buckingham Palace. Her first child had been a girl. 'Don't worry,' Victoria had confidently told the doctor, 'the next one will be a boy.' She was right.

There was, naturally, great rejoicing at the birth. Country-wide, church bells pealed the entire day, and so many military salutes were fired that a wag said, 'My, how they do powder that child.'

The baby was christened Albert Edward, and on his birth inherited the title Duke of Cornwall. Less than a month later, the titles of Prince of Wales and Earl of Chester were also bestowed on the infant. At other times throughout his life, the Prince became the Duke of Rothesay, Duke of Saxe-Coburg-Gotha, Prince of Saxony, Earl of Dublin, Earl of Carrick and Baron Renfrew. But to his family, the much-titled Prince became known as 'Bertie'.

Victoria and her Consort, Prince Albert, were not ideal parents. Victoria was totally absorbed into the life of her adored husband. In a letter to her uncle after the boy's birth the Queen wrote: 'Our little boy is wonderfully large and strong. I *hope* and *pray* he may be like his dearest Papa. You will understand how fervent my prayers to see him resemble his angelic father in *every, every* respect, both in body and mind.' Then Bertie was quickly forgotten, as the Queen returned to her favourite subject. 'I delight in the fact that I possess such a perfect husband. I cannot say what a comfort and support my beloved Angel is to me.'

Already, at birth, the wish for the son to become the father had been formed without regard to the child's temperament and tastes, an age-old recipe for disaster. But the Queen's wishes to create a second Albert were warmly welcomed by other members of the court. This transformation was to be achieved by careful training. Planning for the boy's education was placed in the hands of Albert and a German whom Victoria had grown to trust and rely on – Baron Stockmar. The Baron was a law unto himself at the court, his advice invariably being accepted by both Victoria and Albert.

Prince Albert had, as a boy, demonstrated an unusual passion for academic study. He delighted in the discussion of law and metaphysics with his elders. One year he refused a Christmas holiday because this would have interrupted his studies. An hour-long debate of religious and theological subjects at his confirmation apparently gave the young Albert more pleasure than a Christmas break. This was the lad who was to become Bertie's father.

It was Stockmar who was chosen to vet Albert before his betrothal to Queen Victoria. The Baron was delighted to report that Albert appeared quite uninterested in women, and liked to spend his evenings discussing issues with older and wiser philosophers. This was the man they now intended to recreate through the son. Whilst the rigid, humourless and authoritarian Albert clearly made a good husband, there would be few little boys who would regard him as an ideal father.

Bertie's early years were reasonably untraumatic, although he was denied the company of other children apart from his own brothers and sisters. Albert considered that other boys might pass on bad habits, so the gregarious, friendly Bertie was kept alone in his classroom, studying religion and Latin and similar subjects, or playing four-handed chess with his parents and tutor for relaxation.

From the ages of seven to nine, Bertie's education was placed in the hands of a distinguished scholar from Cambridge University, Henry Birch.

Bertie formed a warm attachment to his tutor, and whether it was the young lad's pleasure at being with Birch, or the considered laxity of lessons which displeased Albert and Stockmar is not known. Whatever the reasons, Henry Birch was dismissed, and a new tutor sought.

The young boy was dismayed at the loss of one of his few friends; he wrote affectionate notes, and left small gifts under Birch's pillow. The young lad's opinion was not even briefly considered.

A recommendation from Sir James Stephen, who was undersecretary at the Colonial Office, brought Frederick Weymouth Gibbs to Stockmar's attention as a replacement for Birch. It was Sir James's nephew, J.K. Stephen, who would be chosen, decades later, as the tutor for Bertie's eldest son Eddy, a choice which would add to the tangled Ripper threads.

Gibbs was considered suitable, and he was engaged to conduct the next stage of Bertie's education. The new tutor quickly assessed the mental capabilities of his royal charge: he questioned the advisability of an intense learning schedule for so unacademic a boy. But Stockmar and Albert were unbending: they wanted a recreation of the father. Perfection was the goal.

Charles Tarver was engaged to teach the boy classics and theology; William Ellis was to give instruction in political economy. But enlightened minds saw the damage which was being inflicted on the young boy's mind. Lord Redesdale wrote of Bertie, 'I can see his poor, bored face even now. It was pitiful.' Bertie began to display signs of violent temper.

After various opinions on the Prince's educational progress were collated, it was adjudged that Bertie, in all spheres of education, was far less capable than his elder sister. 'My son is so stupid,' Queen Victoria is reported to have said. This bombardment of criticism lasted for many years and came from several directions.

The tutor Gibbs quickly became a first-class sneak, relating his charge's every conceivable fault to the royal parents, and keeping his own record of the young Bertie's misdeeds.

'On the terrace, the Prince of Wales quarrelled with and struck his younger brother.' (Prince Alfred).

'Pulled Prince Alfred's hair.'

The complaints are so petty it is difficult to believe that anyone would take note, but Albert considered each misdemeanour carefully. The Prince Consort decided to release some of the fifteen-year-old Bertie's pent-up energy on a four-month tour abroad.

He was surrounded by model all-male company on his overseas journey.

When he was sixteen it was decided that the Prince should now have the weighty task of selecting his own clothes. But even here the heavy hand of Queen Victoria fell. She sent warning notes to her son cautioning him against any extravagance or immodesty of attire.

When, whilst still a teenager, the Prince was given his own home at White Lodge in Richmond Park, a squad of tutors and minders were lodged with him. For their guidance the Queen and her Consort issued a list of instructions. To use the words of the Archbishop of Canterbury's son, E.F. Benson:

'An exhaustive memorandum was prepared in many sections, concerning his dress, deportment, relations with others and conversation. Any tendency towards lounging, loud clothes, frivolity, discourtesy, idleness, vanity, unpunctuality and mimicry must be instantly checked.'

The unfortunate Prince was not allowed the company of boys of his own age, and practical jokes were forbidden.

On Bertie's eighteenth birthday it seemed that relief might be at hand: it was announced that Frederick Gibbs would be retiring. Any joy was short-lived, however. His new 'aide' was to be Colonel Bruce – a dour, humourless man in the familiar mould.

In regard to this new appointment, Victoria and Albert sent their son a directive. 'Your equerries will receive orders from Colonel Bruce. You will never leave the house without reporting yourself to him, and he will settle who is to accompany you, and will give general instructions as to the disposition of the day.' It is reported that Bertie wept when he read this communiqué.

Discipline became even more rigid. Part of Colonel Bruce's timetable for Bertie's studies is recorded:

'Before breakfast, Italian studies. 11 to 12, read with Mr. Tarver. Early afternoon study ancient monuments and works of art. Translate French from 5 to 6. One hour in the evening for private reading and music.'

Baron Stockmar's maxim 'Never Relax' was being faithfully adhered to.

* * * * *

On his eighteenth birthday the Prince had reached his majority as legal heir to the Crown. He was almost immediately enrolled for a short course of study at Edinburgh University. A familiar rigorous schedule of study was drawn up.

Such unremitting application would tax the most studious of minds: for the unbookish Bertie, with a strong personality and even stronger sexual urges, the course must have been nightmarish. Every arrangement for the Prince's stay in Scotland appeared to have been designed to frustrate the young man's personality. He was not allowed to live with the other students for fear that their personalities and habits might contaminate the Royal mind. Bertie was installed at Holyrood Palace with his governor and tutors.

After the term of study at Edinburgh the Prince was moved to Oxford University, and a similar living and working schedule was prepared: however, at Oxford, even working alongside other students was forbidden. Private tutors were engaged for lectures. Meanwhile, Albert made frequent, unannounced visits to the university, in order to check that the educational standards which had been set for his son were being observed.

No advisor appeared to find it ludicrous that an eighteen-year-old Prince should be treated like a ten-year-old boy.

It was at Oxford University that Bertie was introduced to tobacco, but to enjoy his first smoke he was obliged to crouch behind a hedge with a few conspirators, like a schoolboy behind the bicycle sheds.

In a rash moment, Queen Victoria had promised that when Canada furnished an infantry regiment for service in the Crimean War she would send her son on a tour of the Dominions. No doubt Stockmar and Albert decided that the lamentably long university vacation would be the ideal moment to fulfil this promise. There was considerable parental surprise when Bertie's overseas tour proved highly successful.

On his return from overseas, Bertie went back to Oxford for a final term – and for good measure he was also enrolled for a further year of study at Cambridge University.

The pressure of such long and rigid discipline was beginning to place a severe – and evident – strain on the young Prince. His temper became more explosive.

After careful consideration, it was decided that marriage might help stabilise Bertie. Maybe his strong sexual urges had been recognised, although this is unlikely. The shining example of Albert and Victoria's highly successful early union was more likely to have been the marriage catalyst.

The Times discussed Bertie's marital affairs on 5 July 1858:

'To all present appearances, our future monarch's choice of wife is positively limited to exactly seven ladies of Royal blood . . .'

Number five on that list was, 'Princess Alexandra (daughter of Prince Christian) of Denmark.'

Meanwhile, during Bertie's final university vacation, when most students would travel to their homes to relax and enjoy themselves, Colonel Bruce advised that a spell of military training was the perfect way to fill Bertie's long break. This decision was to lead to the first great scandal involving the Prince of Wales.

The Curragh Camp in Ireland was chosen for the Prince's initial military service. The Camp was a remote outpost, where, Colonel Bruce doubtless thought, no youthful, lustful adventures could occur. Colonel Bruce could not have been more mistaken.

Albert and Victoria visited their son in Ireland. Bertie had hoped that for his parents' visit, after a short but concentrated period of training, he might be placed in charge of a battalion of soldiers. But Colonel Percy, Bertie's commanding officer, considered that the Prince's drill and his commands to the men were not up to the required standard. Bertie was made to march past his parents in a lowly subaltern's position.

Queen Victoria noted her son's humiliation without any great sympathy. She wrote to her Uncle Leopold in Belgium, 'Bertie acquitted himself as well as could be expected in the circumstances.'

Fellow officers must have noticed the Prince's harsh treatment, and they decided to give Bertie a special treat. A dark-haired beauty, Nellie Clifton, an actress, was in Curragh in the company of an officer. Nellie was young, healthy and available. The soldiers commandeered her services, then smuggled her past Colonel Bruce, and into Bertie's bed. Bertie appeared to know exactly what to do, and clearly enjoyed himself. Unfortunately for him,

Nellie could not resist boasting of her royal conquest. The gossip spread and news of Bertie's debauchery quickly reached Buckingham Palace.

Albert went into a state of shock. He ordered an immediate inquiry into the affair, and when confirmation of Bertie's actions arrived, the Prince Consort wrote to his son. 'You have caused me the greatest pain I have yet felt in this life. You must not, you dare not be lost. The consequences for this country and for the world would be too dreadful.' Bertie was rushed back to Cambridge, where his father hurried to meet – and to castigate – him.

Returning from this meeting, it was reported that, 'The Consort travelled through cold and stormy weather, and, as a result, caught a feverish cold.' What Albert had really caught was typhoid fever. Bertie was summoned to Windsor Castle, but by the time he arrived there his father was unconscious. Albert died on the night of 4 December, 1861. The effect on Queen Victoria was predictable. For twenty-one years Albert had been her constant and singular joy. 'England, my unhappy country, has lost all in losing him,' she wrote to her uncle.

The devastated Queen wrapped herself in a mantle of grief and stayed cocooned in misery for decades in what could only be termed as 'exhibitive mourning'.

Widowhood would have been the perfect time for Victoria to share the increased burdens of state (which now fell onto her shoulders) with her eldest son and heir, and Bertie could have gained valuable experience for his role as future king; but Victoria held tenaciously on to power. Was that because of a strong dislike which she seemed to have for her son? On one occasion she wrote, 'I shall never look at him without a shudder.' The Queen apparently believed that the shock over Bertie's sexual escapade with Nellie had seriously weakened Albert's constitution, allowing the fatal fever to gain hold. Whatever the reason, the Queen refused to allow Bertie any participation in State affairs: she even refused to allow her son access to cabinet papers which were available to her private secretaries.

Bertie, now of age, was relieved from the smothering burden of education, and, at the same time, he was cut off from any semblance of responsibility. The result was predictable. Freed from all constraints, Bertie launched himself into a life of unrestrained pleasure. Years of educational torment had been wasted. Bertie began to make up for lost time.

* * * * *

Despite Victoria's bereavement it was decided to continue with plans for Bertie to marry. A betrothal of his son and heir had been Albert's last wish, so it would be carried out.

The Times's 'number five' choice of bride, Alexandra of Denmark, had been carefully assessed by the Palace authorities. Despite the fact that a Dane marrying into the British Royal Family would cause great offence to the Prussians (the two countries had been engaged in a bitter territorial argument for years) Victoria decided that as no other suitable candidate was available for her son, the union should go ahead.

Bertie and the Danish Princess had met and liked each other. Victoria had also met Alexandra and they too had warmed to each other. The young Princess had been warned not to smile during this meeting, as the Queen disliked any show of happiness which served to remind her of the golden times with Albert.

An engagement was announced, and the anticipated storm of protest from Prussia was brushed aside. Victoria was, after all, Queen of England, and she could do anything she liked. Bertie and Alexandra were married in St George's Chapel at Windsor Castle on 10 March 1863 at midday. Although a year and three months had passed since her beloved Consort's death, Victoria arrived at the wedding dressed in deepest mourning, wearing an entirely black outfit, even down to the gloves, relieved only by the blue ribbon of the Order of the Garter. This assembly was rounded off by a widow's cap.

Alexandra, glittering with spectacular jewellery, wore a white satin dress trimmed with garlands of orange blossom, covered by Honiton lace; she was surrounded by heralds and trumpeters in brilliant cloth-of-gold tunics. Yet after the wedding Victoria wrote: 'What a dismal affair it was,' forgetting that she personally had not added much cheer. She insisted on sitting in seclusion, dressed in black, occasionally bursting into tears as she looked at the spot on which Albert's coffin had so recently stood, a spot now occupied by his son about to be wed.

There is a wonderfully absurd wedding photograph in which Alexandra, in bridal dress, looks sternly towards the camera, whilst Bertie glowers at his bride: even on this happy occasion no outward show of pleasure was permitted. Victoria is seated in front of the gloomy couple wearing voluminous mourning robes, staring up miserably at a marble bust of her dead Consort. Albert was not going to be left out of the wedding. The portrait is a splendid display of unconscious humour.

Bertie and his wife moved into their own premises at Marlborough House in central London, and, finally, the Prince was complete master of his own destiny. Fun was to be the order of the day. Bertie's love of food was served by endless official dinners. Balls crowded in on each other. Foreign travel, much to Bertie's taste, was undertaken on a grand scale. In Constantinople they were served meals from solid gold, diamond-encrusted plates.

Now that Bertie was free, a set of high-bred rakes became part of his inner circle. Henry Chaplin, Sir Frederick Johnstone and other like-minded hell-raisers, all of whom enjoyed gambling, drinking and seducing women, influenced the Prince, and, after the earlier, dreary company of academics and theologians, Bertie's enjoyment in stepping beyond the bounds of propriety with rakes is fully understandable.

In the days before newspapers had learned the technique of reproducing photographs Bertie's face was recognised by few of the general public. One day the Prince of Wales and the Bishop of Thetford were driving along a country lane when an old woman, carrying a huge basket of cockles, approached the dog-cart and asked the Prince if he would carry the cockles for her. Charmingly, Bertie said that he was unable to do that, but instead, he would give her a picture of his mother. He then handed the old woman half a sovereign. Amazingly, Victoria also frequently went unrecognised by the general public, especially when she was in the wilds of Scotland. This anonymity meant that Bertie was able to dismiss his royal coaches and travel around London in public cabs, visiting clubs with his circle of friends and drinking in bars where no royal personage would be expected to imbibe.

There is little doubt that these activities would have been reported to Victoria – she had her spies everywhere – but now that Bertie was married with his own home there was little she could do about it, apart from sending warning notes and giving motherly advice, most of which Bertie ignored. The days of sending transport to bring the Prince back home had long since passed.

The Prince never missed attending a big London fire if he could help it. Occasionally Bertie and some of his cronies would go every night for a week to Watling Street Fire Station, where they would play at being firemen. Bertie certainly made up for his lack of fun during childhood. One of the firemen who worked at the blaze which destroyed the King and Queen Granaries in London reported:

'Through the height of the fire, his Royal Highness shared the smoke and water with us all, and gave a hand here and there just like one of ourselves. The walls of the place were very high, and as the water soaked the grain, it bulged the walls out till they fell with a terrific crash. Through it all the Prince, who seemed to bear a charmed life, worked with a a zeal and knowledge that would have done credit to any trained fireman, unrecognised by the onlookers, and unnoticed by the rank and file of the Brigade.'

The head of the London Fire Brigade had orders to report any fierce conflagration to Marlborough House. Bertie and his circle would then rush out to view. Clearly the Prince led the most extraordinary lifestyle for a member of the Victorian Royal Family – or any other royal family for that matter.

By the late 1860s Bertie's reputation as a roué and a seducer of women was well established. His close association with the Marquis of Hastings in particular could well have helped corrupt the Prince. The Marquis was young, extremely rich, and intimately associated with brothels and working class clubs. He had a passion for cruel sports, such as cock fighting, and liked to associate with criminals and low prostitutes. Bertie much enjoyed the company of the Marquis, and allowed himself to be led into the nobleman's sordid world. The two friends often travelled abroad together, and it was reported that during a party in Paris a naked courtesan was served up to Bertie on a silver plate.

The Prince of Wales, now much lampooned by cartoons and satirical articles, had become the greatest rake of his time. The foolish educational programme of Prince Albert and Baron Stockmar had backfired, and, totally unwittingly, they had laid the groundwork for the Ripper murders.

Chapter Ten

Eddy

If the Prince of Wales was a first tenuous link in the Ripper murders, then his eldest son, nicknamed Eddy, was a second link. Both these men take us one step nearer to the solution.

For a complete understanding of the puzzle, it is essential that Eddy's background is also fully understood. Eddy was born in the wrong place, at the wrong time, unexpectedly and without preparation; all rare for a royal child.

On 8 January 1864 Bertie and Alix were staying at Frogmore, a royal house in Windsor Park. The weather was bitterly cold and a hockey match, in which Bertie was booked to play, had been organised on a frozen lake in Virginia Water. The royal couple left for the match and Alexandra, whose accouchement was not due for two months, spent a happy time in the company of her husband being pulled around the lake on a sledge.

She left Virginia Water at four in the afternoon in good health and spirits, but when Bertie followed his wife home to Windsor several hours later, he found her in labour, with the royal doctor many miles away. Complete preparations for the accouchement had been made at Marlborough House, but, with the birth not expected so soon, no preparations had been made at Frogmore. A local medic was summoned, and he, with the aid of Alix's lady-in-waiting, delivered Eddy into the world. The baby then had to be wrapped in makeshift clothing.

There was great rejoicing at the birth of a male child, a direct heir to the throne after Bertie. Victoria hastened to Windsor to view her grandchild; he was frail and small, weighing only three and a half pounds. Victoria found him, '. . . a poor little bit of a thing'. That did not stop her, however, from deciding that the boy would be named after her dead Consort. No doubt her mind had been made up from the moment she had heard of the pregnancy. Male = Albert. 'Albert Victor Christian Edward' the Queen announced, much to the dismay of his parents, who thought they should at least be consulted in the choice of names for their first-born. Victoria brushed the protestations aside, declaring that from henceforth, every king who sat on the throne of England must be called 'Albert'. Her obsession did not lessen with time. The boy was christened as Victoria wished, the ceremony taking place in St George's Chapel, Windsor, the scene both of Albert's funeral and Bertie's marriage. Once again the Queen was dressed in deepest mourning.

Although Victoria won initially over the naming of the boy Alix was not without her triumph. From the start she called her son 'Eddy', and this was the name by which he was known to his family and friends throughout his life.

Seventeen months after Eddy's birth a second son was born. He was to be christened George. Being so near to each other in age, the boys were educationally compatible. Naturally, Victoria tried to interfere in the education of both her grandchildren, but Bertie, remembering his own nightmarish tutoring, insisted on a more relaxed programme of study for his sons. He firmly believed that little could be learned from books, and Alix agreed with him, so the Princes were allowed to roam free during their formative years with little enforced education. The result of such freedom was predictable. Victoria called her grandsons ill-bred and ill-trained. 'I can't fancy them at all,' she wrote, yet despite that statement, the Queen was clearly fond of the boys. Eddy was served, from his earliest months, by a personal footman who was also attached to George once he was born, but clearly discipline was not a part of the footman's duties.

Once the boys reached the ages of six and seven respectively it was decided that a firm educational stand must be undertaken. After a short search for a suitable tutor, the Reverend John Neale Dalton, a thirty-two-year-old clergyman, was engaged to educate the Princes privately. Dalton was a brilliant scholar who had graduated from Cambridge University with first class honours in theology, but his high spiritual attainments did not prevent him from emulating the sneaky actions of Bertie's tutor: detailed diaries were kept which noted the boys' behaviour, and a steady stream of letters, assessments and notes outlined his young charges' development. Eddy was considered educationally subnormal. It was reported that he could not concentrate for more than a few minutes at a time: he even lost concentration in mid-sentence, when his words would trail away. He was listless, vacant and prone to prolonged daydreaming. Eddy had, according to Dalton, a weakness of brain, a feebleness and a lack of mental power to grasp even the simplest concepts which were put before him. Although Prince George was more responsive to teaching than his elder brother, his attainments also left much to be desired, and he progressed only slowly.

Alexandra, whose own education had been minimal without any ill-effects in later life, wrote back to say how shocked she had been by the tutor's reports, but clearly she remained unperturbed by the teacher's depressingly negative outbursts.

I cannot help wondering whether Dalton's reports were unconsciously supposed to defend his own position – the case of a bad workman blaming his tools, but whatever his motives, Dalton remained at his post for fourteen years.

Eddy's education was, in many respects, a recreation of his father's schoolboy difficulties, reincarnated in an even more relentlessly negative form. Bertie, however, despite his learning difficulties, must have been aware of his engaging and powerful personality. By contrast, Eddy had no such reserves of assurance on which to rely. He was a languidly beautiful boy inclined towards melancholia, and one must feel sympathy for his predicament: a prince unsuited by temperament and ability for his destiny, he was relentlessly squeezed and moulded by royal forces into a shape thought fit for the highest in the land.

Although Alix suffered from an inherited deafness, only Sir Henry Ponsonby, Victoria's private secretary, thought to wonder whether hearing difficulties might be at the root of Eddy's educational problems. Eddy suffered from otosclerosis, a fusing together of small bones in the inner ear. Being cut off from the tutor's voice and from normal conversation would be enough to make any boy appear educationally weak. And yet, in later years, Eddy proved to be a fine player of whist, a game which requires concentration and mental skill. It is interesting to note that this game requires only sight – a knowledge of the cards held in the hand – and it is best played in total silence. If Eddy's mental powers could concentrate over long rubbers in a card game requiring powers of memory and mental arithmetic, then during his schooling, it was clearly the subjects and teaching methods (which did not recognise Eddy's disability) which had been at fault, and not the quality of the Prince's brain.

A strong bond of friendship and affection existed between the young brothers. In 1877, when the boys were aged twelve and thirteen, it was decided that travel might broaden their minds, and, at the same time, stimulate their desire for education.

Bertie was, at this juncture, deep into his entanglement with the beautiful socialite Mrs Lillie Langtry, an affair of passionate depth. The educational responsibility for two young boys must have interfered with Bertie's insatiable demands for pleasure, no matter how affectionate Bertie's feelings were towards his sons (and there is some evidence that this affection was ambivalent). In Victorian times it was standard practice for wealthy families to send their sons to an all-male boarding school, the payment of fees replacing parental effort. Was there a touch of cynicism when Bertie decided that his sons should tour the world for two years? The Princes were to be accompanied by their tutor.

It was suggested that the boys should be placed on separate ships, but the strong bond of friendship between the brothers made it inadvisable to part them at the start of their teenage years. A further consideration was the fact that George appeared to be the only person who could occasionally rouse his brother from a state of semi-permanent torpor. So the Princes sailed away together as cadets on the naval training ship *HMS Britannia*.

Whilst George, as usual, coped well with his training, Eddy displayed no greater appetite for nautical matters than he had shown for other forms of education.

* * * * *

When he reached the age of sixteen Eddy's mental capabilities appeared as restricted as ever; moreover he had grown into an archetypal 'mother's boy'. Books written in Eddy's short lifetime contain sentimental Victorian statements such as: '. . . he liked to go for long walks at Sandringham, arm around his mother's waist.' Eddy is reported to have said, 'Mama is so nice, she is fond of everything I like. There is nobody like Mama'.

With such an attitude, and with such a low educational standard, Eddy began to draw criticism from his father. Sir Henry Ponsonby had written that whilst accompanying the boys to their training ship before the world tour, the Prince of Wales 'snubbed Prince Eddy uncommonly'. And this cold behaviour was before a two-year parting. It was Bertie who, recognising his son's liking for immaculate dress, unkindly nicknamed Eddy, 'Collar and cuffs,' an appellation which became widely used.

Despite such difficulties however, it becomes clear from documented reports of Eddy's activities and friendships, that by mid-teens, a split between personality and educational ability had occurred. Eddy had grown into a charming and pleasant young man.

It is possible for any person who can listen attentively to conversation to be assigned a degree of intelligence by the speaker: such is human nature – intelligence by association. Perhaps this occurred in Eddy's case. There is no doubt that despite his low educational achievements he was a popular young man amongst those who knew him, and much loved by his family and friends.

Alix, after bearing her two sons, gave birth to three daughters. The girls' education was sadly neglected, but their mother did insist on the instillation of good manners and humility in all her offspring. 'They must not assume attitudes of superiority,' Alix continually ordered the retinues of nannies and tutors. This must have been a difficult lesson for such high-born youngsters to stomach, but Alix's wishes were obeyed: Eddy in particular proved an apt pupil. Any person coming into contact with the young Prince, and expecting perhaps a haughty, regal personality, found instead a self-effacing, gentle and friendly young man. By his mid-teens, Eddy had the ability to instil in his friends a deep sense of loyalty and love: this quality is a far more important talent to any member of royalty than brain power. Eddy's natural qualities, reinforced by his mother's strict training, were invaluable.

* * * * *

After a second lengthy educational tour on board the ship *Baccante*, George, who had developed a passion for life at sea, decided on a naval career. Eddy had to continue his education on land, and so, for the first time in their lives, the boys were parted – a wrench for both the brothers, but more especially for Eddy. Life must have seemed bleak for the nineteen-year-old Prince as he considered the course which had been set for him: study at Cambridge University, competing with the country's finest brains, without the support of his brother, whilst he was being moulded for a future role to which he was quite unsuited. And these trials and tribulations were being undertaken with impaired hearing which would cut him off from a full integration into university life.

To assist Eddy for life at one of the world's finest educational institutions, it was decided that he must have a special tutor who could live with him before his enrolment and help to 'cram' his mind with knowledge. The hunt for a suitable tutor did not take long. The Reverend John Neale Dalton recommended a young man from an excellent family, James Kenneth Stephen. Stephen was interviewed and quickly accepted the post.

It is at this point that the plot thickens.

With James Stephen by his side, Eddy unexpectedly found himself supported by an extremely handsome, highly intelligent and confident young man; he had found friendship in a hostile world; he had found a replacement for his lost brother. This must have seemed miraculous to the diffident young Prince.

Neither men could have known, at their first meeting, that the relationship would eventually prove disastrous for both of them, or that the pairing would mean death for five women.

Chapter Eleven

J. K. Stephen

The next link in the Ripper murders moves us very close to the crimes. Once again a complete understanding of our subject is essential. The Stephen family were descended from farming stock, but within several generations literary talent was in evidence, and a series of books and articles had been written by various family members.

Memoirs, Imprisonment For Debt, A Treatise On Pleading and *New Commentaries* comprised some of the family's literary output. The study and practice of law also became a recurring occupation of successive generations of the Stephen family.

James Kenneth Stephen was born in 1859 (the second son of Sir James Fitzjames Stephen) and in him combined the family's twin talents, writing and the law. He was initially educated at two church schools (in Tunbridge Wells then Banbury) before being accepted into Eton in 1871, where he remained until Easter 1878.

At Eton one of James's tutors was the notorious Oscar Browning, who was dismissed from the College for 'over-familiarity' with the boys. Browning was in his mid-thirties when James (often referred to as J.K.) entered Eton; we now know that he preferred the company of younger boys. Did J.K., a handsome, chunky young man, experience some form of sexual harassment from Browning? A possible answer to this question might lie in one of J.K.'s poems in which a 'Mr. B' is mentioned.

> 'When I had firmly answered "No,"
> And he allowed that that was so,
> I really thought I should be free
> For good and all from Mr.B.,
> And that he would soberly acquiesce:
> I said that I would be discreet
> That for a while we should not meet;
> I promised I would always feel
> A kindly interest in his weal;

I thanked him for his amorous zeal,
In short, I said all I could but "yes".'
I suspect that this poem (written 'From Her point of view')
reminisces about an actual event. The writer agrees to go horse
riding with 'Mr B.', and the fourth verse explicitly describes a
sexual experience, once the couple had stopped, presumably to eat.

'I won't say much of what happened next,
I own I was extremely vexed,
Indeed, I should have been aghast
If anyone had seen what passed:
     But nobody need ever know,
That, as I leaned forward to stir the fire,
He advanced before I could retire,
And I suddenly felt to my great alarm,
The grasp of a warm unlicensed arm,
An embrace in which I found no charm;
     I was awfully glad when he let me go.'

Can we learn about any further intimacies from a wistful verse
from 'The Old School List'?

'There were two good fellows I used to know,
     – How distant it all appears.
We played together in football weather,
And messed together for years:'

James's brother wrote:

'While he was at school he worked hard at such of his studies
as particularly interested him, and as hard as he thought prac-
tically necessary at those that did not. The consequence was
that he distinguished himself greatly as an essay-writer and a
student of history, and did not especially distinguish himself
either in classics or mathematics.'

An appraisal of James's similarly mixed fortunes at various
athletic activities is recorded, but a clearer picture of him at Eton
emerges from one of the contemporary students.

Arthur Christopher Benson, the eldest of three sons born to the
Archbishop of Canterbury, was enrolled at Eton in 1874, three
years behind J.K. Stephen. Despite the difference in their ages
and grades, the boys became firm friends, and later Arthur (less
famous than his younger brother, E.F. Benson, author of the
Lucia books) wrote a volume of short biographies which include

reminiscences of J.K. Stephen:

'I do not remember my first actual sight of him, but he was so entirely unlike other boys that, once seen, it was impossible to forget him. He had a very big head with fine, clear-cut features, large and rather terrific eyes, a strong expressive mouth and a solid chin. He wore his hair, which curled slightly, somewhat long, and parted in the middle. The expression of his face was severe to grimness in repose – it was eminently a judicial face – though it lit up with an irrepressible smile. He gave the impression of enormous strength.'

A contemporary of J.K.'s great-grandfather described that ancestor as, 'a man of volcanic personality – and also a volcanic temper'. Interestingly, Benson mentions J.K. when he was angry: '. . . and on the rare occasions when he lost his temper, the terror of the situation . . .' Clearly J.K. Stephen's temper was also volcanic.

When J.K. left Eton in 1878 to study at Cambridge University, he carried on a vigorous correspondence with the young Benson, who eventually followed his friend to Cambridge.

At Cambridge, James soon gathered around him a coterie of university peers, a group who, according to Benson, 'deliberately made friends with several small boys who seemed inclined to be interested in the same things'. Even at Eton, James had been an idol of young lads for several reasons. 'He played the odd game of football . . . with remarkable skill and endurance, he was extremely good natured, he did very little work, *he defied authority* . . .' (My italics.) As a schoolboy, J.K. also showed signs of a restless energy ('he was never still'), and signs of individuality ('he was eccentric in dress').

In a short passage, Benson states sentiments about J.K. which Eddy might also have experienced in the company of his new tutor:

'I was not, I remember, exactly at ease with him, though I felt it was a great honour to be selected as his friend. I was always overshadowed by a sense of his cleverness, quickness, and ability, and was afraid of not being up to the mark in talk.'

I can imagine Eddy writing those very words.

Benson describes the 'irregular handwriting, the lines sloping at all angles'. To a graphologist, this would be a sign of emotional instability. The passage continues:

'He was of an emotional nature always, but found it hard to express his feelings: and I was aware in those days, especially just before the time came for him to leave the School, that there was some hidden flow of feeling about him, a heartfelt craving which he could not express even to himself.' Then Arthur added some pages later, '. . . he loved close and intimate relationships.'

From Benson's writing alone, a clear picture begins to build up of a mysterious, eccentric, brilliant, highly emotional young man. There was also a sense of daring in the young J.K.. At Cambridge University he broke the rules by running across lawns in full view of the Vice-Provost. He escaped punishment.

At Eton he was once late for an important church service: this unpunctuality could have had serious consequences, so J.K. waited until all the main authorities had closed their eyes and bowed their heads in prayer. He then entered the chapel, walked silently up the aisle and took his place. 'It was exactly timed. Just as he [J.K.] slipped into place, Hornby rose refreshed, wholly unaware of the interruption, and perhaps a little puzzled by the broad smiles of the Collegers.'

Other telling sentences are spread throughout Benson's recollections: '. . . he expanded in an atmosphere of delicate care and caressing affection.' 'He was a strong agnostic.'

The writer then touches on his friend's royal appointment, mentioning Eddy, who, by then, had received a title – Duke of Clarence – from Queen Victoria.

'Then he went for a while as tutor to the Duke of Clarence, and his time at Sandringham proved extremely pleasant and delightful: though I have sometimes wondered whether Jem Stephen's dry art of statement and somewhat impatient quality of mind fitted him to teach a prince of extraordinary amiability and sweetness, but whose intellectual tastes were of the simplest character. They were, however, firm friends: and Jem Stephen realised to the full, as none who knew the Duke ever failed to find, the warm affection and constant fidelity of his illustrious pupil.'

We learn that Stephen once wrote in a sonnet which alluded to Harvey, the discoverer of the circulation of blood:

'What are the habits of this crimson flood
We reek with? Man had questioned many a year.'
This was the eccentric man who became the tutor and the close
companion of Eddy, the Duke of Clarence.

* * * * *

J.K. quickly recognised Eddy's educational limitations. He wrote
to Dalton saying, '. . . he hardly knows the words to read . . .' yet
despite this harsh criticism the two men became close friends, as
Arthur Benson confirms. This friendship was recognised by
Eddy's official biographer, J.E. Vincent:

'. . . he [Eddy] was a member of the Amateur Dramatic Society, to which his by now intimate friend, Jim Stephen,
belonged . . .'

Such a deep friendship holds no surprises: two handsome,
charming young men from illustrious family backgrounds, both
yearning for affection, both highly sensual, both with homosexual
leanings. There could only be one possible outcome: a love affair,
probably of considerable depth and passion, between Prince Eddy
and J.K. Stephen.

One can imagine James beginning to weave his spell over the
royal pupil, perhaps by pointing out that kingship requires not so
much intellectual power – one can always employ brilliant minds
– but the very qualities of charm, compassion and friendliness
which Eddy possessed in such abundance.

Benson in his memoirs recounts how J.K. Stephen would
clown around and his antics could quickly convulse an audience
with laughter. Doubtless the tutor, who liked to be the centre of
attention, brought a sense of the ridiculous into Eddy's life, a
dimension which the Prince would not have previously experienced. From Eddy's reactions Stephen must have been aware that
he was slowly gaining power and ascendancy over a future King
of England. What dreams of glory may have built up in the
ambitious tutor's mind?

J.K. Stephen accompanied Eddy to Cambridge, a university
which J.K. had left only a year earlier. He would therefore have
known intimately many of the students and lecturers, including
Oscar Browning. Browning, despite his overtly homosexual bent,
and despite the nature of his dismissal from Eton, had been
engaged to teach history at King's College, Cambridge, arriving

there in 1876. Browning had not changed his ways – he was known to be friendly with the rich and perverted Baron Houghton, who enjoyed holding orgies and was a famous voyeur (although to be fair, W.E. Forster did say of the Baron, 'I have friends who would be kind to me in distress, but only one who would be kind to me in disgrace.').

It was into this kind of company that Eddy was to be led. And the reserved Prince would have relied on his knowledgeable companion and friend, James Stephen, to choose and make any introductions. All the Prince's early contacts at university would have been vetted and approved by the new royal tutor.

Eddy's entire life, from the first moment, had been controlled by outside forces: every decision had been made for him by a string of advisers, tutors, and, of course, powerful members of his family, not least Queen Victoria. Knowing that total control and supervision from a minder would have been routine for the Prince, J.K. could have gained an easy and complete mastery over his royal charge, and Eddy would have appreciated being led and manipulated.

We have seen J.K.'s propensity to gather around himself an admiring throng of younger men, and we have learned of his ability to dominate such a group. But James's power had been modest up to leaving university. He had, in the past, dazzled young boys with his football skill, and he would, in the future, start his own magazine and thus rule a small but select band of distinguished writers. But as tutor to Eddy, undreamt of power might lie at hand. J.K. Stephen must have given this fact much thought. There is no reason why the ambitious James should not have been planning a glittering future for himself as the power behind the throne, once Eddy was King – a monarch fully trained to listen to Stephen's advice and guidance, and to act on such wisdom. J.K. would have been in the position of a dictator – one of the world's most powerful men. Similar dreams of power have, throughout the ages, led to disaster. J.K. while at university, had been raised in an atmosphere of intrigue. Oscar Browning, in his memoirs, asserts that jostling for power and position at the university was normal practice, carried out in an atmosphere of corruption. And the above assertions are not based purely on speculation. Stephen's brother, H.L. Stephen, wrote of his friend,

J.K. Stephen

Montague John Druitt

The Prince and Princess of Wales with Prince Albert Victor

The Duke of Clarence

Miller's Court

29 Hanbury Street

Sir Charles Warren

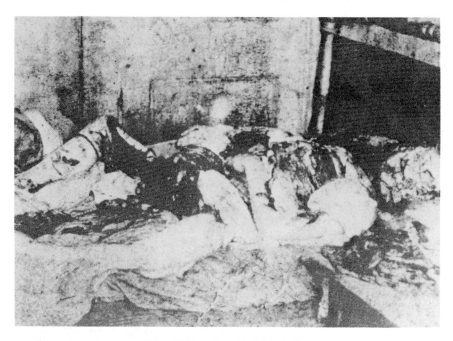

Mary Kelly as found in Miller's Court

Mortuary photograph of
Catharine Eddowes

Reconstructed image of Liz Stride

(by the artist Peter Fry)

Reconstructed image of Annie Chapman

(by the artist Peter Fry)

Harry Wilson, the man who regularly corresponded with Eddy: '. . . if the Duke of Clarence had not died in 1892, Harry would have been his private secretary.' This clearly proves that Eddy's close friends had already worked out suitable positions of power for themselves once the time came.

It was into this atmosphere of intrigue that Eddy moved, carefully guided and watched over by his new tutor. It is easy to imagine Stephen manipulating his royal charge, weaving his web of influence, pointing out, perhaps, that Eddy had no choice in his destiny – he could not even choose a career for himself, a basic liberty allowed to the lowest commoner.

So it is distinctly possible that, as Eddy succumbed to his tutor's powerful personality, dreams of a splendid destiny would have grown stronger in Stephen's mind. However, in seeking to dominate, it is possible for the powerful partner himself to become ensnared. The aphrodisiac of complete control over an important person is addictive, and the breaking of powerful dreams can cause mighty explosions. Neither James nor Eddy could have known that the seeds for a string of terrible murders were being sown.

Chapter Twelve

Who? And Why?

There is now only one more Ripper player to examine in detail. But first, let me pose an important question. Is it possible that members of the Royal Family and the son of a distinguished father, can be linked, however indirectly, to five penniless East End prostitutes and to their subsequent murder? And if so, how?

One renowned theory, that of Stephen Knight, links Prince Eddy *indirectly* to the crimes. This basic assumption is correct but the details of Knight's theory are wrong, as I will show later. Dr David Abrahamsen in his book *Murder and Madness*, first published in America by Donald I Fine Inc. in 1992, accuses Prince Eddy of *direct* involvement. This is not true, but it has been, in the past, a widely-held theory.

Eddy became a direct suspect in 1970. Dr Thomas Stowell, CBE, was an experienced medical man, born in 1885. He was a specialist in industrial medicine, and the holder of several honorary diplomas, which gained him prestigious private and governmental posts – clearly a distinguished man; a man whose word one would tend to trust.

In 1970 Dr Stowell claimed to have read the private papers of Sir William Gull. Gull had been born the son of a barge owner and had been raised in straitened and humble circumstances. He was, however, clearly gifted and intelligent, and applied himself diligently to medicine, winning prizes and honours, before gaining a teaching post at the prestigious Guy's Hospital in London. Gull's path to honours and fame was made possible in 1871 when he attended and helped to cure the Prince of Wales, who was close to death from typhoid fever. Gull was swiftly promoted to the post of Physician in Ordinary to Queen Victoria.

Dr Stowell caused an international sensation when he wrote in *The Criminologist* that Gull's papers had contained confidential matters which hinted that Queen Victoria's grandson might have been Jack the Ripper. This is a matter which we will examine in later chapters. For me, the interesting fact is not who Sir William Gull surreptitiously named as the killer: the interesting fact is that Sir William thought he might know the murderer's identity at all. Why, when the entire London police force was apparently baffled by the murders, should the Queen's Physician, with no obvious link to the crimes, think he knew Jack's identity? Is this further evidence of high involvement? Nigel Morland, the founding editor of *The Criminologist*, claimed that during a meeting with Inspector Frederick George Abberline, the noted detective had told him not to look for Jack the Ripper at the bottom of London society but a long way up. This assertion would make it appear that Abberline knew the identity of Jack the Ripper. Interestingly, the famous detective did not, like many other leading policemen, write his memoirs.

Stephen Knight sincerely believed that he had solved the Whitechapel murders. He maintained that Eddy had met and fallen in love with a Catholic shopgirl, Annie Crook. The couple secretly married and a child was born. The Establishment learned of this liaison and took Annie Crook into custody, where William Gull performed a brain operation to make her forget her past. Mary Kelly, who had been engaged to care for the Prince's child, Alice, escaped with the little girl into the East End. Here she foolishly revealed the explosive secret to four prostitutes; the five ladies then decided to try and blackmail the Establishment. But the powers behind the throne decided that the English crown might not survive such a scandal if the truth became widely known, and the women were all killed to silence them: death was the Establishment's assurance of absolute silence.

I was closely involved professionally with Stephen Knight during the writing of his book, and eventually dramatised the story. As my own theories occasionally skirt close to those of my late friend's, let me analyse the above statements.

1) Prince Eddy married Annie Crook. I consider this highly unlikely. Eddy was timid and terrified of his family, especially Queen Victoria. He was also used to being led and advised, and tended not to take the initiative himself. He would not, therefore, have secretly married a shopgirl, and certainly not a Catholic shopgirl, knowing what the consequences would be once his secret wedding was discovered. And with Victoria's network of spies he

must have known that any marriage would eventually be revealed.

2) There is documentary proof linking Eddy to homosexual activities (his discovery in a homosexual club), but no direct proof that he ever indulged in heterosexual couplings. He was reported to have been in love with several women, including his fiancée May of Teck, who eventually married his brother, George, but these feelings could have been merely cerebral. There is certainly no documentary evidence that Eddy was ever involved with prostitutes. Given his known sexual proclivities, his known circle of friends and his known character, a love affair with a woman which drove him beyond all control is highly unlikely.

3) Mary's flight with the child. Why escape to the East End, where she and her charge could easily be identified and picked up by the authorities? An escape to France, a country with which she was apparently familiar, would have made far more sense. And where would Mary have kept the child in the East End? There is no record of her being with any infant in Miller's Court – quite the opposite. And why did she tell the other prostitutes her secret? Mary was an intelligent woman. In order to obtain money from this affair she would have followed the code of all blackmailers. The very basis of extortion is secrecy; to reveal any confidential information undermines the power of the blackmailer. Mary's friends were frequently drunk: Mary would have known as well as anyone else that drink loosens tongues. She would have been very stupid to share her valuable knowledge and to risk her secret becoming widespread.

* * * * *

My own theory will reveal that Mary did indeed try to extort money from the Establishment, but not through a secret involving Eddy: the secret involved Eddy's father, the Prince of Wales. Bertie was the Victorian royal most closely associated with sexual adventures, and his philanderings ranged far and wide. As we have seen, Bertie explored an amazing variety of sordid adventures under the influence of his wild friend the Marquis of Hastings, amongst others. Only a few stories from these vice dens were ever recounted, but these antics were guided by just one principle – female beauty. A young woman's riches, social standing or marital status were not of prime importance, only a lady's looks and figure counted.

The notorious Victorian rake Frank Harris, who used to tell the Prince of Wales dirty jokes ('the filthier the better') recounts (in his autobiography, privately published in 1920) some of Bertie's sexual adventures. Several of them are so outrageous they do not bear repeating. Harris tells how Bertie would indulge in sexual adventures in the back of cabs whilst being driven around London. The Prince dallied in the bedrooms of various friends' houses, in clubs, and, on one occasion, whilst in Scotland, overcome by lust, he tumbled one lady friend in the open in the heather. But these high-jinks took place in the main with middle class or aristocratic ladies: could Bertie, even briefly, have been involved with an East End prostitute? Once again, the answer is, 'Yes'. I will shortly provide facts to support that assertion.

In Victorian times, amongst men, these antics would have been considered the behaviour of a full-blooded male – understandable heterosexual high-jinks no doubt much admired by his cronies.

Even when the King was old and too infirm to mount, a special chair was constructed for the stout Edward to enable easy oral stimulation of the monarch by prostitutes.

Bertie's dedication to sexual gratification was life-long, and he may well have taken a special delight in adventures with women far removed from his own social standing. Throughout history this has not been an uncommon trait, whatever the sexual predilection of the upper-class roué. Oscar Browning was drawn towards young, uneducated males, and was frequently known to entertain young carpenters and labourers all night in his rooms at Cambridge.

Links between royalty and commoners, including prostitutes, are well recorded throughout history. Given Bertie's wild behaviour and known enthusiasm for loose women, a link with Mary Kelly becomes a distinct possibility. But where could he have met her? At a wild West End party? Mary had confided to Joe Barnett that before arriving in Whitechapel she had worked in a high-class West End brothel. There is no reason why she should not have maintained contact with people and friends whom she had known a few years previously. Victorian research shows that Mary was not a coarse girl but a well educated woman who had a temper and a wild adventurous spirit – just the kind of personality which might have appealed to Bertie. However, Bertie and Mary probably did not meet in the West End. During my researches I have uncovered the extraordinary fact that Bertie, along with Sir George Chetwynd, Lord Richard Grosvenor and several other wild friends, rented a flat in the East End bordering on the territory around which Mary solicited. (The address of this flat and further details will be discussed in the last chapter.) This is a natural link between the prostitute and the royal. As the Prince, or one of his wild friends, or all of them together, travelled incognito towards Whitechapel, it is highly likely that they had spied Mary, who would have been natural prey to such men.

Bertie's wild behaviour, including his infidelities with countless women, had become widely known over a long period and his lifestyle had gained general acceptance. Given this fact, his consorting with an East End prostitute might have raised some eyebrows and unfavourable comment, but it would not, in itself, have required drastic action by the Establishment. However, a liaison with a low class woman, or even a high class woman, would have raised the greatest of alarm amongst the powers behind the throne if two joint complications had arisen: *pregnancy* and *Catholicism*.

Even pregnancy by itself was not a desperately dangerous affair. There were many claims that the Prince had fathered illegitimate children, and, given the number of affairs into which Bertie plunged, this is not unlikely. It was strongly rumoured that Lady Susan Pelham-Clinton, who was a close friend of the Prince of Wales, had given birth to his child. One of the Lady's advisers is said to have kept the Prince of Wales regularly informed about the progress of Susan's pregnancy. But for Bertie to sire a child with a titled lady was one thing; for him to sire a child with an East End prostitute was a different, possibly dangerous matter. However, the most explosive issue of all would be for a member of the Victorian Royal Family to sire a child with a Roman Catholic, low-class whore or not. That would be dynamite waiting for a match to be struck. It cannot be too strongly expressed how unpopular such a coupling would be in Victorian times.

An attempt in the eighteenth century to emancipate the Catholics led to violent rioting in London, led by Lord George Gordon. Both the Government and the Magistrates were intimidated, and troops had to be called out onto the streets. Hugh Walpole, writing from his house in Twickenham, recounted the riots in a series of letters:

[On 8 June, 1780]: 'Lord Mansfield's house was just burnt down, and at night there were shocking disorders.' [And on 9 June]: 'Yesterday was some slaughter in Fleet Street – they have exacted sums from many houses to avoid being burnt as Popish . . . Kirkgate saw men and women lying dead in the streets under barrows as he came home yesterday . . . whole families ruined, wives that tried to drag their husband out of the mobs.'

During betrothal arrangements between Queen Victoria and Albert the question of Catholicism had been discussed. There was a rumour that the forbidden religion was not unknown in Albert's family tree so Victoria wrote anxiously to her beloved on 22 November 1839 asking, on behalf of Lord Melbourne (the then Prime Minister), for a short history of the House of Saxe-Coburg. Her letter continues:

'. . . he wishes to hear this in order to make people here know exactly who your ancestors are, for a few stupid people here try to say you are a Catholic . . .' (He was not).

Violent demonstrations against Catholicism had taken place during the 1850s, and an Anglican vicar was attacked for merely placing candles on his altar and dressing his choirboys in surplices: such actions were construed as being a step towards Catholicism. Even that extraordinary royal servant John Brown was occasionally heard to mutter, 'Nasty beggars, those Catholic clergy.'

In 1890, a betrothal between Eddy and the Princess Hélène d'Orléans was seriously discussed, but the lady was a Catholic. When the Prime Minister, Lord Salisbury, was asked whether Princess Hélène might retain her religion after marriage to Eddy, provided that any children would be raised as Protestants, Salisbury warned that the country's anger against such a union might endanger the position of the throne. Let me repeat the Prime Minister's authoritative decision: the marriage of a Victorian royal, even to another royal, *might endanger the position of the throne*, (my italics) merely because the high-born lady was a Catholic. This was the opinion of the Prime Minister; clearly the throne would be in the greatest of danger if, through even a casual liaison, the lady in question was an East End Catholic whore.

Bertie caused a stir when, during a Declaration at his first opening of Parliament on 14 February 1901 he made a protest against the uncivil crudeness of the repudiation of Catholic doctrines. As King, he trod in quicksands when, on a foreign tour in 1903 he expressed a wish to pay his respects to the Pope, Pius X. Such a request came under close diplomatic scrutiny.

It is perhaps difficult to understand in the 1990s the deeply-rooted fear of the Church of Rome by the nineteenth-century Protestant population – a fear and hatred passed down in slightly lessening degrees from decade to decade, century to century. But nonetheless, in the 1880s the fear of Catholicism amongst many sectors of society was still very real, fed by a knowledge of the Catholic Church's unquenchable zeal (dating back to the Middle Ages, and still not forgotten) for hunting down heretics and for crushing, if possible, all opposition to religious power by the Church of Rome.

Even today Catholicism would impede a union with a member of Britain's Royal Family. So given the above facts, it is clear that the Establishment would be alarmed in the extreme if it believed that Bertie could be linked to a pregnant, Catholic East End prositute, and that news of this union might leak out; especially given the vacillating feelings towards the Crown in Victorian times. Indeed, the Establishment's fears are confirmed by no less a person than Queen Victoria herself. William Gladstone (a Prime Minister who did not endear himself to Her Majesty), at the Queen's request, wrote to tell Bertie that the throne of England was safe only so long as the nation had confidence in the personal character of the sovereign. Yet the nation clearly did not have that confidence. In 1871 a pamphlet entitled *What Does She Do With It?* referred to Queen Victoria's rapaciousness. In late September 1871 Gladstone saw an advertisement for this work, and re-marked, 'Things go from bad to worse.' He then commented that, 'The Queen is invisible and the Prince of Wales is not respected.' Clearly, from time to time, the Government feared for the Crown's stability, as did the Crown itself. As late as February 1888, just months before the commencement of the Ripper murders, the *East London Observer* opined, 'There is grave reason to fear that a social revolution is impending.'

Contemporary opinion, at all levels, signalled the deepest social discontent amongst some sections of the population; the Queen's unpopularity took firm root after she had gone into seclusion following the death of Albert. There were six attempts on her life, culminating in an unemployed Scotsman, in 1882, firing shots at her on Windsor Station.

On her few public appearances, Victoria was, from time to time, hissed at or booed. The *National Reformer* commented that: 'Her Majesty, by doing nothing except receiving her civil list, is teaching the country that it can get along quite well without a monarch.'

E.F. Benson, writing in 1933, summed up anti-monarchy feeling succinctly:

'. . . the report [of a breach of neutrality in the Franco-Prussian War] fanned public feeling against them both [Victoria and Bertie], and there was widespread agitation for the establishment of a Republic in England. Further fuel was piled on from other sources of discontent with the monarchy: the Queen's continued seclusion, already extremely unpopular, was added to the blaze and speakers in newly-founded Republican clubs all over the country produced figures to show what the country spent on a sovereign whom her subjects never saw, and who must be laying by enormous sums contributed by taxpayers who received no benefit whatever from her existence. The Prince similarly had an income from the country of over £100,000; certainly he, unlike his mother, spent it all, and was supposed to be heavily in debt. But the manner of his spending was as objectionable as his mother's saving, for it was all poured down the sink of his private life, and went in gambling and in betting . . . With a sovereign who was never seen . . . and an heir-apparent who appeared too often where he should not, England would do very well to be rid of them. And all this was not merely gutter-talk; Mr. Gladstone, the Prime Minister, told both the absentee mother and the too-frequently-present son that he was seriously disturbed about it.'

Even today there is widespread debate regarding the future of the Monarchy, with some of the above problems being discussed, and this is with a popular Queen on the throne, a lady whose devotion to duty is unquestionable. How much more intense that discussion must have been in Victorian times, when the Queen had only periods of popularity with the masses, periods which alternated with moods of the opposite humour. In 1870 Bertie was enveloped in a scandal which resulted in his appearance in a court of law – a scandal in itself. Sir Charles Mordaunt sued his wife for divorce. The indiscreet Lady Mordaunt had, in a fit of guilt, confessed to her husband that she had been unfaithful to him. The Prince of Wales was named amongst a string of lovers, and he was subpoena'ed to appear as a witness. As Bertie had indeed been engaging in frequent sexual intercourse with the lady (presumably dodging the other lovers) he was in a difficult position. However, in the witness box, and under oath, he denied any improper relationship with the lady, thereby committing perjury.

On this occasion the Royal Family were saved by Lady Mordaunt's father, Sir Thomas Moncrieff: with ruthless ingenuity he had his daughter certified as insane when she made the allegations. Temporary insanity was confirmed by leading doctors, the judge accepted this evidence, and thus Mordaunt lost his case. This is a blatant example of one member of the Establishment lying in order to save fellow members of the Establishment, even to the extent of vilifying a daughter and breaking the Hippocratic Oath. Plainly no sacrifice was too great for Queen and Country.

The case naturally increased gossip about Bertie's private life. It was alleged that he was heavily in debt to French money-lenders and that they were beginning to harass him for repayment. He was hissed at and booed during public appearances. On one occasion rotten fruit was thrown at him. Cartoons began to lampoon the Prince mercilessly, and a satire was published, *The Coming of K.* which was clearly based on Bertie and his pursuit of actresses, society ladies and prostitutes.

It was not until a year after the Mordaunt affair that public sympathy was regained by the Prince. He became seriously ill with typhoid fever and was thought likely to die. Bertie's recovery signalled a wave of popularity, but subsequent scandals, including a second appearance in court (in a slander case over cheating at cards) led to a further dimming of the public's affections.

In the 1870s virulent outbursts of Republicanism must have alarmed the many members of the Government who had warned about the dangers of such movements. One leading Republican declared that the monarchy was 'the master of fraud that shelters all others'.

The death in 1883 of the much-favoured royal servant, John Brown, renewed speculation about his true relationship with the Queen. Persistent rumours that Victoria and John had been secretly married and that the union had produced a child did not add to the Monarch's popularity.

On 8 February 1886 a series of meetings and marches were organized to highlight, amongst other things, the plight of the unemployed. After parading through the heart of London the marches were to culminate in Trafalgar Square, where a mixture of leading Socialist and Marxist speakers would address the crowd. This meeting, which became known as Black Monday, led to a series of violent disturbances and a not unexpected confrontation with the police. Queen Victoria wrote to her Prime Minister, Mr Gladstone:

'The Queen cannot sufficiently express her indignation at the monstrous riot which took place the other day in London, and which risked people's lives and was a momentary triumph of socialism and disgrace to the capital. If steps, and very strong ones, are not speedily taken to put these proceedings down with a high hand, to punish severely the real ringleaders, and to 'probe to the bottom' as Mr. Gladstone has promised, the whole affair, the Government will suffer severely. The effect abroad is already very humiliating to this country.'

If Queen Victoria was so outraged by the 1886 disturbances the serious riots one year later, known as Bloody Sunday, must have been even more distressing to her.

In 1887 Sir Charles Warren decided to ban meetings in Trafalgar Square, which had become a favoured venue for political gatherings. Socialists and Marxists could draw the crowds to this large, central meeting place, to listen to fiery messages of revolution.

Large crowds decided to ignore Warren's ban and converged on central London, but were prevented from entering Trafalgar Square by baton-wielding police. Despite this, the Square eventually filled up, and armed guards and mounted police were ordered into action against a crowd of 100,000. In the ensuing battle hundreds of civilians were injured and two were killed. Memories of this battle soured relations between the working classes and the police for decades.

In 1888 the centenary of the French Revolution was approaching and the national newspapers would have been commenting on the affair. This thought may also have alarmed the powers behind the throne. There was also the rise of Communism to contend with. Eleanor Marx was repeating her father's famous slogan:

'. . . [Communist] ends can only be attained by the forcible overthrow of all existing social conditions. Let the ruling class tremble at the communist revolution. The proletarians have nothing to lose but their chains. They have a world to win. Workers of all countries unite.'

These powerful words were reinforced by the blazing voice of George Bernard Shaw who, along with other committed and vociferous socialists, had pledged solidarity with the communists.

Only one year earlier, in 1887, Lenin's brother Alexander – despite stirring speeches during his trial – had been executed in Russia for an attempt on the Czar's life. The Czar was, of course, closely related to the British Royal Family. With such violent contemporary events and with disturbed social forces to brood over, the possibility of further insurrection in the land would have greatly alarmed the Establishment, and there are few forces more ruthless than a powerful State when it feels threatened and has to protect its own interests.

It was in this atmosphere of massive discontent and civil strife, with a growing voice for Republicanism, that the Establishment found itself embroiled in 1888. It is my contention that during this disturbed period, Mary Kelly, an East End Catholic prostitute, selected a reliable contact (to be discussed more fully later) and announced that she was carrying the Prince of Wales's child. Given the above considerations, if the Establishment thought that there might be any reason whatsoever for believing this statement, it is easy to see that panic might have ensued throughout the corridors of Power. And given Bertie's record of affairs with so many women, and given his extraordinary East End accommodation arrangements with his wild friends, there would be every reason to believe such a story.

So: leaving aside the question of parentage, was Mary pregnant? Many recorded opinions say 'yes'. Caroline Maxwell said that she remarked to Mary (on the morning following Mary's 'death', when Mary said she had been sick), 'I pity your feelings'. Many people think this remark interpreted the nausea as morning sickness.

The highly-regarded Ripper authority Donald Rumbelow, a former policeman, boldly states in his book *The Complete Jack the Ripper* :

'Kelly, not quite three months pregnant and probably feeling the effects of morning sickness, was generally too unwell to solicit for much custom.'

We must remember that if Mary Kelly's pregnancy dated from some time in April, then she would have been over six months into her condition during the alleged conversation with Mrs Maxwell: plenty of time for her to be feeling the full effects of pregnancy. Yet it was established that the body found in Miller's Court was *not* pregnant, despite rumours to the contrary. An obvious conclusion is apparent. Was the body found in Miller's Court a substitute corpse? We shall see.

* * * * *

Let us recapitulate:

Question. Is there any evidence of an official cover-up during the Ripper crimes? **Answer.** A considerable amount. The press remarked on an official cover-up several times. Vital witnesses were not called into court to give evidence, and facts were suppressed. During Mary Kelly's inquest the law was broken, official papers were not signed and the affair was rushed through in one day and closed with indecent haste.

Question. What class of person would merit such an extraordinary bending of the law? **Answer.** Only the very highest in the land, meaning a member of the Royal Family or possibly one or two very senior politicians. But from this group, the only person known to be actively associated with, and to use the services of, prostitutes was the Prince of Wales.

Question. Given the above evidence of a cover-up by the authorities, is it possible that Mary might have met with Bertie, and might sexual relations have taken place? **Answer.** Considering Bertie's known tastes, we can give an emphatic 'yes' to the last part of the question. And if Mary and the Prince did meet (and given his rented flat in the East End on the very edge of Mary's soliciting area, such a meeting is distinctly possible), then a capricious, unpredictable girl such as Mary would have attracted the Prince. (Bertie was also capricious and unpredictable.). Indeed, given a meeting in private between the Prince and the prostitute, sexual relations would almost certainly have taken place. This was the usual experience of any pretty girl in Bertie's company.

Question. Would there be any need to protect the Crown from deep scandal by so drastic a measure as a cover-up? **Answer.** Given the abundant evidence contained in this chapter regarding the Crown's precarious position, an official cover-up at any cost would be vital.

Question. Is it likely that high authority would dare to sanction a manipulation of the law? **Answer.** Yes. We saw an example of this manipulation during the Mordaunt divorce scandal. The Victorian age was a time of far less accountability than today, when we have the powerful, often intrusive, investigative press, and probing television programmes. In 1888 East Enders knew little about politics; they did not even recognise their Royal Family in person. Authority and the upper classes, within certain limits, carried on as they pleased. In 1888 the Police Force had only been in existence for around six decades. This was enough time for it to become a law unto itself without becoming accountable for its actions. Recently a serving police officer (who has studied the history of the Police Force since its founding by Sir Robert Peel) said to me, 'Until 1972 no one – not even serving officers, and certainly not the public at large – dared to question the decisions of the higher authority in the police force. Whatever was said or done went unchallenged.' Such unquestioned and dangerous power would have applied even more strongly in the nineteenth century.

* * * * *

If Mary Kelly became pregnant soon after meeting Bertie it need not have mattered whether the Prince, or one of her clients, or Joe Barnett was the real father. Being intelligent, Mary would have realised the vast opportunities which involving Bertie in a plausible paternity suit could bring. The authorities' actions indicate that they believed Kelly's story, so let us, for interest's sake, consider all the various possibilities inherent in this situation.

1) Kelly, knowing Bertie's reputation, might have dreamt up a promising blackmail plot. The Prince was, of course, a prime target for extortion: in later years there was at least one documented blackmail attempt against the Royal Family when, after Bertie's death, indiscreet love letters to his mistress, the beautiful Frances, Countess of Warwick ('Darling Daisy') fell into the wrong hands.

2) Mary might have been to a party at which the Prince of Wales was present without actually meeting him, but, from this experience, she dreamt up her pregnancy story.

3) Mary might have been to the Prince's East End flat and engaged in sexual intercourse with Bertie *without* becoming pregnant. In Victorian times, prostitutes must have been adept at avoiding pregnancy.

4) Mary might have been impregnated by one of her clients or by Joe Barnett, but, with a stroke of cunning, after relations with Bertie, she might have devised a plan whereby she could convincingly claim that the child belonged to the Prince of Wales.

If Mary approached the Establishment in the hope of money on any of the above four pretexts, then she would have been guilty of blackmail. But, as we have already mentioned, it is a distinct possibility that Mary did indeed meet Bertie in intimate surroundings; if so, sexual intercourse would almost certainly have taken place, and the prostitute might (perhaps deliberately) have become pregnant.

In this case, if Bertie *was* responsible for impregnating Mary, then her demands for support would not have been blackmail in the accepted sense of the word. Any woman in a similar situation would have expected to be cared for lavishly. It is my contention that Mary *was* genuinely carrying a royal child and felt entitled to some support, as any woman would. So in what way could she have approached the Establishment with her demands?

Chapter Thirteen

Montague Druitt

The last link in our Ripper puzzle involves one Montague John Druitt. Druitt was born in Wimborne, Dorset on 15 August 1857, and, like J.K. Stephen, he came from an eminently respectable family. His father, William, was a highly-regarded surgeon and a Justice of the Peace; he is described in the *Wimborne Guardian* as having been 'a strong churchman', which might indicate that Montague had been raised in a repressed religious atmosphere. William married his wife Ann in 1854, and the union produced seven children – a first son (named after the father), then Montague, then five more offspring. Ann brought her own wealth into the partnership, and the couple, with their seven children, lived in spacious comfort in one of Wimborne's finest houses.

Montague displayed intellectual ability early in life, when, aged thirteen, he won a scholarship to the prestigious Winchester College, whose students were known as 'Wykehamists' after the founder, William of Wykeham. At Winchester, Montague would have been subjected to the typical harsh regime which was prevalent at Victorian public schools. Conditions at Winchester during the 1820s were outlined by F.D. How:

'Chapel was at 6.00 a.m. Morning school at 7.30, after which an excursion had frequently to be made to the top of St Catherine's Hill, an apparently useless process to which the conservatism of Winchester clung, and which went by the name of "Morning Hills".'

Strict discipline was maintained at the school during Montague's time. A contemporary describes Dr George Moberly (headmaster until a few years before Montague's arrival) taking studies in classical literature. He asked a pupil to translate a section of work by the great Roman poet Horace. The boy's efforts to read the verse, 'Decende caelo et dic age tibia,' produced 'Come down from heaven and give us a tune'.

Dr Moberly was outraged by this vulgar lack of learning, and ordered the boy to be flogged. There was a set routine for this procedure. The boy was made to kneel down, his clothing was rolled up as high as the waist, and a rod with four long apple twigs attached was used by Dr Moberly to administer from four to six lashes.

Pupils at Winchester were raised in a strongly religious atmosphere, and they were made to submit to the infamous 'fagging' system. Flogging, both from the masters and from the senior students at the college, was prevalent. However the harshness of public school life did not seem to deter Montague: he achieved success in his studies, he was clever in debates, and he became an excellent and devoted cricketer. A memorable anecdote, found in Tom Cullen's book *Autumn of Terror*, records that Druitt: '. . . championed Wordsworth against his detractors, finding it a great merit on the part of the poet that he was a *'bulwark of Protestantism.'* (My italics.)

After gaining distinction at Winchester, Druitt was awarded a scholarship to Oxford, from where he graduated with a B.A. in 1880. After a break, Montague decided on a career in law, which meant a further period of study. To underwrite his legal examinations for admittance to the Bar, Montague was forced to borrow from his father. From this borrowing there might be hints that the son did not find complete favour with the father; when William (senior) died, he left an estate of over £16,000, a large sum in the 1880s. The main assets were shared between Ann, the three daughters and William junior. Montague, along with two brothers, received comparatively little; his share was an ungenerous (from so large an estate) £500, and deducted from this sum was any money which Montague had been forced to borrow against his educational expenses. This rider was a niggardly gesture on the part of William senior, especially when one considers that in Victorian times it was considered mandatory for rich parents to pay for their sons' education.

Montague became a registered barrister in 1885, and a few months later rented chambers in the Inner Temple at 9 King's Bench Walk. We have Stephen Knight to thank for pointing out that at this address Druitt was in the close proximity of two of J.K. Stephen's brothers: Harry Lushington Stephen at 3 King's Bench Walk; and Herbert Stephen, whose chambers were opposite King's Bench Walk in Paper Buildings. Might J.K. Stephen and Montague Druitt have been introduced to each other by one of J.K.'s brothers? Near to King's Bench Walk is Lincoln's Inn, where J.K. himself had chambers, so he would almost certainly have maintained regular contact with his siblings.

Montague's legal career did not flourish, a not unusual state of affairs in the 1880s. A contemporary of Druitt, George R. Sims, a journalist and dramatist, wrote that only one in eight who were called to the Bar made a living from the law: '. . . the life of men who have come enthusiastic to the law and have utterly failed would fill as many pages as are contained in a complete set of law reports.'

This is confirmed by my own researches. *London Souvenirs*, written in 1899 by C.W. Heckthorn, contains an anecdote on the above subject:

'Success at the Bar comes to barristers in the most capricious manner. In this profession, as in many other pursuits, modest merit but slowly makes its way. Manners maketh the man, but impudence an advocate; without this latter quality even high connections and powerful patronage often seems ineffectual. Earl Camden, the son of Chief Justice Pratt, was called to the Bar in his twenty-fourth year, and remained a briefless barrister for nine long years, when he resolved to abandon Westminster Hall for his College Fellowship . . .'

Montague Druitt kept his chambers until his death, and although he was one of the many luckless barristers who received no briefs, and although he was without any appreciable inheritance from his father, much of his bequest presumably having been used on heavy educational expenses, Montague appeared to enjoy a comfortable life-style. He had had the foresight to provide extra earnings by taking a teaching job in a private school at 9 Eliot Place, Blackheath in 1881. It is clear, however, that his schoolmaster's salary did not allow the accumulation of savings, as, in 1882, as we have seen, he was borrowing against his inheritance to pay for his legal training.

The owner and Headmaster of the successful school at which Druitt taught was George Valentine. Unfortunately little information about the school, and no information about Druitt's life whilst he taught there, can be unearthed: but we do know that in

1881 Druitt indulged his passion for sport by joining the Morden Cricket Club in Blackheath, where he became treasurer. It has been a generally accepted fact that Montague received no legal work whatsoever once he was empowered to practise law, but Paul Begg discovered that the law lists of 1887 cite Druitt in employment as a 'special pleader'. Pleading was an occupation mainly undertaken by law students who were not yet fully qualified to practise at the Bar. The job mainly entailed advisory work and assistance in civil cases. In pleading, a writ outlining the harm which a plaintiff has suffered is sent to the defendant, who, in reply, returns his defence. In Druitt's time the position was between counsel and attorney; special pleaders no longer exist, but in late Victorian times, the work provided a good grounding for students before they were called to the Bar. But Montague *had* been called to the Bar. Perhaps he was especially short of cash in 1887 when he took on work which was clearly below his abilities and his status as a barrister.

Puzzlingly, Druitt was able to save a considerable sum of money whilst he was teaching. When he died in December 1888 his estate amounted to around £1,300 cash, which he personally must have earned, apart from any small sum left over from his father's legacy. Further money was added to the estate posthumously by his mother's will.

In late Victorian times £1,300 was a considerable sum. The Bank of England informed me that the pound in 1888 would now be worth £44.90, based on figures worked out at the end of 1992. This means that, in today's money, Druitt left around £58,000 cash in his will. Yet his salary as a teacher would have been around £200 per annum, and we know that he was penniless in 1882 as he was forced to borrow against his inheritance.

Let us examine Druitt's savings more closely. The cheque for £16 found on his body might well have represented one month's wages – this would fit in with a salary of £200 per annum. There was, of course, his work as a pleader. I have tried to ascertain from a number of sources how much Druitt might have earned from pleading, but it has proved impossible to quantify accurately. The amount would have depended upon the nature of the case being tried, the eminence of the barrister involved, and, of course, on the number of jobs Druitt was able to undertake. The pay for such work would have been reasonably generous, but as Druitt was a full-time school teacher, with a considerable number of evening and weekend responsibilities at several sporting clubs, it is difficult to know how much time he could have spent at his extracurricular legal activities; surely, however, not enough time to accumulate considerable savings. And, of course, had the pleading work been regular and lucrative, Druitt would surely have given up teaching and followed his chosen profession.

We must now consider why Druitt took up pleading in the first place? The obvious reason would be that by 1887, he was short of money. So short that he was willing to accept work for which he was over-qualified. There were rigid social barriers in Victorian times, and for a barrister to accept a pleader's job must have meant some loss of face. The fact that Druitt found and accepted such work indicates an urgent need of extra income during 1887. This would make sense. From the time that Montague was called to the Bar he had had the expense of setting up his legal practice (very costly); the expense of maintaining chambers at King's Bench Walk; the expenses of day-to-day living; lodging expenses if he was not resident at Eliot Place; travelling expenses; clothing expenses, and expenses relating to his many cricketing activities. Could this full financial load, along with considerable savings, have been achieved on the modest income of a school teacher? Almost certainly not; so it is not surprising that Druitt accepted extra work – any kind of work – to supplement his regular income. But this creates another puzzle. It is inconceivable that Druitt could have saved the equivalent of, in today's money, £58,000 during the last two years of his life, even with the pleader's job. Therefore, the large estate left in his will should have meant that he was already financially comfortable in 1887, with large cash savings. If that was the case, why did he need to accept further work? There seems to be no logical explanation for Druitt's fortune. Could there be sinister reasons behind his nest egg?

After the death of her husband the mental health of Ann Druitt began to deteriorate. By July 1888 she required full-time treatment for her problems at an asylum in Clapton, East London. It was only one month later, at the end of August, that the first Ripper murder was committed.

At the end of November 1888 Montague's career at Eliot's

Place, Blackheath, came to an abrupt end when he was summarily dismissed from his teaching post by Mr Valentine. Reports of this affair are sketchy, and we have details of the dismissal mainly from testimony given by William junior at his younger brother's inquest. William told the coroner that after he had been informed that Montague appeared to be missing, he had gone to the school in Blackheath where he was told that his brother had 'got into serious trouble and had been dismissed.' Clearly, William had heard of no trouble brewing in his brother's affairs, which would indicate that the dismissal was peremptory.

The most common speculation for this discharge has been that Montague had an improper relationship with one of the boys at the school, but this is only inspired guesswork. Druitt's previous record of behaviour does not indicate the likelihood of such conduct, although a sudden and forbidden uncharacteristic passion cannot be ruled out, and it is difficult to think of any other reason for so abrupt a termination of employment without, one assumes, any notice whatsoever.

The first positive indications that Druitt might be involved in the Ripper murders came from Sir Melville Macnaghten. He was clearly fascinated by the Ripper case and wrote extensively on the subject, as we saw from the highly-placed police officer's comments in Chapter Four. Macnaghten stated that: '. . . the Whitechapel murderer had five victims and five victims only . . .' There are two available versions of Macnaghten's confidential report on the murders, one version still on Scotland Yard files and one version which was copied by Sir Melville's daughter, Lady Christabel Aberconway, from her father's original notes. After discussing the case of a popular suspect, Thomas Cutbush (who enjoyed lightly stabbing ladies around the buttocks), Sir Melville wrote:

'. . . I may mention the cases of three men, any one of whom would have been more likely than Cutbush to have committed this series of murders:-

1) A Mr M.J. Druitt, said to be a doctor and of good family, who disappeared at the time of the Miller's Court murder, and whose body (which was said to have been upwards of a month in the water) was found in the Thames on 31st Dec. – or about 7 weeks after that murder. He was sexually insane and from

private info I have little doubt but that his own family believed him to have been the murderer . . .'

M.J. Druitt was, of course, a barrister, but he came from a medical background, and Sir Melville was writing some years after the events (in 1894), from memory. It is quite clear that his suspect was Montague. And clearly, the remark 'from private info' means that Sir Melville had been told more than he was prepared to reveal: what could that have been and why was he not prepared to reveal it?

Sir Melville's second choice falls on 'Kosminski, a Polish Jew', and his third candidate is 'a Russian doctor, Michael Ostrog'. However, by 1914, the year in which Sir Melville's memoirs were published, the two latter suspects had been dropped and his opinions had focused sharply on to one man:

'I incline to the belief that the individual [Jack the Ripper] who held up London in terror resided with his own people; that he absented himself from home at certain times, and that he committed suicide on or about the 10th November, 1888.'

Despite the incorrect minor detail (Druitt did not live at home), and despite the incorrect date in the memoirs (December would have been more accurate; Montague died in the first week of December), it is clear that Sir Melville was referring to Druitt. Macnaghten's proud boast of 'working from memory' would account for the errors. So we must wonder again what the highly-placed policeman's 'private info' could have been? And why would he not reveal it? There was no compunction about discussing the case in detail in every other respect. Who was being protected?

Sir Melville was not the only one to suspect Druitt. William Bachert, who by 1890 had taken over the chairmanship of the Vigilance Committee, continued to pester the police over the Ripper case. There are claims that, after being sworn to secrecy, Bachert was told that the murderer had drowned at the end of 1888. Why were the authorities so certain? In 1924 Sir Basil Thomson, who had access to the records of Scotland Yard, stated that the police believed Jack to have been an insane Russian medical student 'whose body was found floating in the Thames immediately after the last of the outrages.' This is clearly a garbled version of Druitt's death. J.F. Moylan, CBE, writing about Scotland Yard in 1929, stated that there was public anger against the police and the CID because of their failure to arrest Jack the Ripper. It is now certain that the murderer, Mr Moylan maintains, '. . . escaped justice by committing suicide at the end of 1888.' Clearly Druitt was a favourite police suspect, but this was kept secret from the public for a great many years.

Hargreave Lee Adam, a former member of the CID turned crime writer, wrote in the introduction to his 1930 book *The Trial of George Chapman* that three leading policemen, (Dr, later Sir, Robert Anderson, Major Henry Smith and Sir Melville Macnaghten) had all told him that the police knew the identity of the Ripper. Macnaghten had added that he had documentary proof of the killer's name, but that he had burned the papers, which, if true, is the most extraordinary behaviour for a policeman in his position: but then, as we shall see in the final chapter, an inordinate amount of official material which referred to Jack the Ripper was burned. The *Acton Chiswick and Turnham Green Gazette* of 5 January 1889, gives a full account of events concerning Druitt's death:

'FOUND DROWNED. Shortly after midday on Monday, a waterman named Winslade, of Chiswick, found the body of a man, well-dressed, floating in the Thames off Thornycroft's. He at once informed a constable, and without delay the body was at once conveyed to the mortuary. On Wednesday afternoon, Dr. Diplock, coroner, held the inquest at the Lamb Tap, when the following evidence was adduced:- William H. Druitt said he lived at Bournemouth and was a solicitor. The deceased was his brother, who was 31 last birthday. He was a barrister-at-law, and an assistant master at a school in Blackheath . . . witness heard from a friend on 11 December that deceased had not been heard of at his chambers for more than a week. Witness then went to London to make inquiries, and at Blackheath he found that the deceased had got into serious trouble at the school, and had been dismissed. That was on 30 December. Witness had deceased's things searched where he resided, and found a paper addressed to him (produced). The coroner read this letter, which was to the effect:- "Since Friday I felt that I was going to be like mother, and the best thing was for me to die." Witness continuing, said deceased had never made any attempt on his life before. His mother became insane in July last. He had no other relative . . .'

There are several curious features in this report. Firstly, there is the statement by William that Montague had no other relative. This is patently untrue. Montague was one of seven children, and he was the first one to die, so why did William, himself a solicitor, stand in a court of law and lie quite blatantly? And is there any significance in the statement: '. . . witness had the deceased's things searched where he resided . . .'? Might not William have been expected to search through his brother's things personally, or did he want an independent witness to find Montague's suicide note? The Gazette continued with a report on the finding of Druitt's body:

'. . . Henry Winslade was the next witness. He said that he lived at No. 4, Shore Street, Paxton Road, and that he was a waterman. About one o'clock on Monday, he was on the river in a boat, when he saw the body floating. The tide was at half flood running up. He brought the body ashore and gave information to the police. PC George Moulson, 216 T said he searched the body, which was fully dressed, excepting the hat and collar. He found four large stones in each pocket in the top coat; £2.10s in gold, 7s in silver, 2p in bronze, two cheques on the London and Provincial Bank (one for £50 and the other for £16), a first-class season ticket from Blackheath to London (South Western Railways), a second-half return Hammersmith to Charing Cross (dated 1 December), a silver watch, gold chain with silver guinea attached, a pair of kid gloves, and a white handkerchief. There were no marks of injury on the body, but it was rather decomposed. A verdict of suicide whilst in unsound mind was returned.'

This appears to be a full and highly detailed report of the proceedings. Yet Montague had been dramatically dismissed from his post, and such a sacking may well have affected the balance of his mind which would help to explain the suicide. He was dismissed from the school on 30 November, which was a Friday, obviously the day referred to in his suicide note. It is, therefore, surprising that the coroner did not want to know why Montague had been dismissed; though one can understand William not volunteering such information if the details were sordid. As this was an article for a provincial newspaper, which would have been only too eager to deal in scandal, it is unlikely that the reporter would have failed to include details of Montague's dismissal if they had been discussed in open court.

It has generally been accepted that Druitt died on 3 December, but, as the invaluable *The Jack the Ripper A to Z* points out, the death might have occurred on 1 December, a date which would be confirmed by the return ticket found on the body.

Druitt's known actions paint a strange picture of a man in a suicidal state of mind. After writing a note plainly indicating that he intends to take his life, Montague keeps in his pocket a large sum of cash and several cheques for impressive amounts. He dons his gold chain and silver watch, and collects a pair of fine gloves. Then he walks to Blackheath Station and travels to London (Charing Cross). Here, if we accept the date of his death as 1 December, he must have bought a *return* ticket to Hammersmith. He then travels to Hammersmith and throws himself into the Thames, although there is a long stretch of the River only one minute's walk from where his journey from Blackheath had ended. And why did Montague travel into London to find a river in the first place? I frequently visit friends at Blackheath; the reaches of Greenwich are not too far distant. If Montague had walked across the Heath and down Croom's Hill, he would have reached a long stretch of the Thames into which he could have jumped. There is an unreal air about a person who, having decided to commit suicide, dresses himself in all his finery, keeps very large sums of money on his person, then takes two train journeys to his death. Even given the fact that an insane person's actions cannot be explained, a long, solitary walk seems a more likely choice for a man with deep suicidal urges than a long train journey to a specific spot.

As the diligent and intelligent Ripper researchers Martin Howells and Keith Skinner (who, cleverly, without the advantage of my proof, half-solve the Ripper mystery in their book *The Ripper Legacy*) comment:

'. . . are we to assume that he [Druitt] wished to prolong his life just long enough to jump off his favourite bridge? The hypothesis is ludicrous, and yet if we are to accept William's statement, that is what we must believe. At the very least, we can see how imperative was the coroner's need to ascertain the last person to see Montague alive; the fact that he did not even try, when a report about this barrister's death was being prepared for the Home Office, is highly suspicious . . .'

Precisely. Here is further evidence of irregular conduct in a court of law, and once again the death of a subject linked to the Ripper murders was not fully investigated. Why? And what was Sir Melville Macnaghten's evidence which convinced him that Montague's own family suspected their relative, and why was that evidence not stated in court during Montague's inquest? William, the brother, a solicitor trained in the ways of law, had ample opportunity to speak out.

As we have seen, the whole ambience of Montague's last journey was that of a man travelling to a pre-arranged meeting, probably somewhere in Hammersmith; could he therefore have been murdered? And if so, by whom, and why?

One further puzzle – the cheque for £50 found on the body. Translated into today's money that sum would equal £2,250. Who gave him a cheque for that amount? It is unlikely that a part-time job as a lowly pleader would have provided such a huge sum. Even the £16 cheque represents over £700, and he was carrying well over £100 in cash. In all a sum equivalent to over £3,000 in today's money was on Druitt's body when it was recovered from The River Thames. What was going on? Druitt's life and death contain many mysteries which I will examine in greater detail in a later chapter.

First, for clarity's sake, let us once again list the main points in this complicated story.

* * * * *

On Friday, 31 August, 1888, in the middle of the night, a middle-aged prostitute, Mary Nichols, was murdered and mutilated. She was found lying sprawled on her back on a London pavement. Although people were spending fretful nights in houses overlooking the murder site no unusual sounds – no cries or scuffles – were heard.

One week later another middle-aged prostitute, Annie Chapman, who resided mainly at an address only a few minutes' walk from Nichols's favoured doss-house, was discovered at dawn in the back yard of a common lodging-house. Annie had been murdered and mutilated. Her pocket had been cut open and rifled, and its contents had been carefully laid out in a heap beside her body. Although the yard was in constant use, both day and night, no one saw the murderer at work and no cries for help were heard. Three weeks later the body of Liz Stride was found, huddled in a passageway leading to Dutfield's Yard with its throat slashed from ear to ear. A witness, Israel Schwartz, testified to the police that he had seen an initial attack on Liz; she had been thrown to the pavement by a man outside Dutfield's Yard, but Schwartz was frightened away by a second man, possibly a look-out. Despite this vital and unique evidence – Schwartz possibly being the only man ever to have seen the Ripper about to begin his work – he was *not* called to give evidence at the murdered woman's inquest. Why not?

Stride was almost certainly seen being attacked at 12.45 a.m. and she was murdered close to 1.00 a.m. What happened to her and where was she in those missing 15 minutes?

Forty minutes after the discovery of Stride's body a second murder victim, Catharine Eddowes, was found dead and badly mutilated, lying on her back on the pavement of a London square. Eddowes was known to use the name 'Mary Kelly' from time to time. On the night of her death Catharine was many hours late for a meeting with her lover. She had disappeared penniless and sober at 2.00 p.m. and for over six hours there is no recorded trace of her movements, despite massive publicity after her death. Yet Catharine had obtained enough alcohol during the afternoon and early evening to inebriate herself. Did she get the money for drink through soliciting? If so, why did someone not see her touting for custom? All the other prostitutes had been spotted in the middle of the night, but Catharine would have been at work for six hours during the day. She was arrested at 8.30 p.m. and taken to Bishopsgate Police Station. There, after some hours in custody, and despite the fact that the police themselves had warned that women should not go out at night, the duty officers at Bishopsgate Police Station released Catharine into the heart of the Ripper territory at 1.00 a.m., despite the fact that they must have known she was penniless. Did they expect her to walk the streets all night? Surprisingly, after being released from custody in the early hours, presumably suffering from a hangover, and possibly still unsteady on her legs, the middle-aged woman did not turn in the direction of her partner's lodging-house to try and get in touch with him, although she had remembered her earlier broken promise to the effect that she would be back soon: instead, she headed towards Mitre Square, and somewhere along the way she met Jack the Ripper. Mitre Square was a respectable business centre on the fringes of the City of London. Why would Catharine have been so far from home in such an area? No one heard a sound nor saw anything suspicious in this fourth Ripper murder. Jack, as usual, had melted away.

After the double murder the police became uncooperative with the press. As one paper reported: 'The police are extraordinarily reticent with reference to the Mitre Square tragedy.' A second paper said: 'The police apparently have strict orders to close all channels of information to members of the press.' Why? Even embarrassment at their lack of success should not have forced the authorities to clam up; they should have been busy making excuses and explaining how much effort they were putting into the murder investigations.

Almost six weeks after the double killing a fifth murder occurred in 13 Miller's Court, part of a London lodging-house. Here the victim, named as Mary Kelly, was slashed beyond recognition. The corpse had been mutilated, eviscerated and partially skinned. Apart from a cry of 'murder' (which might not have referred to the affairs in Miller's Court), no sound was heard. No suspect could be pinpointed and, therefore, no arrest was made.

On the morning after the fifth murder the supposed 'corpse' was sighted by three independent witnesses, many hours after her 'death'. One witness, under oath, swore that she had had a conversation with Mary Kelly, although Mary was supposed to have been murdered by this time. This will be discussed in the next chapter.

The inquest on this final victim was presided over by an experienced ex-police surgeon, Roderick MacDonald, who was well versed in the rules of procedure on such occasions. Yet the inquiry headed by MacDonald broke several basic legal requirements. Vital facts concerning the injuries of the victim and the weapon used to inflict those injuries were not ascertained. Little notice was taken of Mrs Maxwell's sensational sighting of Mary Kelly after her supposed death, and Maxwell was not recalled to give further evidence. The inquest was rushed through at break-neck speed; it opened and was closed in one day. This haste meant that there was insufficient time to trace Kelly's Irish relatives, who could possibly have helped identify the mangled remains found in Miller's Court. Kelly's lover of 18 months, Joe Barnett, said that he could only identify her by the ears and the eyes, but as the face had been slashed to pulp, it must have been difficult to see the eyes mixed amongst the mashed flesh, and the ears had been partly removed. After the inquest official papers relating to the affair were not signed by MacDonald. Despite the highlighting of these inadequacies by national newspapers no new inquest was called.

As soon as Kelly's inquest was closed an important witness, George Hutchinson, approached the police and said that he had seen a man pick up Mary Kelly on the night she was murdered. Hutchinson then gave an incredibly detailed description of Kelly's companion – a man who might have been Jack the Ripper.

Inspector Frederick George Abberline, the officer in charge of the basic Ripper investigations, thought that George Hutchinson's evidence was important, but the police did not re-open Kelly's inquest in order to include this new material officially, along with the extra sightings of the supposed victim.

The actions of the Metropolitan Police Commissioner, Sir Charles Warren, were extraordinary. Graffiti had been discovered on a wall, over the spot where a piece of blood-smeared apron had been thrown away. Later tests proved this snippet to be part of Catharine Eddowes's apron, which meant the graffiti had most probably been chalked by the murderer. On hearing this news, Warren rushed into the East End in the middle of the night and personally removed the writing.

Sir Charles had been responsible for the use of bloodhounds in the murder investigations, although it must have been obvious to the dullest of minds that in a dirty, smelly, overcrowded area such as the East End, no dog could ever be successful in tracking a particular odour. The dogs proved useless, yet, despite that failure, the final murder victim (and the murder site) was left unattended for most of the morning, whilst the advisability of calling in dogs to Miller's Court was debated.

Warren must have been informed about the final murder im-mediately. He must have known that policemen were awaiting orders about the use or otherwise of bloodhounds, and that the murder site was unentered; yet instead of issuing orders to sort out the chaos, he resigned. And it later transpired that no bloodhounds were available to be brought to Miller's Court even if they *had* been needed.

At the inquest into the death of Montague Druitt, a famous Ripper suspect (and justly so, as I will prove), vital facts were again withheld from the proceedings.

Sir Melville Macnaghten said that he had been given private information which led him to believe that Druitt's family believed Montague was the killer; the family would presumably be in a position to know the truth of this matter, and clearly they had succeeded in convincing a highly-placed police officer that their suspicions were well-founded. Yet Macnaghten took the matter no further, which is distinctly odd. William Druitt, on hearing of his brother's disappearance, did not go to Montague's lodgings personally, but delegated the task to outsiders, who found a suicide note. This stated that Montague thought he had been going insane since the Friday (three days earlier) – yet his family believed him to be Jack the Ripper, which means he should have thought that he had been mad for about four months. At the inquest into Montague's death, no efforts were made to find witnesses to the deceased's final hours. No attempt was made to find out why he had been dismissed from his teaching job, although this could have had vital bearings on his death. The victim's brother told blatant lies to the court by claiming that there were no other brothers or sisters. These questionable events brought no murmur of protest from the authorities.

Druitt's suicide also raises questions. I have been assured that suicides frequently dress in their best clothes, but why the very large amount of money; why the *return* railway ticket; why the long and unnecessary journey to a distant part of the River Thames to end his life? Could Druitt's death have been murder and not suicide? If so, who would have wanted him dead? And why? This set of circumstances is so strange and so bizarre a story it would hardly be accepted as a work of fiction, yet the above details are strictly factual. We must now attempt to weave a scenario which can provide a solution to this most extraordinary of tales.

Chapter Fourteen

Do The Suspects Fit The Crime?

In the final chapter of this book I will prove the identity of Jack the Ripper and I will prove *why* these terrible crimes took place; 'why?' is equally as important as 'who?' in the Ripper mystery. However, although identity and motive will be solidly established, the actual *modus operandi* of the five murders can only be based on informed speculation founded on facts which are known about the case.

As a starting point, let us accept that Mary Kelly had indeed been made pregnant by the Prince of Wales – probably during high-jinks in the communal East End flat which Bertie rented with his upper class cronies. Unless she were careful it might be difficult for a prostitute to know who had impregnated her; did Mary therefore deliberately entrap the Prince?

Once Mary's plans were laid she would have been faced with the problem of approaching the Establishment; an Establishment which, when faced with a Catholic prostitute who might be able to prove that the Prince of Wales had bedded her, would have panicked – even without the claim that she was pregnant from her royal encounter.

I will prove that Montague John Druitt was involved in the murders along with a partner in crime. How did the apparently pleasant young barrister become involved in so sordid an affair? To answer that question we must remember that Mary Kelly mixed with a wide range of social classes. If she had been bedded by the Prince of Wales she may also have been bedded by his aristocratic friends. She was known to have been taken to France by a rich lover and she was known to have had many West End contacts. With this range of associates there is no reason why Mary should not have learned of, or even met, Montague Druitt perhaps through some society or school function.

Kelly undoubtedly did approach the Establishment, and she must have used some link to do this; as Druitt was involved in the murders, it is a reasonable speculation that Druitt was that link. He was the man approached professionally by Mary Kelly with her delicate problem. Montague was highly accessible. He had contacts in cricket clubs, in the legal profession and, of course, being a full-time school teacher, he would have had a great many contacts with parents of his pupils. It was also a well known fact that J.K. Stephen had been the tutor and friend of Eddy, heir to the English throne. Might Mary have known, perhaps through socialite gossip, that Stephen was acquainted with Druitt, giving her direct access to royalty?

I will prove that M.J. Druitt and J.K. Stephen knew each other, and knew each other well enough to join together in a partnership which needed daring and total trust. Before revealing that proof however, let us first examine the likelihood of such a partnership.

Male bonding, allegiance and loyalty are found in many parts of society. Such a bonding between men of all sexual persuasions appears to be an inherited form of tribal behaviour. Men's clubs abound. In 1991, a famous West End club voted to continue to uphold its century-old rules – men only, no women. Many of these clubs are essentially masculine places where the mutual support of various members is unwaveringly maintained by a rigid, frequently tacit code of conduct. Public houses were (and still are) another kind of favoured regular meeting place for men. It is only comparatively recently that the presence of women in public houses has become tolerated and completely accepted by male drinkers.

Then there is the most influential loyalty of all, the 'old school tie' which will chain young males to each other in an absolute allegiance. Friends who were educated together in celebrated public schools will frequently protect each others' interests, no matter what the crime and no matter what the consequence. We can see this ethic clearly demonstrated in a recent famous spy cadre, when privileged men banded together in secret and betrayed their country but kept an unwavering loyalty to each other. James Kenneth Stephen was raised in an environment that encouraged this kind of loyal behaviour; at university he had been a member of the Apostles.

The Apostles were a Cambridge University-based secret society, one important enough to be the subject of a book by Richard Deacon. This collection of like-minded young men was a traditional and recognised part of life at Cambridge University, but its workings were cloistered and its agenda secret. However, the Apostles' unofficial motto was, 'the love of man for man is greater than the love of man for woman', which is very revealing, although many of the more recent members of this society have been indisputably heterosexual.

H.F. Wilson (who, after leaving the university, retained a lively correspondence with Eddy) and J.K. Stephen were both members of the Apostles, and both were close friends of the Duke of Clarence. James was raised amongst secret intimate male relationships, and there is no reason to believe that Montague, considering his education, was not equally versed in similar ties; all Victorian public schools had analogous traditions. George Broderick, remembering his days at Eton during the 1840s, writes of: '. . . a strange and subtle instinct of honour . . .'. This was an unwritten code of conduct at the College. James was an Etonian and Montague a Wykehamist, but both men would have understood the public school code of loyalty and honour. Moreover, it is possible that the bond between these two attractive young men might initially have been based on sexual attraction. There was certainly the closest of trust, as I will prove.

There are other points to consider. James Stephen and Montague Druitt had remarkable similarities:

1) Both men came from the same social background.

2) Both men came from families which, up to that date at least, had had a history of mental illness. (James's father and Montague's mother and grandmother suffered from periods of insanity.)

3) Both men were trained in law.

4) Both men were renowned for their debating skills.

5) Both men were skilled and enthusiastic sportsmen.

6) Both men had the same sexual proclivities, if one accepts that Sir Melville Macnaghten's assertion that Montague was 'sexually insane' meant, as Victorians usually meant by that phrase, that he was homosexual.

7) Neither man attained the eminence which early talent had indicated.

8) Both men were involved in murder.

But how did two such advantaged and presumably pleasant young men become involved in a series of revolting and savage acts of homicide? And would such educated and refined minds be likely to rampage around the East End committing barbaric acts?

To answer the second question first – even the most apparently sane and refined of minds can commit callous acts of cruelty, often as a considered matter of duty.

It does not require any specialised training or knowledge to be able to recognise the double standards of normality and barbarity which can exist comfortably side-by-side in the most apparently civilised of minds.

No doubt the men who conducted the Spanish Inquisition considered themselves fine, upstanding citizens, faithful friends, happy to play with children and take part in all civic duties. Yet these devout men would torture and inflict indescribable cruelties on their victims, all in the name of religion and love. Examples of political terrorism are too numerous and too well-documented to need repeating. Absolute loyalty to a cause appears to paralyse the human conscience. Pleasant young men from all cultures will plant bombs with not a jot of remorse or sympathy for the consequences of their actions to their victims or to themselves.

* * * * *

Let us return to the narrative, reiterating that we can only, at this point, attempt informed speculation. Mary has now solved the problem of how best to approach the Establishment – through Montague Druitt. His chambers at King's Bench Walk, EC4 could be easily reached on foot from the East End.

So this is my reconstruction: Mary Kelly calls and sees Montague at his chambers in the Temple, where she breaks the news about her pregnancy and the alleged father of the expected child. Mary would have asked for Druitt's professional advice, but, being smart, she probably would not have left a forwarding address. Mary would only have pledged to call again after Montague had had time to consider her case.

Montague, realising the enormous repercussions which this information could have in the ranks of the Establishment, goes immediately and sees J.K. Stephen, who was a noted friend of royalty. James would have been readily accessible either at his parents' home in De Vere Gardens, Kensington, where he lived, or at the West End offices of *The Reflector*. This was a magazine which J.K. had founded, an enterprise on which he lavished his entire attention. The magazine was to be printed on the best possible paper, and its contents would be either political or literary.

Druitt, although he was not a noted royalist, might well have met, and possibly have liked, Eddy. There were a number of links between Eddy and Druitt. J.K. Stephen was one link of course, and one of Druitt's brothers served in the same regiment as Eddy's equerry; Stephen and Eddy were friends; Stephen and Druitt certainly knew each other, as I will prove, so why should they not all have been acquainted? They were all of the same sexual persuasion, and in the Victorian era, when homosexuality caused such horror, men attracted to each other banded together in the tightest of groups.

So Druitt visits Stephen and relates his startling news. It is easy to imagine the fury aroused in James's sick mind on hearing about Mary Kelly's 'royal' pregnancy. His first thought might have been directed towards the consequences which such a situation might bring about if it were to become public knowledge. Did James visualise a popular uprising? Or, more likely, did he think of the possible destruction of his own dreams and ambitions? The Crown was, as we have seen, widely unpopular in many quarters during the 1880s, and a royal scandal of massive proportions might well have toppled the monarchy. Such a fall would have smashed James's own considerable ambitions to be the force behind the Heir Apparent, once Eddy, Duke of Clarence, was settled into a position of power. James would have seen the possible disintegration of the things most dear to him – the State, the Crown, his beloved friend, and his own glowing future – all threatened by a worthless woman. Any illegitimate child would be a half-brother or sister to Eddy, and this child would link, by blood, the Royal Family to a Roman Catholic East End prostitute.

A tidal wave of anger must have swept through James Stephen's sick mind. We have read A.C. Benson's account of this man's terrifying fury as a young, healthy fellow. We need only read through *Lapsus Calami*, a collection of Stephen's poems, to realise the inherent violence in the man. We know for certain from medical reports still on file at St. Andrew's Hospital, Northampton, that J.K.'s mind was beginning to become unhinged in 1888. James's troubles were reputed to have started with an accident to the head from which he never fully recovered, although experts have expressed doubts that this accident would have been any more than a contributory factor to the severe mental problems which followed. In the foreword to *Lapsus Calami*, James's brother writes:

'In the winter of 1886–7, while paying a visit at Felixstowe, he accidentally received a very severe blow on the head. He did not lose consciousness but was badly cut. The wound healed, but I do not think he ever enjoyed perfect health again.'

Following a line of reasoned speculation based on facts, are there any pointers which indicate that J.K. Stephen was mentally disturbed shortly before the murders? There are definite indications that this was the case. At the end of April 1888, about four months before the murders started, James closed his magazine. From the text of his final editorial, it is quite clear that the man's mind was troubled. Most writers on the subject of *The Reflector*'s demise state that this was caused by financial pressure. J.K. sets out a range of possibilities to explain the magazine's closure. Revealingly, he keeps on referring to the magazine's demise as his own.

Was it towards the end of April when Montague brought news of Mary's bombshell? Excerpts from J.K.'s last editorial in his magazine (21 April 1888) may prove instructive: I have a strong suspicion that J.K. Stephen was obliquely accusing the Prince of Wales for what was about to happen. It is certainly the most extraordinary diatribe:

'Ladies and gentlemen, it is with a mixture of regret and satisfaction that I inform you that this is in all probability the last time I shall address you. One never knows for certain what is going to happen; . . . moreover, it is not unpleasant to sink mysteriously into that unknown abyss from which (such as I am) I not less mysteriously arose. *Mystery is a mighty thing*;' [my italics] '. . . from trifles grave consequences sometimes spring . . . out of the ashes of the dead Reflector may arise a marriage, *a murder* or the regeneration of mankind.' [My italics] '. . . (accursed calendar, you cannot harm me now) . . . I do not pretend – I will be frank with you – that the King of Terrors has claimed either the publisher or the editor as a subject . . . "But why, sir, have you come to this sudden decision?" Aha, my friends, do not press me too nearly . . . Prudence and diplomacy seal my closing lips . . . Anyhow I owe an account to no living man or woman, and "the rest is silence," as another moribund gentleman is reputed to have exclaimed. Not quite silence either. I know that some of you, who are more nearly unemployed than I could wish you to be, will not spare my memory the probings of inquisitive speculation. Questions will be asked, and answers will be given. *Even in the jaws of death I smile, superior to the conjectures of others on a problem whose solution I am about to carry undivulged into a world whence no questioner returns to enlighten his companions in ignorance* [my italics] . . . Others, perhaps, will more charitably infer that, although not a ruined man, fearful of sheriff's officers, *and apt to toy significantly with deadly weapons in hours of solitary despondency*, I am, nevertheless aware that the limit of expenditure which I am willing to incur is within measurable distance, *and that I prefer instant death, while my proportions are still bulky, and my printing and paper beyond reproach, to the horrors of a lingering end* [my italics] . . .'

There then follows an extraordinary passage addressed to the 'Postmaster General'. Clearly there had been a contretemps about postal rates, but could the 'Postmaster General' be an oblique reference to another person? In the next passage, which is placed three-quarters way through the long, final editorial, an underlying message is loud and clear:

'But hold! There are a few whose guesses on this melancholy problem have a personal character, and to them a word in season may be spoken. Yes, sir: you the Postmaster General; I mean you. Skulk not behind the pretence of being too much occupied to give ear to what I say; you shall not escape being gibbeted before my readers. Doubtless you think that your unjust refusal to recognise that I, too, am a newspaper, has either drained my coffers dry, that your wine and wheel-taxing colleagues may revel in halfpence which belongs by right to me, or has blasted my faith in mankind, and destroyed my interest in life. I will not undeceive you, tyrant: *even if you hereafter*

should govern colonies, or perhaps sway the destinies of an empire,
even though you continue to be my representative and that of my
betters in the Commons House of Parliament, this weight shall hang
for ever around your guilty neck for anything that I will do to
remove it.' [My italics.]

That is an extraordinary passage. Would the Postmaster
General, Henry Cecil Raikes, ever govern colonies or sway the
destiny of an Empire? Not if his past record was anything to go
by.

Raikes, born in 1838 at Chester, stood for election to Parliament in 1865, contesting his home town seat. He lost. In 1866 he
contested an election at Devonport and lost. In 1868 he finally
became an MP winning the seat for Chester, but he lost that seat
again in 1880. Two years later, Raikes once more became an MP,
representing Preston, but less than a year later he resigned the
seat. Raikes became Postmaster-General in 1886, and died five
years later in 1891. Clearly the Postmaster-General, with such a
chequered career, would never 'govern colonies' or 'sway the
destinies of an Empire'. But Bertie would. '. . . though you continue to be my representative and that of my betters in the
Commons House of Parliament.' Clearly James is not referring to
postage any more. So what was on his mind? The key words are,
'. . . this weight shall hang around your guilty neck.' What
weight? Mary's pregnancy? And the added words, '. . . this
weight will hang around your guilty neck for anything that I will
do to remove it . . .' speak for themselves. James is clearly writing
on several different levels. A further passage from the final editorial states:

'My death will, perhaps, involve the non-appearance of some
literary gems . . .'

James's writing is full of phrases such as 'mystery, death and
horrors'. His editorial finishes with the words:

'In conclusion, I can but wish you all such species of good
fortune as may be to your taste, and declare that for myself I
crave the only blessings which can now avail me aught – a
kindly epitaph, and reluctant oblivion. I am, Ladies and
Gentlemen (or shall I say I have been?) Your obliged, humble
Servant, The Reflector.'

These are extraordinary words which betray a maelstrom of

emotions. In this writing I can find several hints which say that Mary's bombshell may well have been dropped towards the end of April 1888 and no reason to think that this was not the case. We must also consider the strange fact that the murders occurred only at weekends during a period when J.K. Stephen was free only at that time.

After winding up his magazine in the summer of 1888 James was appointed (by his father) Clerk of Assize for South Wales, giving him light circuit duties (duties which, by all accounts he did not carry out efficiently). Michael Harrison, in his book *The Life of the Duke of Clarence and Avondale 1864–1892*, reveals that James was in Wales on weekdays during the period when the Ripper murders occurred. Could this account for all the murders taking place only on a weekend; dates when Stephen could be in London? Medical notes reproduced in Dr David Abrahamsen's book *Murder and Madness* indicate that Stephen's mental collapse began around this period. Laurence Humphrey, MD, the noted doctor who attended James at St Andrew's hospital in Northampton (where James eventually died in 1892) diagnosed that his patient had been suffering from mental disease since 1888. Throughout his stay in the mental hospital James Stephen thought that a warrant had been issued for his arrest. Why should James think that he might be arrested? Even though the man was by this time insane, the fact that he felt so constantly guilty and feared retribution is still an interesting observation.

* * * * *

The potential threat to the Establishment which Kelly posed could have elicited a strong response from the most normal and controlled of minds, and, as we know, J.K. Stephen's mind was far from normal during the summer of 1888. This is well documented by A.C. Benson (J.K.'s schoolfriend), who writes:

'. . . he accepted a legal appointment – a Clerkship of Assize – which gave him light circuit duties and a competence. But now his behaviour began to be marked by a curious eccentricity. It all seemed so deliberate, and his mental powers were so preternaturally acute and brilliant, that it was supposed and hoped that it was a passing phase. He became very restless in mind, taking up such pursuits as drawing and even music, for which he had no aptitude whatever. I remember his showing me a number of water-colour pictures of the most grotesque kind, which he assured me were portraits; *one in particular, of a female figure in a long brown coat sitting on the rail of a stile, in a kind of twilight, with a low moon in the distance, and a curious suggestiveness about it.*' [My italics.]

Mary Nichols was murdered on the second day of the moon's last quarter, and the night was fine. She was wearing a long brown topcoat.

As has been mentioned, James's reaction to possible danger to the Crown would be a complex one, with the overriding consideration probably one of ambition mixed up with his passion for Eddy. Proof of this deep-seated feeling (on the part of James anyway) is available, as we shall see later. Let us consider the circumstantial evidence first of all – the poetry. In the lampoon *The Coming of K.* 'K' was the symbol used to represent Bertie. Amongst James's poems is an ode which also uses the symbol 'K'. Could this poem, with its distinctly erotic language, have been based on experiences shared between the Duke and Stephen? The second verse is headed by the words 'Placid K.' Few were more placid than Eddy.

TO A.T.M.

See where the K. in sturdy self-reliance,
Thoughtful and placid as a brooding dove,
Stands, firmly sucking, in the cause of science,
Just such a peppermint as schoolboys love.
Suck placid K.: the world will be thy debtor;
Though thine eyes water and thine heart grow faint,
Suck: and the less thou likest it the better;
Suck for our sake and utter no complaint.

In stanza's three and five of his poem, it may be that James was egotistically mentioning himself in the words, 'Near thee a being, passionate and gentle, Man's latest teacher, wisdom's pioneer' and – 'Lo! with a voice unspeakably dramatic, Lo! with a gesture singularly fine . . .'. A.C. Benson relates James's over-dramatic but effective acting performances.

To complete the poem, here are stanzas three to eight:

Near thee a being, passionate and gentle,
Man's latest teacher, wisdom's pioneer,
Calmly majestically monumental,
Stands: the august Telepathist is here.
Waves of perception, subtle emanations,
Thrill through the ether, circulate amain;
Delicate soft impalpable sensations,
Born of thy palate, quiver in his brain.
Lo! with a voice unspeakably dramatic,
Lo! with a gesture singularly fine,
He makes at last a lucid and emphatic
Statement of what is in that mouth of thine.
He could detect that peppermint's existence,
He read its nature in the book of doom;
Standing at some considerable distance;
Standing, in fact, in quite another room.
Was there a faint impenetrable essence
Wafted towards him from the sucking K.?
Did some pale ghost inform him of its presence?
Or did it happen in some other way?
These are the questions nobody can answer,
These are the problems nobody can solve;
Only we know that Man is an Advancer:
Only we know the Centuries revolve.[1]

There is passion in the above poem, but might the friendship between Eddy and J.K. have weakened by 1888? In 1885 Eddy had been drafted into the 10th Hussars as a lieutenant; his father was Colonel of the regiment. During this period Eddy maintained a spirited correspondence with H.F. Wilson, but there is no record of any letters between Eddy and J.K. Stephen. Any correspondence might, of course, have been destroyed. As we shall see, an alarming amount of written material belonging to characters possibly associated with Jack the Ripper was subsequently burned. Perhaps James, in his torment, might have thought that by taking dramatic action in the Kelly affair he would demonstrate his

---

1   *The Reflector*, 1888

continuing love for Eddy in no uncertain manner, and so strengthen the ties of friendship once more. James would mastermind the removal of Kelly, and then maybe Eddy would learn of – and appreciate – the danger which J.K. had been willing to face in order to protect the Crown. Of James's love there can be no doubt: solid proof of that deep affection was clearly demonstrated by his reaction to Eddy's untimely death from influenza-related pneumonia on 14 January, 1892. As soon as he heard of the demise of his friend James refused to eat, and, over the following weeks, starved himself to death.

* * * * *

So, to return to a reconstruction of events:

Montague has now related Mary's story to J.K. Stephen; we have already considered Stephen's reaction. Obviously his first move would be to recruit Druitt into the murderous plans which must have formed in his mind. Given James's hypnotic personality and gift of overpowering persuasion, involving Druitt as a support is likely to have required little effort, but was there also the added bait of money? Montague would have had little to lose, protected by the powerful forces of State, and he had much to gain. By 1888 Druitt's legal career was moribund, and he was trapped in a schoolteacher's post in a successful but unimportant South London school, forced to take part-time legal work below his capabilities: not a happy outcome for a man whose early achievements promised a glittering future. In addition, around April, his mother's mental health was showing signs of deterioration. Ann Druitt had attempted suicide in early 1888 and, later that same year, in July, she was placed in the Brooke Asylum, Clapton, where she was certified insane.

Besides these family worries, Montague had, as we have seen, considerable financial commitments. The idea of combining help to the Establishment with a large reward would have been seductive. This could account for Montague's puzzling wealth discovered after his death. As for James – he could combine his love of State and the monarchy (and of Eddy in particular) with his misogyny. This hatred of women is clearly expressed in the much-quoted stanzas from two of J.K. Stephen's poems, both published in February 1891.

A THOUGHT

If all the harm that women have done,
Were put in a bundle and rolled into one,
Earth would not hold it,
The sky could not enfold it,
It could not be lighted nor warmed by the sun;
Such masses of evil
Would puzzle the devil,
And keep him in fuel while Time's wheels run.
But if all the harm that's been done by men
Were doubled and doubled and doubled again,
And melted and fused into vapour and then
Were squared and raised to the power of ten,
There wouldn't be nearly enough, not near,
To keep a small girl for the tenth of a year.[2]

and

IN THE BACKS

As I was strolling lonely in the Backs,
I met a woman whom I did not like.
I did not like the way the woman walked:
Loose-hipped, big boned, disjointed, angular.

After a long, unflattering description of the woman, her clothing and her possible character, the poem ends with the lines:

I do not want to see that girl again:
I did not like her: and I should not mind
If she were done away with, killed or ploughed.
She did not seem to serve a useful end:
And certainly she was not beautiful.[3]

There is little ambiguity in the above stanzas regarding Stephen's feelings for both men and women. The decision to kill Mary Kelly would certainly fit this man's personality. He was a

---

2   *Granta*, Feb. 1891
3   *Cambridge Review*, Feb. 1891

fellow of massive self-confidence who tended to disregard authority, even whilst still at school. He was a man of wild passion and great physical strength, a man with theatrical urges and a misogynist. When such a man saw all that he loved and respected threatened by an East End prostitute, murder would be an almost inevitable course of action.

A first move would be to check the basic truth of Mary's story. Was Bertie in London around March and April 1888? He was, and, moreover, he was celebrating heavily. The 10th of March 1888 marked Bertie and Alexandra's silver wedding anniversary. There was a State Ball at Buckingham Palace and a family dinner party at Marlborough House. Queen Victoria, after leaving this function, drove through the West End to see the illuminations.

Such an anniversary would have been the ideal occasion for Bertie's friends to give him the kind of entertainment which he loved most – wild parties, naturally without his wife, possibly at the East London flat. Alix's deafness would have contributed to her preference for quiet nights in the bosom of her family, which must have suited Bertie very well.

So let us assume that Bertie and Mary Kelly met and intimacy occurred. As we have seen, the attractive prostitute might well have been in the habit of robbing sailors during the course of sexual bargaining. This was common practice. So could Mary have stolen a memento from Bertie for later use against him? I shall eventually prove that this was indeed the case. Mary had a cool, calculating nature, and the opportunity to gain proof of her association with the Prince must have been too good an opportunity to miss. Was this memento the object the murderer was searching for when he mysteriously rifled the pocket of Annie Chapman? Several polished coins were discovered at Annie's feet. Was a royal portrait on the face of the coins uppermost? This would be a subtle but barbed clue from the murderer, linking the murders to the Royal Family, and pointing to a fury which was directed at Bertie, if the lines from the last edition of *The Reflector* did indeed (as seems likely) refer to the prince ('. . . this weight will hang around your guilty neck for anything that I will do to remove it . . .'); the coins might have been James's insane expression of disapproval – a clue which would have been recognised by very few, apart, perhaps (and hopefully on James's part), from Bertie.

But if the death of Mary Kelly was the murderer's sole objective, and many writers have believed that it was, then why were four other prostitutes killed? Here we must delve deeply into the realms of speculation. Could the four earlier murders have been a clever smoke-screen? If even a hint of Mary's story – linking her sexually to Bertie – had leaked out, and she had then been mysteriously murdered, gossip might have quickly flared up and inflamed the East End. (The Los Angeles riots of 1992 were a contemporary example of how quickly insurrection can arise and engulf a city.) But if Mary's death appeared to be only one in a string of unrelated murders, no particular attention would be drawn to it. This seems tenable, yet there is a flaw in such an explanation. As Stephen Knight pointed out, the murdered women all lived within a minute's walk of each other. This is a list of their last known addresses:

MARY NICHOLS
The day before she was murdered,
Mary was staying at: 56 Flower and Dean Street
LIZ STRIDE
On the day before she was murdered,
Liz had been at: 52 Flower and Dean Street
CATHARINE EDDOWES
On the day before she was murdered,
Catharine had spent the afternoon at: 55 Flower and Dean Street
ANNIE CHAPMAN
On the night she was murdered,
Annie had been trying to pay for a bed at: 35 Dorset Street
THE FINAL MURDER TOOK PLACE AT: 29 Dorset Street
(13 Miller's Court was the back part of this house)

This was no random selection. The five victims of these attacks all lived very close to each other, three in one street, two in another street, both streets almost adjoining.

There were, according to Metropolitan Police estimates, around 1,200 prostitutes in Whitechapel in 1888. But, of course, not all of these women would have lived around Dorset Street. Many lived in the other East End areas which comprised Bethnal Green, Mile End, Bromley-By-Bow, Limehouse, Spitalfields, Old Ford, Shoreditch, St George's in the East, Poplar, Whitechapel,

Stepney and Bow.

Now if the five Ripper victims had not known each other, and had lived in different districts, but had been murdered on the one spot, then the murders could possibly have been random: there would be nothing to link the women to each other, except the fact that a murderer had become fixated by one small area, and killed any woman who happened to be in that place at a suitable time for murder.

If the five victims had all lived together in one room, but had been murdered at different sites, on different times by totally different methods – one stabbed, one drowned, two strangled, one beaten – then the murders could possibly have been random killings committed by different men, all using different methods of homicide.

But the five women we are discussing all lived almost next door to each other, they knew each other, they drank and talked together and they were all killed by the same method and by the same man; three were named Mary (counting Catharine's alias), and two of the women used the name 'Mary Kelly'. This makes the odds astronomically high that the Ripper murders were not random killings. *The women were hunted down as part of a pattern.* However, this fact creates a new puzzle. What would be the purpose of hunting down a group of penniless, pathetic prostitutes? My theory alleges that Kelly was demanding money to support an unborn royal child, and, as we have already mentioned, if this were the case, Kelly was intelligent enough not to involve four alcoholic, gossipy prostitutes in her plans.

It might be advisable, at this juncture, to ask whether there is any indication that Kelly was expecting a large sum of money: if she were, then this would reinforce the extortion theory. In this respect, there is the leading question of her rent at Miller's Court. If Mary had *not* been expecting money, then it is difficult to understand why she had been given three months' credit on the rent of her room – a favour unheard of in the East End, when sick, middle-aged women were turned out in the middle of the night because they did not have fourpence. Could the young, attractive Mary have paid her rent by offering sexual favours to the landlord, Mr McCarthy? From all accounts, McCarthy was a respectable businessman, married with four children. This outward respectability might not preclude such an arrangement, but as we have seen, it was his wife, Mrs McCarthy who collected the rents, and she was a stickler for prompt payment. So Mary must have been able to convince the woman that she would soon have an ample amount of cash. Maybe she showed Druitt's business card to Mrs McCarthy and convinced her (without giving any details) that a large settlement was soon due, as, indeed, Mary might well have had every reason to believe.

To return to our original problem, if the murdered prostitutes did not share a deadly secret with Mary Kelly, then what thread grouped them together as women who needed to be eliminated? And was there any particular reason why the murders began with Nichols?

* * * * *

Once Kelly had contacted Druitt, it would have been easy for J.K. Stephen to track her down. He might have been on good terms with some of Bertie's East End companions with whom he could check the prostitute's story, or he might have had Mary followed after a visit to Montague, but most likely Stephen would have used powerful contacts – friends who had influence with the East End police (to whom Kelly was well known) to discover the prostitute's address; given the high-level cover-up, some trusted members of the police force must have been involved in the affair, probably at an early stage. Once Kelly's address was known, a delay would be inevitable. The Victorians did not have sophisticated pregnancy tests: proof could only be discovered by physical signs. If Mary had become pregnant at the beginning of April, it would have taken some time for the condition to become obvious. Was it perhaps this final proof of the prostitute's pregnancy – a slightly swollen stomach – notably evident around July, which roused Stephen to his first bout of murderous fury? Or did he receive a doctor's report to that effect?

Either way, once J.K. Stephen had been convinced that murder was necessary, it would not have been difficult to talk Druitt around to the same point of view; Kelly had to be eliminated. Stephen might even have persuaded his friend that he had personally obtained agreement, tacit or otherwise, from a leading member of the Establishment, and, as we shall see, maybe he had. But probably the most powerful persuasion offered to Druitt was that of money. Druitt's large estate would support this theory.

Once murder had been decided upon by the two unbalanced young men, logistics had to be worked out and plans had to be laid. Two pleasant-looking, well-dressed, clean young men would have been highly visible in the East End of London, but that could easily be overcome. Nondescript clothing would not be difficult to arrange, and James would enjoy wearing clerkly apparel; this would appeal to his highly developed sense of theatre, and, as we have seen, the murders do have a distinctly theatrical character. The display of the mutilated bodies was itself obscenely theatrical; the corpses were laid out as though for view, one woman with her possessions neatly arranged on the ground. There was an element of, 'Look at what I've done' in Jack's grotesque games – and we know from documentary evidence that J.K. enjoyed being the centre of attention, displaying his many talents before his peers at various educational establishments. Such a personality may well inject a theatrical element into his crimes. And if we accept that even one of the Ripper letters was genuine – or that the piece of posted kidney was genuine, or the chalked message – then we must accept that the murders were performed with a gloating air of theatricality. As we have seen, it was easily proved that the blood-smeared piece of apron, so dramatically thrown away in Goulston Street, was genuine. The murderer could easily have kept this gory souvenir of his crime along with his knife, or he could have thrown the fragment away in a hidden corner; but the blood-smeared piece of cloth was left at the foot of a much used public stairway, where it could not fail to be noticed – an incident which added to the mood of public panic. James Stephen fits perfectly the psychological portrait of the murderer.

* * * * *

The two men must now have worked out detailed plans for their proposed crime. Rumours that Jack the Ripper used a coach have been current for a number of years. But a coach and horses would have been as much out of place in the slums of Whitechapel as well-dressed young men. The one form of transport which would not raise a second glance would be a horse and cart, the cart perhaps covered by a tarpaulin, under which a change of clothing, wet towels, and even a long knife could be hidden. In the days before motorised travel, such a method of transport could be easily purchased, and there was a plethora of stable yards throughout London. In the light of this theory, might it be significant that Mary Nichols's body was discovered lying outside the gates of a stable yard in Buck's Row? If several of the victims had been lured onto the back of a cart, where they were strangled whilst being driven through dark areas, then no sounds of murder would have been heard. This would explain the absolute silence of the attacks: no cries, no grunts, no scuffles as the unfortunate women fought for their lives.

This is my thesis on the first murder: on the night of 30/31 August 1888, J.K. Stephen, his mind dangerously unbalanced, set out with Montague Druitt on a journey to the East End. At this moment Druitt would also have been suffering from intense mental strain, since only a month earlier his mother had been declared insane and placed in an asylum. Dr Abrahamsen asserts in his *Murder and Madness* that murderers in general share one common characteristic – intense personal torment; a tenet fully justified by Stephen's and Druitt's mental states. Driven by a mixture of conflicting emotions, the couple, having discovered Kelly's address, must have travelled to the East End to search her out, with murder on their minds.

Let us surmise. In the yard at Buck's Row (site of the first murder) the two men could have stabled a horse and cart. To repeat – equipment such as a change of clothing, wet towels, and a long, sharp knife could have been hidden under a tarpaulin. After harnessing the horse Druitt now drives them both to Dorset Street in search of Kelly.

At Miller's Court Stephen dismounts and goes into the Court to check out the scene. At this moment Mary Kelly might have glanced out of the broken window and seen a stranger staring at her premises. After having approached the Establishment she might have been expecting some trouble. With this in mind, suspicious and intelligent, she decides to test the stranger. She pulls on a bonnet and leaves her lodgings to go to her local bar, *The Britannia*, on the corner of Dorset and Commercial Street. Although Mary did not usually wear a hat the remains of a burnt bonnet was found in the grate at Miller's Court after the mutilated body was discovered.

On her way to the bar Mary must have realised that the stranger was following her. As we saw in Chapter 7, Mary, when in trouble, was in the habit of changing clothing with friends.

In *The Britannia* Kelly could have met a regular drinker, Mary Nichols, and persuaded her to wear maybe a large and distinctive shawl and a distinctive black hat.

Nichols's hat was certainly a recent acquisition. We have that information from the doss-house deputy from whom the penniless Nichols tried to cadge accommodation on the night she was murdered. He said that he had not seen the hat before, and the victim's last reliably recorded words were: '*I'll soon get my doss money. See what a jolly bonnet I've got now*' – words which clearly indicate recent ownership of the hat. How else would Nichols have acquired her bonnet if not by loan? We know that she was penniless; no one gave expensive presents in the East End; if Nichols had stolen the hat it would have been pawned to buy drink – as we've seen, John Kelly even took the boots off his feet to pledge them. And Mary would not have bought the headwear; money has only one purpose for an alcoholic – to buy drink. On the day that she died, Nichols confessed to her friend, Ellen Holland, that she had earned her doss-house money three times, but on each occasion the cash had been spent on gin. An alcoholic will spend money on drink before he or she will pay for lodgings, buy food, and certainly before they will buy clothing. Indeed, if Nichols had owned the bonnet whilst the pawn shops were open earlier in the day, it would, no doubt, have been pledged. Facts indicate that she received the headwear only a short time before her murder.

To continue the scenario: Nichols, proud of her new outfit, leaves *The Britannia*. Up to this point in time, of course, no Ripper murders had taken place, so Nichols would not have been feeling nervous. J.K. Stephen and Druitt see the hat and shawl, which they associate with Kelly, leaving the public house. Although Nichols was a few inches shorter and a bit slimmer than Mary Kelly, Victorian clothing was voluminous; layers of material reached from the chin down to the ankles, and if one looks at old photographs of the poorer women, their clothing was often similar. High fashion was not known in the poorer parts of London – long, black outfits were. Finally, a peaked bonnet would hide the face, especially in badly lit streets. It would have been easy to fool the two men; to them, the distinctive outfit, or maybe only the distinctive hat, was Mary Kelly, either returning home or going to solicit.

The murderous duo now follow Nichols. Most likely Stephen jumped from the cart and trailed his prey on foot, still thinking he was following Kelly. 'The hat and coat' would not have had far to go, as *The Britannia* was close to Flower and Dean Street.

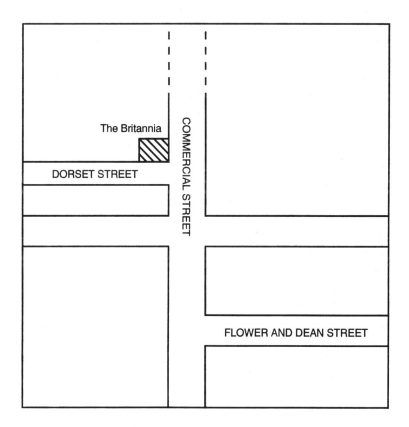

J.K. would have assumed that 'Mary Kelly' was calling on a friend, in which case she would sooner or later leave the Flower and Dean Street doss-house to return to Miller's Court or *The Britannia* – at which point she could be waylaid.

Nichols left the doss house sooner than J.K. would have dared to hope. Within seconds the prey was back on the streets, having been refused entry to the premises. One wonders why Nichols even tried to get lodgings without having money in her pocket when she must have known the strict doss-house rules.

James now only had to follow Nichols into one of the many dark side streets. An approach by a stranger would not, of course, appear strange to the prostitute. On the contrary, it was a regular occurrence. Maybe he asked, 'Is your name Mary?' Surprised by the question, Mary would have answered, 'Yes. How did you know?' Stephen is unlikely to have had doubts about the woman's identity, as this would already have been confirmed by Druitt on the basis of the distinctive hat, or the shawl, or both. Kelly was, of course, Irish, although she'd been brought up in Wales, but there was no reason why James Stephen would know this and he had never heard Kelly's voice or her brogue. And, in the badly lit, or even unlit street, late at night, with his prey wearing a peaked bonnet, it would have been difficult for Stephen to judge the woman's age or looks, although, as has already been mentioned, Nichols's father and a journalist both remarked that she looked at least ten years younger than her real age when they saw her in the mortuary. Moreover, in Stephen's roused state of manic fury, rational thinking would have disappeared. There are certainly examples of this kind of murder – for instance, Lord Lucan was accused of killing his children's nanny in mistake for his wife.

Bargaining would have been speedy. The cart was near and Nichols might have been delighted at having a comfortable trysting place, nestled amongst canvas as opposed to standing up against a wall. Druitt, as he had met the supposed victim and would not want to be recognised, must have kept his face muffled and looked straight ahead to hide his features. Nichols would have climbed eagerly on to the back of the cart and allowed herself to be partly covered by the tarpaulin, and, I repeat, as no Ripper murders had taken place by this date, she would have had no fear.

As Druitt drove off, J.K. (who, as A.C. Benson tells us, was physically very strong) would have strangled her into a state of unconsciousness.

It would not have taken long for Druitt to drive to Buck's Row and into the stable yard. And people living nearby would have been so used to the sound of horses' hooves that they would not have noticed a late cart, any more than people nowadays living near a multi-purpose garage would notice the late arrival of a car.

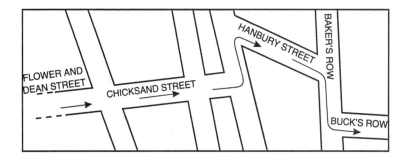

After reaching the stable yard, and after checking that no pedestrians were approaching, the men could easily have rolled Nichols's body from the back of the cart, after which James might well have been overcome with feelings of repulsion and loathing for his victim. Still unaware that he had attacked the wrong woman, and appalled by the thought that a royal baby – a foetus which could bring ruin and disgrace onto his beloved Eddy – might be nestling in the crumpled heap at his feet, Stephen (whilst his partner stabled the horse) viciously cut Nichols's throat, then lifted her skirt to slash at the vagina, the focus of his hatred and disgust.

Had the murderers seen any pedestrians approaching, they could easily have dodged back into the stable yard. This killing had been achieved in perfect safety.

Their job completed, the duo could have returned home either by taking a train from Whitechapel – although they would have had to wait for the rail services to begin at around about 5.00 a.m. – or they could have walked back to Druitt's chambers in the Temple, or, as we shall see, they might have had a safe house near to the scene of the crime.

Over the weekend, it would have become clear from the co-pious press reports that they had murdered the wrong woman, but Stephen's reaction to this mistake is more likely to have been fury than remorse.

On the Sunday evening, 2 September, James would have left

London for his Assizes in Wales, and Montague would have returned to his teaching post.

Meanwhile, Mary Kelly would have been deeply disturbed. She could have had no absolute proof that the murder was personally connected to her; the killing of Nichols whilst wearing Kelly's clothing might well have been a curious coincidence, but Kelly must have had her suspicions. Erring on the side of caution, might she have boldly called on Druitt during the week, possibly at Blackheath? Kelly might have decided that there was only one way in which she could protect herself, apart from running away, and it would have been difficult for a penniless prostitute to dig up her roots and move. Anyway, the lure of substantial sums of money from the Establishment would have kept Kelly in place; and in any case she must have felt that she had the upper hand. So did Kelly, for protection, tell Druitt that she had stolen a memento from Bertie – as she had done, as we shall see.

We know that Bertie carried mementos. Lillie Langtry, one of Bertie's many mistresses, delighted in giving friends souvenirs, as she recorded in her autobiography *The Days I Knew*. The beautiful Lillie even named the shop from where she purchased her gifts, and records the delight of the young Eddy when it was his turn to receive a memento from her.

Mary would have been feeling invulnerable as she explained to Druitt that Bertie's stolen item, along with its history, had been passed on to a friend who lived close by for safe keeping. (Chapman frequently lodged a few doors away, at 35 Dorset Street.) And did Kelly even name that friend as Annie Chapman? If Annie were subsequently attacked, then Mary would be absolutely certain that she herself was the target for murder, and she could have made further plans for her safety.

Such defiance would be construed as a challenge by J.K. Stephen, and a man of his inflated ego would have been driven into a manic fury by such hubris from (to his way of thinking) an East End slut. And he may well, in his manic state, have been suffering from delusions of grandeur, an aberration whereby the person feels totally invulnerable and above all law and authority: the Ripper's behaviour did indeed indicate such a state of mind, as a distinguished Australian psychiatrist, Dr Anthony Orsmond, pointed out to me.

Let us now return to my version of events before Annie Chapman's death. If Kelly had indeed spun a cunning plot to protect herself by naming the unfortunate Annie Chapman, then the unbalanced and infuriated James, on his return to London from Wales the following weekend, could easily have determined on a further murder. He might have decided that Annie must also be eliminated. If he could retrieve the souvenir much of Mary's power would be taken away.

Once James had decided on another murder I believe he reasoned that if the killing were savage enough Mary Kelly might be so stunned and frightened by the event that she would be terrified into silence and obedience. Such reasoning is not new. Primitive tribes have long used this method to keep members of their communities under strict control. In the past, several native American tribes, in secret initiation ceremonies for boys passing into manhood, used to perform acts so terrifying and dramatic that the youngsters were shocked into a state of permanent fear of the elders. Masks used during this type of tribal ceremony are frequently grotesque and frightening. The brutality of the Ripper murders display the same basic intent to terrify.

To return to my theory: the week after Nichols's killing, J.K. Stephen and Montague Druitt were once again in the East End and Annie Chapman was now their target.

On the night of her death we know that Chapman was drinking in a public house – probably *The Britannia*. Frederick Stevens, a fellow lodger at Annie's usual doss-house, reported to the newspapers that he had been drinking with her in the early hours of the morning on which she was killed. Chapman had left the public house at around 1.00 a.m.. The murderers would then have re-enacted the Nichols's affair. Let us again speculate. J.K. Stephen might have tracked Annie down to *The Britannia*. Glancing through the window, he could have asked a woman who was leaving whether Annie Chapman was inside. The woman might have pointed out J.K.'s intended victim. As soon as she left *The Britannia* Annie could have been followed around the corner to Dorset Street, where she attempted to find lodgings without having the money to pay for them.

Somewhere around 2.00 a.m. Chapman was turned out of the doss-house. She was seen by a night-watchman, John Evans, as she turned into Paternoster Row.

The time of her death was officially estimated to be around 4.30 a.m., although with imprecise Victorian medical calculations there are variations on this time. However, it is clear that Annie could not have been attacked immediately after leaving the Dorset Street doss-house. She might, of course, have met a client there and then, which would have kept J.K. and Montague at bay. She might have gone back to a man's room for a couple of hours – such an arrangement was frequently made, the prostitute charging more for her prolonged services. Or maybe, feeling ill, she reported to an all-night infirmary for more treatment. Pills from previous infirmary visits were still on her body when she was killed.

Wherever Annie Chapman went after leaving Dorset Street J.K. and Druitt were not far behind, waiting for the chance to kill her. Finally J.K. would have found the right opportunity; when no pedestrians were around Chapman was approached.

As Annie was feeling unwell (and little wonder, as she was, as we have seen, dangerously ill, probably near to death from natural causes) she might have declined an offer to climb into the back of the cart. But a convenient yard was close at hand. This venue would not have worried James. He was not local; he did not realise that the yard was in constant use; he was armed with a sharp knife, and a horse and cart was standing nearby which provided a convenient and safe hideaway; if anyone should use the yard during the murder then James would have been able to hack his way out and disappear on to the back of the cart. *The Times*'s view, that, '. . . the assassin, if not suffering from insanity, appears to be free from any fear of interruption while on his dreadful work,' was near the mark. Planning had replaced the need for luck.

With Annie lying dead on the ground at his feet James could now search the body for any souvenir which Kelly might have entrusted to her friend for safe keeping. He would have known, as everyone knew, that poor people tended to keep valuables on their person, their precious possessions often sewn into lining or the hem of their clothing.

A quick examination of Annie's dress would have revealed no hidden valuables. The pocket was then discovered, perhaps tightly tied with string. This pocket was slashed open and the contents examined: James would not have found any goods which might have belonged to Bertie. Chapman was the only victim to have her possessions examined.

J.K., in a further display of arrogant contempt and self-confidence, then carefully arranged Annie's few pathetic trinkets on the ground. We know that Annie was penniless earlier in the evening. If she had earned money from a client it would have been at least fourpence if not more. Did J.K. personally provide the polished farthings which were found carefully laid out at her feet?

Finally, as a further display of rage and disgust, and maybe as an attempt to signal to Mary Kelly the kind of fate which she might possibly expect, the organ most central to the Ripper affair, the uterus, was cut out and taken away. This would have been a clear warning to the pregnant prostitute.

It has always been assumed that Jack cut away the vital organs from his victim then stuffed them into his pocket or into a bag, but this method of transporting human tissue would allow blood to seep from it which might be noticed by any number of people. According to my thesis James had only to wrap the bloody pieces of flesh in a piece of oilcloth, perhaps reinforced by newspaper or a towel, then slip his dreadful souvenirs under the tarpaulin on the back of the cart. His own bloodstained clothing could have been changed at the stable yard or even under the tarpaulin, his task unseen during the dark ride through unlit side streets. Blood could have been wiped from his hands by a damp towel, also kept on the cart. This explanation would solve the mystery of Jack's legendary invisibility.

As we have seen, a cover-up by the authorities must have started as early as the inquest into Annie Chapman's death.

We are now faced with the problem of Mary Kelly's reaction to these grim proceedings. We know from Joseph Barnett's testimony at Mary's inquest that she was frightened not only by the murders (the whole East End population was paralysed with fear for that reason), but also of 'someone'. Here is Barnett's evidence again:

Coroner. Have you heard her [Mary Kelly] speak of being afraid of anyone?

Barnett. Yes, several times. I bought newspapers and I read to her everything about the murders, which she asked me about.

Barnett also said that Mary was not afraid of any particular individual, but we know, through a friend of Kelly's, Lizzie Albrook, that Mary wanted to leave the country. Clearly, without funds, this was not possible, and Kelly was trapped. She had still not received any money from the Establishment and she was in serious debt to her landlord. Despite her fear, the alluring prospect of cash and great comfort must still have loomed large in her mind – riches for the taking, if she could only keep her nerve and outwit her adversaries.

* * * * *

Is it possible that at this juncture in the proceedings Queen Victoria interfered, and that this interference provided a new complication? Queen Victoria took a great interest in the Ripper murders, as her notes on the subject to her then Prime Minister, Lord Salisbury, show. The following theory must be only suppositional – much of the Ripper solution has to be – but I am selecting facts which will fit in with my proof of the murderers' identities, which I shall reveal in the last chapter.

* * * * *

That Victoria had spies everywhere is a solid fact. She knew all the Court intrigues, and all the gossip, knowledge which caused one of her exasperated ministers to ask, 'Where *does* she get her information from?' It is almost certain that news of an illegitimate royal child would quickly come to the Queen's attention. Any such baby would be Albert's grandchild, by blood if not by ties of marriage, and Victoria's passion for her dead consort still raged. Given this continuing passion, the idea that a direct descendent from Albert might be killed, even before birth, would have aroused the Queen's fury, and this could be a fearsome emotion.

Did the Queen insist that Kelly's foetus be fully conceived and delivered? Such insistence would fit in with the Queen's other actions towards her dead consort – actions which could hardly be called mentally balanced. Each day Albert's bed was made up, even his chamber pot was scoured. Victoria, when faced with problems, would 'consult' her dead husband, by holding one of his treasured possessions and waiting for his thoughts to be directed to her from heaven – she even took Bertie and Alix, on the night before their marriage, into the dead Consort's mausoleum, so that Albert could bestow his approval and blessings on the union – such behaviour borders on the psychotic. Victoria's unhinged passion for Albert – and no doubt for his blood-line, may well have overcome possible feelings of hatred and disgust for the child's mother.

We must now consider how the Establishment would have viewed the Queen's interference. The high authorities most likely to be concerned with the matter were the police commissioner, Sir Charles Warren (who was certainly part of a cover-up); Sir William Gull (whose notes indicated that he had private information about the murders); Inspector Frederick George Abberline (who was in charge of the ground forces during the murders); and possibly the Prime Minister, Lord Salisbury, as the holder of the highest office in the land. They would have had their own safety to consider if insurrection swept the country, and, as we saw earlier, the Catholic prostitute represented a great threat to the State – and thereby to themselves. It had so far proved difficult to murder Kelly, and now such a course of action was being forbidden by Queen Victoria, at least until her grandchild had been delivered.

Even if Mary just disappeared, and if she did indeed possess proof of her liaison with Bertie, then awkward questions might have been asked. And, once the child was born, Mary would be even more dangerous. The prostitute held powerful cards in her hand and she must have now been treated with a new respect by the Establishment. The best plan would be to try and consult with Kelly – to lure her onto their side, then she might be persuaded to help during this crisis.

My own choice as a negotiator for any deal would be Sir William Gull. Having been born in humble circumstances he presumably had the 'common touch' and he certainly had the best interests of the Royal Family at heart. A contract between Mary and the Establishment might have been in the process of negotiation when a new complication arose. Catharine Eddowes, who frequently called herself 'Mary Kelly' (Kelly being the surname of her common-law husband), started to spread the news that she knew the identity of Jack the Ripper. A much-delayed reward had been offered for information which could lead to the serial killer's arrest, and this money attracted Catharine. As we saw in Chapter Five, the Superintendent of a casual ward related (in an October interview with the *East London Observer*) how Catharine had told him she was about to claim the reward money; she knew Jack's identity. Such a claim would almost certainly have been repeated to other people.

Once news of this statement became known (even if Catharine were mistaken, or was only boasting) the Establishment might have been worried that Mary Kelly, perhaps whilst drunk, had hinted at, or had actually discussed, her deadly information. This, like many other Ripper mysteries, can only remain the subject of speculation, but I believe that it fits the known facts.

To recapitulate – news has now reached the Establishment that a woman is claiming that she knows the identity of Jack the Ripper, which might mean she knows the reason behind the killings. J.K. Stephen decides, either unilaterally or with the consent of the powers behind the throne, that Eddowes must be silenced. I see no reason why Stephen, when he had free time, should not have personally wandered around the East End during daylight hours, picking up gossip and information. As I have said earlier, Paul Begg mentioned to me the puzzle of 'the unidentified stranger' seen with Mary Kelly in Miller's Court two days before her death. This stranger was described, by Thomas Bowyer, as being smartly dressed, aged around twenty-seven or twenty-eight, with 'very peculiar eyes'. That could have been J.K. Stephen, or, even more likely, Montague Druitt. The 'smart dress' is interesting. Clearly, when the men were not on a murdering mission, they did not mind standing out from the East End crowd; or perhaps this was a clever calculation – they wanted to be remembered as smartly dressed during the day, so that more fitting clothing, worn at night, would not help in any identification. J.K. Stephen appeared to have the kind of mind which would think of everything, but, unfortunately for him, the ploy did not work with Liz Stride, who, irrespective of any change of clothing, must have recognised the couple when she met them at Dutfield's Yard.

I strongly suspect that Kelly was, by now, on the side of the Establishment. It is not difficult to imagine her being seduced by her new power and by her meeting with a man such as Sir William Gull. There is a natural tendency for underlings to believe and trust implicitly the word of someone in a position of the highest authority. To be told that Queen Victoria was taking a personal interest in the safety of the child, and, of course, in its mother, could have been a powerful drug. Kelly must have been convinced that the child was her passport to safety and luxury, in which case she would have been only too willing to help out in any way that she could.

The need to commit a new murder might have provided the authorities with an opportunity to entrap Kelly. Are there any pointers to Kelly's involvement in the later murders? We know that she was allowed to run up a huge debt in the months before her 'death' (or disappearance) which means she was probably able to convince her landlords that she was expecting cash. The former CID officer turned crime writer, Hargrave Lee Adam, wrote in his introduction to *The Trial of Dr Lamson*, published in 1912, 'If you wish to discover the motives of a cunning person, you must apply common sense to his actions. Every man has a motive for his smallest action; if his actions are not governed by custom and habit, then he has an ulterior motive.' Interestingly, Mary Kelly stopped going to her usual haunt, *The Britannia* about one month before her own 'death'; that is around the time of the double murder of Stride and Eddowes.

Maybe Kelly was made to believe that it would be best for everyone, herself included, if, at some point, she should 'disappear'. Maybe clever talk by clever people convinced her that if her own identity could be exchanged with that of someone else, she could then melt away into a life of luxury and ease. And maybe she did just that. Here it is useful to repeat the strange fact that not one member of her family turned up before or after her funeral, despite proceedings being delayed whilst a search was made for them. Did they know that Mary had been spirited away whilst maybe not knowing the reason behind the disappearance?

Many writers and authorities have claimed that Mary Kelly was the key to the Ripper affair, and it is indeed an extraordinary coincidence, much remarked upon, that two women using the same name should be targets of the killer. Perhaps Gull convinced Kelly that if Eddowes really did have knowledge of Jack's identity as she claimed, and freely talked about it, then she would be a danger not only to the Establishment but to Kelly herself. Recruiting Kelly into their murder plot would have been a most cunning move on the part of the Establishment. If she could be persuaded to help in silencing Eddowes then that complicity could be used as counter-blackmail. Kelly, entrapped, would have to tread even more cautiously. Death by hanging for the crime of murder was commonplace in Victorian times.

Considered detachedly from a modern viewpoint, such planning might seem complicated, but one has only to recall modern instances of State plotting to realise that a scheme to involve Kelly in murder was relatively straightforward. A fairly recent example of State plotting which leaps immediately to mind is the removal of an exile by the Bulgarian authorities. Georgi Markov, a forty-nine-year-old defector, whilst walking along the Strand was stabbed by the tip of a specially prepared umbrella which inserted a deadly pellet of poison into Markov's leg, causing his death. This sounds more like a fictitious method of assassination but it actually happened. Then there is the history of the 'Watergate' affair and the many puzzles surrounding the assassination of President John Kennedy. When powerful people in government have much to lose, State plotting, of the kind which involved Mary Kelly in murder, has proved, over the years, to be fairly routine.

* * * * *

As we have seen, Catharine Eddowes's behaviour on the day of her death was distinctly unusual, a day during which she disappeared without trace for around six and a half hours. Catharine and her partner John Kelly appear to have been a devoted couple despite personal defects, so why did she lie to John on the eve of her death? and why did Eddowes not go straight to him after being released from custody in the early hours of the morning?

As we have already mentioned, it might be reasonably expected that someone would have reported seeing her around and about before her arrest. No one did. It must therefore be assumed that Catharine drank in someone's house, or in an area where she was totally unknown. But going 'out of the area' was out of character. East Enders had their favourite watering holes to which they tended to stick. So where did Eddowes go to get drunk? It is my belief that she was with Mary Kelly, who, setting her friend up for death, must have pumped alcohol into Catharine until she was paralytic; then Mary left Eddowes in Aldgate, ready to be picked up by the murderers on their horse and cart. But Eddowes began to cause a disturbance. The police got to her before the murderers could. Alternatively, a highly-placed contact at Bishopsgate Police Station might have been drafted into the arrangements, with Catharine's arrest being deliberately engineered by the authorities. Kelly, under instructions, might have deliberately left her friend on a policeman's beat. Under this arrangement the murderers would have known exactly where Eddowes was and when they could reach her. Policemen on the beat, and even coroners, would have followed any instructions from their superiors without question and without needing an explanation for the orders. In Victorian times workers did as they were told, in a chain of command which passed downwards from the top echelons.

Whatever actually happened, it is certain that Catharine did not spend a normal day in the hours before she was murdered and her movements and motives are still shrouded in mystery. There is no reason to think, when Catharine told John at 2.00 p.m. that she would be back no later than 4.00 p.m., that she did not believe that herself. Whatever Catharine was planning, wherever she intended to go, she must have calculated that several hours – between two and four o'clock in the afternoon – would be sufficient time to complete her business. Clearly it was not.

Intriguingly, once in police custody, Catharine's name was registered as 'Mary Kelly', although she herself is reported to have said that she was called 'Nothing'. So who named her?

As we have seen, Eddowes was released from Bishopsgate Police Station in the early hours of 30 September at exactly 1.00 a.m. – a precise timing which hints at a possible pre-arrangement.

Catharine's arrest had been witnessed by one of her friends who reported the event to John Kelly. He immediately, and sensibly, assumed that the police would detain Catharine for the entire night so he did not worry about her continued absence. Even a lowly market porter had enough common sense to believe that no woman would be released in the middle of the night into Whitechapel. The police force (in general) was desperate to prevent any more murders, especially as their lack of progress in catching the killer had reflected very badly on the force's efficiency. In the case of Eddowes the police seemed to be positively inviting further violent crime. Why?

Let us return to my version of events. After Mary Kelly had become embroiled in the conspiracy, she must have been given sufficient money to cover the expenses of a day's carousing: maybe she took Catharine to an out-of-the-way drinking place where neither of them were known. And what stories might Mary Kelly have confessed to her friend? Dreams of riches if they both unmasked the Ripper perhaps – any lie would do whilst Catharine drank herself into a trap.

As I have said, the arrest of Eddowes was most probably pre-planned, Mary having been instructed as to where she should abandon her friend. As we have already speculated, the police (or even the police-surgeon and the coroners Roderick MacDonald and Wynne Baxter) would only have needed a set of instructions from higher authority on how to proceed; an explanation for that course of action would be neither expected nor given.

So after approximately four hours in custody Eddowes was released at exactly 1.00 a.m. On gaining her freedom she, along with every other East End woman, would have been suspicious of an approach by a stranger: her clear intent (indicated by her words, 'I'll get a damn fine hiding when I get home') was to head for the lodgings of her common-law husband. And this objective could have been achieved with just a few minutes' walk. Part of the plan, therefore, must have been for Mary Kelly to meet Catharine 'accidentally' on her release from Bishopsgate Police Station. Common sense tells us that a woman, on a cold night, who remembers her promise to hurry home, a woman suffering from a hangover and suffering from Bright's Disease, which causes lethargy, must have been waylaid to have ended up in Mitre Square, in the opposite direction to, and some distance from, her lover's lodgings. Being hailed as she left the police station by the lady-friend who had supplied her with drink for the whole afternoon would be a very plausible explanation for Catharine's actions after being released from custody; and that delay, which prevented her from reaching the safety of her lover's lodgings, would have set her up as an easy target. Meanwhile Kelly, by allowing herself to be used as a decoy, would have been enmeshed even further into the web which the Establishment was weaving.

It was reported that the police officer on duty watched Eddowes leave the station after her release. He saw her turn to the left, away from Flower and Dean Street. This action would fit in perfectly with the fact that someone may have called to her as soon as the station door was shut behind her. Kelly, I believe, had been waiting for her victim to be released.

* * * * *

We must now try to work out the killers' timetable on the night of the double homicide. It would appear, from the timing of the murders, that James and Montague were back in the East End at around half-past midnight on 30 September 1888 both prepared for violent action.

It is highly likely that Stephen and Druitt changed their stable yard throughout the ten-week Ripper operation. They would not wish to become known in any one area so it would have made sense to move venues to different locations, perhaps several times.

Dutfield's Yard provided limited stabling facilities. It is, therefore, possible that by late September Stephen and Druitt were using the yard for their operations. No one would have made any enquiries about, or paid much attention to, two indifferently-dressed young men. In the yard, horses would have arrived and departed constantly, and no one would have linked Stephen or Druitt with the murders. Jack was thought to be a lone man.

Let us try and follow the scenario through using part of Israel Schwartz's statement to the police – as recorded by Inspector Donald Swanson – as a rough guideline. 'He saw a man stop and speak to a woman, who was standing in the gateway [where the murder was committed]. The man tried to pull the woman into the street . . .'

The murderous duo must have gone to their new stabling quarters at Dutfield's Yard where the pattern of murder suddenly changed. If Hargrave Lee Adam is correct there has to be an ulterior motive for that change. The Stride murder is different from the other four homicides in two main respects. Firstly, the body was not mutilated, and secondly, the place of the murder was not a deserted spot. Indeed, the area outside the Working-men's club and around Dutfield's Yard in general was fairly busy on the night of the double murder, which means that Jack took a definite risk, which, we now recognise, was not characteristic; he was even spotted by Schwartz about to begin work. So what made him change his usual working pattern – that of only killing in dark, deserted places where there was minimal chance of being seen? Obviously he was forced, for some reason or other, into a murder which, unlike the others, he had not planned. What could that reason be? Could it be that, unlike Nichols, Chapman or Eddowes, Liz Stride recognised her attacker? There had to be some reason for Jack to kill in a relatively busy street with so many people coming and going. And Liz Stride's actions show fear towards at least one of the men, which means she recognised danger. Why?

We should also note that Schwartz's description of the two men involved in the struggle with Stride (given witnesses' notorious mistakes in regard to the identification of suspects) could easily fit Stephen and Druitt: '. . . the first man who threw the woman down:- age about 30; ht., 5ft 5in; comp., fair; hair, dark, small brown moustache . . .' (There are photographs of Druitt in which he has grown a small moustache.) '. . . second man: age 35; ht., 5ft 11 in; comp. fresh; hair, light brown; . . .'

To repeat Schwartz's words yet again: 'The man tried to pull the woman into the street . . .' But why should Liz Stride resist a personable man's advances? She was waiting to be propositioned. If Liz had not been frightened there would have been no need for Druitt to use force. A prostitute, confronted by two fine-looking young men, would have been more than willing to go into a dark corner with them.

We know that Stride had decided to defy fate and solicit late at night in the Ripper's territory so she was not the nervous type. And, as mentioned, Victorian theories depicted the killer as a solitary, depraved man, stalking the streets alone. There was no hint in newspapers of the time, in interviews or in published police reports, that more than one man might be involved. Liz, therefore, should have had no reason to suspect and so repulse two customers. Many young fellows would have wanted sex and that was the commodity which Liz supplied, so why did she resist and scream? If the men had ignored her advances that in itself would not alarm her: many men doubtless did. So what was all the fuss about?

If Stephen and Druitt had pre-planned Liz's murder they would have continued their *modus operandi* and lured Liz on to the cart without any commotion, to be taken to a dark, deserted place. The prostitute would have been only too delighted to have quietly melted away with what seemed to be two personable young fellows, so clearly some foreknowledge about the men alarmed Liz, and her reaction to that alarm forced the normally cautious murderers to take unnecessary risks.

It is interesting to note that, according to Israel Schwartz's evidence, the man watching was peacefully lighting his pipe. J.K. Stephen smoked – he wrote a poem to 'The Grand Old Pipe', which includes the line, 'My pipe was my one consolation'.

Might Liz have met Druitt – or Stephen – on one of their fact-finding missions into the East End? Could she have seen either one talking to Mary Kelly in a local public house, and did she overhear snatches of their conversation and become suspicious? Maybe Kelly, during her meeting, noticed Liz listening and mentioned her name to Druitt. Maybe Liz recognised him as the man who had been enquiring after Annie Chapman on the night of her murder. Again, we can only speculate, but clearly something about the men who approached her outside Dutfield's Yard frightened her. She knew *something* about them – she realised they were dangerous. The intriguing possibility that the men knew Liz's name was raised by my editor Roderick Brown.

Let us yet again examine part of Israel Schwartz's invaluable statement. 'The man who threw the woman down called out, apparently to the man on the opposite side of the road, "Lipski".' We must ask ourselves why. The man on the opposite side of the road clearly was not a casual passer-by, as Schwartz tells us that he stood '. . . lighting his pipe'. People who watch a violent incident do not casually light up tobacco whilst observing the scene. But why would the attacker call out 'Lipski' to his confederate? This was a term of abuse for Jews. Schwartz was a Jew and a foreigner who spoke no English, but as he appeared to know the word 'Lipski', he may well have been subjected to the insult. Mr Brown acutely observed that 'Liz Stride' called loudly and quickly, may well sound like 'Lipski' to foreign ears, especially to a man who spoke no English and who, perhaps, half-expected to hear such an insult.

A friend of mine, William Pearson, the distinguished writer of *Tornado Down* went a step further along this line. William suggested that 'Lizzie' was even closer to 'Lipski'. The prostitute would, very likely, when introducing herself to men, use her

Christian name ('I'm Lizzie'). Schwartz could well have heard 'Lizzie' being called out, and not 'Lipski'. This would well and truly make Stride a specific victim. Speculating once more, it is possible that both Druitt and Stephen had spoken to Liz and learned her name whilst making various enquiries during daylight sorties into the East End posing as respectable young friends.

Now they came face to face with her late at night and Stride suddenly realised that they were not the innocent men she had initially thought them to be. Druitt, recognising who they had come across, called out to his confederate, who was busy with his tobacco, the reason for his actions. He was explaining to Stephen who the woman was and why he was attacking her; something on the lines of, 'good grief, look who's turned up here. "Lizzie".' A word easily translated to the alarmed foreigner's ears as 'Lipski'.

On his return from chasing Schwartz, Stephen must have found that his friend had already silenced their prey by strangulation to stop her screaming. The autopsy report stated that Stride had been asphyxiated prior to having her throat cut. But, perhaps, just as J.K. returned to the entrance of Dutfield's Yard he noticed that Mrs Mortimer had appeared at her doorway. The men now had to get rid of the inert body. She was not originally part of the murder plot but she now had to be killed, as, once Liz had regained consciousness, her knowledge would make her dangerous. But she cannot be murdered on the spot; singing is coming from the Workingmen's Club; someone could appear at any moment; a woman is standing on the pavement a few doors away – this is a busy spot. There is an easy solution to the problem. The cart is close at hand. Hoisting the body between them (she would look like a drunk being helped if anyone appeared) Stride is taken towards the cart. If Schwartz was two or three minutes late in his timing and Joseph Lave (see below) a few minutes early, the time would be almost exactly 12. 45 a.m.

Once the murderers had the unconscious body on their cart further difficulties appeared. Joseph Lave testified that he had left the Workingmen's Club and walked about for five minutes to get some air. He had then groped his way back along the dark passageway. Fortunately for the murderers Lave did not stay in the yard for long. Stephen and Druitt were in a hurry – to get to the prearranged meeting place and pick up Catharine Eddowes and her decoy, Mary Kelly; and now, as it was getting so late, they could not risk taking the body with them in the hope that they would find a suitable dark and deserted place in which to kill and dump Stride. Fortunately for them Lave does not stay out in the open for long. But they would not wish the cart to be seen by Mrs Mortimer – perhaps they could be traced from their stabling arrangements. One of the men, probably Druitt, therefore went to the end of the passage to peer out, unseen, into Berner Street. After a few more minutes, at 12.55 a.m., Mrs Mortimer went indoors. Druitt must have hurriedly returned to the stables where Stephen was now on the cart ready to drive away. The coast is clear.

The men now drive from the stable into the yard, and, with the pressure of time, they decide to dump and murder Stride in the dark of the passageway. Now it is Druitt's turn to murder. He has to climb down from his side of the cart and help to roll the body on to the ground before quickly slitting the throat. To the two men Stride would not have represented a human being but merely an object which threatened the most important forces in their lives – the State, the Monarchy and Prince Eddy. The couple, like many other fanatics, would have felt no remorse, only complete justification for their brutality.

This reconstruction provides a complete solution to the missing 15 minutes between Stride's attack and her actual murder. The theory also explains Stride's injuries – injuries which differed from those of the four other Ripper victims who were probably killed by J.K. Stephen. A short, broad knife with a bevelled edge was used to kill Stride: the other victims were dispatched with a long, narrow-bladed weapon. (Clearly both men were armed.) The body had fallen onto its back, feet pointing in the direction of the gates. Dr Phillips, who examined the body, believed that the slash to the throat began on the left side. Stride was found with her face towards the wall. Phillips's observation would tie in with Druitt standing over her and drawing his knife straight up across her throat.

Such differences in the style of murder led Edwin Thomas Woodhall (who wrote *Jack the Ripper: or When London Walked in Terror*) and Chief Inspector Walter Dew (in his memoirs) to protest that Stride might not have been a Ripper victim. The lack of mutilation on her body has given rise to further speculation in this direction, but the mutilations were, I believe, Stephen's special trade mark, and, as the men's true rendezvous was with Catharine Eddowes they would not wish to appear covered in blood, besides which there was no time for anything other than straightforward murder.

A retired detective from New Scotland Yard, Arthur Butler, writing about the Ripper killings for *The Sun* in 1972, also thought that Liz was not a Ripper victim. The hue and cry which was going on over the discovery of Stride's body in Berner Street would have kept Jack off the streets, Mr Butler argues; but transport by a horse and cart, and with Mary Kelly acting as a decoy, would give the time and the opportunity to commit both murders without detection. (Interestingly, Butler also states that he knew that Mary Kelly had told acquaintances that she was pregnant and that she was getting rid of the child.)

During the killing, which would only have taken Druitt seconds, the horse and cart would have blocked any interruptions from Dutfield's Yard, and singing from the Workingmen's Club would have drowned out any noises. Louis Diemschutz drove right past Mrs Mortimer's house and she heard him, but the murderers would have driven away from number 36, the noise of their cart being drowned out by the community singing.

The killing of Stride must have wrecked the men's tight schedule. It would have been a few minutes before 1.00 a.m. when Stephen and Druitt drove away from Dutfield's Yard and rounded the corner of Berner's Street, just as Louis Diemschutz in his pony and trap was rounding the opposite end of the street, shortly to find the murdered body of Liz Stride, her throat still oozing blood.

Meanwhile, as prearranged, Mary Kelly had waylaid Catharine Eddowes after Eddowes's release from custody. They would have chatted, Catharine probably complaining about her detention and maybe mentioning the 'damn fine hiding' she would get from John for being so late home. If the couple walked slowly towards Flower and Dean Street Mary could easily have kept her friend chatting until, as planned, Druitt and Stephen drove past. Mary would now wave to the two men as though they were old friends. She tells Eddowes that she knows the men, she knows their likes, and she knows that they pay in sovereigns, not shillings.

As Eddowes is hopelessly late anyway, and as it might mollify John if she were to arrive home with a handful of money, it would not have required much talk to persuade Catharine to climb on to the back of the cart with Mary, alongside Stephen: and, as the cart trundled off, Eddowes, waiting for her embrace amongst the canvas, is, instead, quickly choked into unconsciousness. Perhaps it was at this point that Stephen raises her dress and slices at Eddowes's stomach and vagina (probably without completing the mutilations) telling Mary Kelly that she will receive the same treatment if she mentions a word of her secret to anyone else. Mary, shaken, her hands covered in blood from Catharine's wounds, is then allowed to climb out of the cart near to Dorset Street. This sequence of events would solve another abiding Ripper mystery, one which has already been mentioned in Chapter 6 and is now considered anew.

Major Henry Smith, Acting Police Commissioner for the City of London, had been awakened and told of the murders and of the graffiti at Goulston Street. He hurried to the site only to discover that Sir Charles Warren had washed the chalked message from the wall. The Major then continued his own investigations. He sleuthed around the East End and eventually found a sink near Dorset Street where bloodstained water was still gurgling down the drain. Major Smith remained convinced that he was only minutes behind the Ripper. But Eddowes's body had been found much earlier. Did Smith think that the murderer would have lingered in the area, covered in blood, only bothering to wash when the police had been fully alerted and were wandering around Whitechapel in large numbers? Many writers have commented on the fact that, as the sink was remote and set back from the street, the Ripper must have known the territory well. But Mary Kelly *lived* in Dorset Street. Given the long delay, a much more likely explanation is that *Mary* was responsible for the bloodstained water which Major Smith found still gurgling down the sink. It is highly likely that, once indoors, Kelly noticed a piece of her own clothing was bloodstained. Few East End Victorian houses had their own water supply so Mary might well have slipped out and rinsed the blood from her clothing; this would link her even more strongly to the murder of Eddowes whilst they were both together on the back of the cart.

The invaluable Paul Begg has explained to me that there is now some doubt about Major Smith's testimony as his memoirs have proved unreliable. Perhaps, however, the Major changed his timing of the 'bloodstained sink' discovery after realising that it would not tie in with the Ripper's probable schedule on the night of the double murders. He would have had no reason to know that the timing would tie in with Mary Kelly's actions.

Druitt and Stephen, after leaving Mary Kelly near to Flower and Dean Street, must have driven along Goulston Street, where, perhaps, they intended to deposit the body. Stephen would have delighted in thinking about the sensation which a disembowelled body, lying at the bottom of a public staircase, would have caused. Large crowds quickly would have gathered to view the body and onlookers would have been terrified by so theatrical and terrible a scene. Such a thought would have delighted Stephen. But before the body could be moved from the cart the murdering duo were disturbed; maybe a lamp was lit in a nearby room, maybe someone shouted, or maybe, by a startling irony, the duo were disturbed by burglars – a daring robbery had been committed near to Mitre Square whilst the Ripper murders were taking place. Could the robbers have dashed along Goulston Street as Stephen was about to move the body? Mayhem truly ruled in the East End that night.

Stephen, disturbed for whatever reason, must have quickly driven off to the more secluded Mitre Square where the body could be easily deposited on the pavement within seconds thus solving the magical appearance of the corpse during the few minutes when Mitre Square was not under police observation. As no sound whatsoever was heard by residents of the Square the body could have been carried from the cart the few yards from Mitre Street into the Square, before being dumped in the dark corner. Stephen perhaps then completed his trademark by cutting away parts of Eddowes's body, if he had not already done so. Again, this final operation might only have taken a few minutes.

The two men were now on the edge of the City boundaries, and with all available policemen swarming around Berner Street and Goulston Street, they could have melted away into the night, leaving behind them a baffled, bewildered, distraught, terrified populace.

This would explain how the Ripper managed to move so

quickly between the two murder sites (Berners Street and Mitre Square) meeting, murdering and mutilating Eddowes on the way, without being seen or heard. His feat was a conjuring trick, seemingly impossible if one does not know how it was done. And so, with the extraordinary double killing, a further myth was added to Jack's reputation.

* * * * *

By this stage possible witnesses and those who might embarrass the Establishment had been eliminated to some degree but the central problem still remained – Mary Kelly. Her condition must by now have been noticeable although because of layers of voluminous Victorian winter clothing the pregnancy might still not be obvious in public. I believe that with Queen Victoria insisting that the child be born events would have to move swiftly, and this need for haste perhaps contributed to James's lurid, absurd plan, which he, no doubt, considered brilliant.

* * * * *

There is now the overriding difficulty of explaining away the violent events at Miller's Court. A body, its face slashed beyond recognition, had been identified as that of Mary Kelly. Then, some hours after her supposed death, Kelly was seen and recognised by three independent witnesses, one of whom had a conversation with her. How can so bizarre a scenario be explained away? The above events have been recorded many times with few theories being put forward; and indeed, an acceptable solution is hard to find, but for factual happenings there has to be an explanation and I must try to provide one.

Mary Kelly could not be killed physically by order of the sovereign, but once she was installed in luxury for the birth of her royal child gossip surrounding the accouchement would have been intense and dangerous. So why not figuratively destroy Mary Kelly then substitute a corpse in her place? Such a scenario seems extreme, but let me repeat – the extraordinary 'murder' of Mary Kelly; the mutilation of the corpse at Miller's Court; the strange inquest, during which one witness testified under oath to having spoken to the 'dead woman'; all of this is strictly factual, again making truth appear stranger than fiction.

J.K. Stephen's wild reasoning does make some kind of sense. If Mary Kelly, on the sovereign's unbalanced orders, could not be killed, but if she could also not be allowed to live why not have the best of both worlds – life and death, a figurative murder? If Kelly did not officially exist any longer, if her death were to be so sensational that every person in the land would discuss it, then later talk and gossip that Mary was living in luxury whilst she awaited the birth of Bertie's child would have been treated as nonsense no matter how intense or how informed the speculation might be: everyone would know that Mary Kelly was officially dead and dead women do not give birth to children.

Stephen, in his unbalanced state, would have found this plan feasible and clever, as indeed it proved to be. And with his forceful personality and clever use of language he probably had little difficulty in selling his plan to both Kelly and Druitt.

Both would probably have received plausible offers of great wealth. It would have been easy to believe even the most outlandish promises from people of power and prestige who are usually thought of as honourable, especially in the days of Queen Victoria.

Druitt and Kelly would have been made to believe that they were now important members of the Establishment, and, as such, they would have worked vigorously towards any end which their masters dictated. Once their tasks were completed it is my belief that both of them were then murdered; to repeat, death would have been the absolute guarantee of silence.

Mary would feel no wrench at being parted from her family after she had been persuaded that she must disappear. Although, as we have seen, she had occasional contact with her brother and possibly her mother, she did not appear to be especially close to either of them. Or maybe, as none of the family appeared at the funeral, they had been told that for undisclosed reasons it was necessary for Mary to 'disappear'. There had to be some reason why no relative was ever discovered despite an intensive search being made by the contemporary press.

Druitt would have needed little convincing. And for Mary, the idea of being destroyed then reborn as a new woman, with no ties of family or low-class East End friends, must have had strong appeal; especially if she were given proof that Queen Victoria was taking a personal interest in her. The idea that the Establishment would not want her trailing friends from her old life, or even her family, into the higher echelons of society would have made perfect sense. Even today the idea of completely wiping out the past and of changing one's role in life for a position of money, power and privilege would appeal to many people. Within the last few decades a former British cabinet minister, John Stonehouse, attempted to create a new character and life for himself by leaving the now legendary 'heap of clothes on a seashore'.

Kelly's actions before her own 'death' would tie in with preparations for a disappearance. Let us re-examine some of those actions again.

After living with Joe Barnett for over a year Kelly must have known her lover's character. She must have known that Barnett would object to her bringing prostitutes back to the cramped single bedroom: she must have known that such actions would drive Joe away; yet, as we saw in Chapter 7 this is precisely what she did. Why would Mary want to drive Joe Barnett out of the flat? Maybe because she wanted to hide her pregnancy for a while longer? Although Mary tended towards stoutness her condition, at just over six months, would soon have been starting to show.

On the night of her death, when, after the double killing of Stride and Eddowes, most prostitutes with any common sense (and Mary was not short of sense) had stopped soliciting in the middle of the night, Kelly, according to George Hutchinson, strolled around the East End in the small hours with impunity.

There are several reports of Mary mentioning her lack of money directly before the Miller's Court murder. Such complaints make me suspicious that she was trying to hide the opposite state of affairs. All East Enders were continually short of money; it was a fact of life and there would be no need constantly to draw attention to it. Yet on the night of her 'death' Mary spoke to a young woman (reported only as Margaret) and said that she had no money and intended to 'do away with herself'. She then met George Hutchinson and said, 'I must go and look for some money'. This sounds urgent, but why would she want money in the middle of the night?

Earlier in the small hours she had gone to her room, presumably with a client, where she began to sing loudly for about an hour. This was obviously not a regular occurrence because the singing upset a neighbour, who was tempted to complain. Then Mary went out soliciting again, although she had had her fill of clients and beer for the night and should have gone to bed. Then, shortly after giving every indication that she was extremely drunk, Mary solicited around Commercial Street, where she had a lucid conversation with George Hutchinson and where she picked up another client.

These events have an air of exhibitionism about them as though they were being staged in order to create a dramatic effect. A particular scene was being set.

* * * * *

Mary's uncharacteristic habit of sleeping with women before the day that she was 'murdered' would indicate that she herself had chosen the prostitute who was to die in her place.

* * * * *

Could George Hutchinson, that purveyor of detailed information to the police and to the press, possibly, maybe even unknowingly, have been a part of the plot? Hutchinson, at various times, mentioned a gold chain, a horseshoe shaped tiepin, and a large seal with a red stone. Was he signalling that an objective (regaining Bertie's possessions) had now been achieved? Certainly a 'large seal with a red stone' might be the kind of official object, an object of great importance, which Bertie would carry.

In the book *The Ripper and The Royals*, the author, Melvyn Fairclough, and Joseph Sickert, enterprisingly interviewed George Hutchinson's son Reg, a gentlemen now in his seventies. Reg reported that his father had information about the crimes but wouldn't reveal it. However, George believed that the Ripper crimes were 'more to do with the Royal Family than ordinary people', which is extremely interesting. Reg also said that his father was given 100 shillings but George would not say why. Reg, naturally, stressed his father's excellent character and I have no reason to doubt otherwise. George may well have followed instructions without knowing the purpose behind the orders, and, no doubt, as an honest working Victorian man, he would have been glad of the money – no questions asked, and who could blame him?

* * * * *

For the final part of the drama, as I see it, we must assume that Mary Kelly callously left her chosen sacrifice – possibly someone who facially resembled her – asleep in Miller's Court. She let in the murderers, Stephen and Druitt, probably at some time around 4.00 a.m., then left the premises, maybe to wait on the cart, rolled up safely in the canvas.

But the murder and mutilations at Miller's Court must have taken a considerable time, probably longer than had been anticipated. At 5.45 a.m. a resident of Miller's Court heard a man's footsteps leaving the court. The public houses were open by this time. Kelly, after her long wait, must have found that the tensions of the night, and the events which she knew were taking place in her rooms, too much to bear. And perhaps – just perhaps – she might have been experiencing some remorse at the thought of her friend's fate. It is easy to imagine that such mental pressures might become overwhelming, so I suggest that Mary, unable to overcome the craving for a drink, climbed down from the cart and went to a local public house. The original intention might have been to visit the bar for one quick gin. Her 'murder', taking place indoors in the middle of the night, could not be precisely timed, so it would not matter if she were spotted. But for a lady who liked alcohol, and especially for a lady who was suffering from intense stress, one quick gin can lead to several more. Then with the comfort of alcohol (and Mary could now afford as much as she liked) she could quickly have lost track of time – maybe even of reality. Events of the night might have appeared, through the curtain of drink, to be a nightmare from which she would eventually awake. Whatever the explanation (and the above seems most likely), Mary's craving for drink overcame her common sense, and she went to her local public house, *The Britannia* where she was seen; and, having tasted alcohol, she stayed much longer than was wise.

* * * * *

Druitt and Stephen, their dreadful work completed, would have returned to the cart only to discover that Mary had disappeared. The men must have been covered in blood, so initially they would have had to clean up and probably change their clothing, then they would have gone looking for Mary.

She in the meantime, dazed by stress and drink, and not thinking rationally, now returned to Miller's Court, perhaps expecting to find Druitt and Stephen waiting for her. This action, as we have seen, was backed by contemporary press reports of witnesses seeing her the following morning. To recapitulate, *The Times* in November 1888 stated that a tailor, Maurice Lewis, said that he had seen Kelly leave her room then return to it at 8.00 a.m. on the morning following her 'death' (no heavy object behind the door). This statement would be consistent with the above scenario. But Mary's actions were incautious to say the least. I can only assume that the dreadful murder must have sent her into shock. Few people, even hardened characters such as Kelly, could easily overcome the sight of a former friend literally slashed to pieces before their eyes without some kind of extreme reaction.

Half an hour later Mrs Caroline Maxwell had her reported conversation with Mary. Given that both Lewis and Maxwell might have been slightly inaccurate in their recall of time, it is possible that Mary spent between 15 to 25 minutes in her room with the mutilated corpse. It is not beyond the bounds of possibility that shock and drink caused her to faint. Then, after recovery, but still overcome by alcohol and the night's events – all on top of her pregnancy – she rushed outside and was sick, after which the conversation with Mrs. Maxwell occurred. To repeat:

Maxwell. 'Why don't you go to "The Ringers" and have a pint.'

Kelly. 'I've been there and had it, but I've brought it all up again.'

It would now have been essential for Mary to think quickly. She was in a dangerous position – the Establishment could prove her part in the murder. Maybe she suddenly realised that she had been trapped but, buoyed up by alcohol and dazed by shock, beyond caring, she went out drinking once more – the last sighting of her was around 10.00 a.m..

Stephen and Druitt, now both cleaned up, might have known Mary's usual haunts. After finding their prey with difficulty they must have quickly spirited her away and taken her to a safe place where the baby could be born. After that Mary's fate would be completely in the hands of the Establishment.

The authorities now had in their power a woman who did not legally exist any longer, and, therefore, a woman whose baby did not exist. All other legal niceties would be completed by the law. A hasty inquest with a sympathetic coroner was rushed through. The corpse was declared to be that of Mary Kelly. Witnesses were swiftly dealt with; any awkward evidence was ignored. The affair was hastily, and irrationally, completed within a day.

But, perhaps, with the last vestiges of duty lingering in his mind, the coroner, Roderick MacDonald, could not bring himself to sign a legal document which put his final stamp of approval on the proceedings. Negligent conduct in court – breaking the law by failing to establish the precise wounds and the weapon which caused death – this was certainly professional misconduct, but, in the circumstances, could be overlooked. However, a signature on a legal document has always been viewed with the utmost seriousness. Perhaps Roderick MacDonald's conscience was not entirely corruptible.

The case of Mary Kelly was now finally closed, and the threat to the Establishment had, in the most spectacular fashion, been averted. Perhaps the new Ripper puzzle should be – 'What happened to Mary Kelly?'

* * * * *

One year after the killing of Annie Chapman a woman's torso was found under a railway arch in the East End's Pinchin Street. The legs and head had been hacked off. The womb was missing. Legend has attributed this murder to Jack the Ripper.

Was this the fate of Mary Kelly?

Every nuance of the complicated Ripper events will, of course, never be known, but my resolution of the affair does explain away many of the abiding mysteries:

1. The silence of the murders.

2. The actions of the authorities.

3. The rifling of Annie Chapman's pocket and the laying out of her goods on the ground.

4. The difference of the wounds which killed Liz Stride.

5. The strangely detailed information supplied by George Hutchinson.

6. The blood in the sink at Dorset Street.

7. The timing of the double murders.

8. Catharine Eddowes's mysterious wanderings, before her arrest and after her release from custody.

9. The missing 15 minutes between Stride's attack and her murder.

10. And, strangest of all, the reappearance of Mary Kelly on the morning after she was presumed dead.

* * * * *

There has been much speculation about the reason for the Ripper file remaining open at Scotland Yard until 1892, four years after the last Ripper murder was committed. The reason for that fact is clear and convincing. *J.K. Stephen died in 1892.*

But let me repeat, the evidence presented so far regarding J.K. Stephen and M.J. Druitt being involved in the murders is circumstantial. Although so many of the facts clearly provide a powerful case against the two men there is no incontrovertible proof. I am, however, in a position to supply that proof: without doubt J.K. Stephens and M.J. Druitt were a combined Jack the Ripper team. The following chapter will explain why I can state such a fact so positively.

Chapter Fifteen

The Ripper Revealed

The double murder occurred in the early hours of 30 September between approximately 1.00 a.m. (Liz Stride in Berner Street) and 1.45 a.m. (Catharine Eddowes in Mitre Square). Berner Street was not within central London's boundaries, and the area was, therefore, under the jurisdiction of the Metropolitan Police Commissioner, Sir Charles Warren. Mitre Square, however, was just within the City of London boundaries; this meant that Major Henry Smith was in charge. Out of the five Ripper victims only the murder of Catharine Eddowes took place within the city.

1888 newspapers record that it was immediately after the discovery of Eddowes's body in Mitre Square that a summons was sent to Major Henry Smith, as he was Acting Commissioner of The City of London Police. Major Smith, in his memoirs *From Constable to Commissioner*, published in 1910, writes about the event:

'The night of Saturday, 29 September, found me tossing about in my bed at Cloak Lane Station, close to the river and adjoining Southwark Bridge...suddenly the bell at my head rang violently. "What is it?" I asked, putting my ear to the tube. "Another murder sir, this time in the City." Jumping up, I was dressed and in the street in a couple of minutes. A hansom cab - to me a detestable vehicle - was at the door...'

Other less-important City of London police officers, such as Superintendent Alfred Foster, were also summoned, in the middle of the night, to the murder site in the Square. Clearly, judging by this documented activity, the homicide of Liz Stride at Berner Street, which had happened 45 minutes before Eddowes's attack, would have been immediately relayed to Sir Charles Warren. Berner Street was, I repeat, within the Metropolitan Police boundaries.

Major Henry Smith also relates in his memoirs how, having been informed of the murders, he visited Mitre Square; he then proceeded to spend a busy night visiting the morgue and rushing around the area as a whole. Let me repeat that although Warren must have been summoned after the discovery of Stride's body, he did not put in an immediate appearance, which is not surprising. Stephen Knight confirms that although the two earlier murders (of Mary Nichols and Annie Chapman) had occurred in areas under the control of the Metropolitan police, Sir Charles did not bother to visit either murder site at any time. But when he was informed, well before dawn, about the graffiti which had been found in Goulston Street, he inexplicably rushed to the site. Let us examine the matter of the graffiti once more.

On the night of the double murder PC Alfred Long walked his Goulston Street beat. Goulston Street was another dreary, over-crowded thoroughfare, although efforts at improving the street's housing stock had been made. Brick tenements, euphemistically named Wentworth Model Dwellings, had been erected in the street. Sets of flats in the Model Dwellings were served by a series of open entrances which led to communal stairs.

Nothing out of the ordinary caught the constable's attention as he plodded his beat back and forth past the Model Dwellings. On his 2.20 a.m. round all was quiet. However, on his return beat, just before 3.00 a.m. the constable noticed a piece of torn rag on the ground near the base of a common staircase leading to apartments 108-119 of the dwellings. Chalked on the wall above the torn cloth were the words:

> The Juwes are
> The men That
> Will not
> be Blamed
> for nothing

At the time of the murders a considerable amount of graffiti was chalked around the East End. As the above message does not make obvious sense, and as it does not mention murder, there was nothing to link the piece of blood-stained cloth directly to the words. Slaughter houses around the East End could easily have been the source of the remnant. However, common sense indicated to Constable Long that this could be an important find. Detectives were called to Goulston Street.

In the meantime Catharine Eddowes's body had been taken to the mortuary, and it was noticed that part of her apron was missing. Once reports of the Goulston Street blood-smeared rag had filtered through to the authorities they compared it to the apron on the body and found a perfect match. Obviously, with Victorian transport, it must have taken at least a few hours to link the torn rag to Eddowes's apron; and this matching proved that Jack had indeed paused in the entrance to the block of dwellings, where he had thrown away his memento. Such a discovery now made the chalked message supremely important. Possibly it was the only direct clue ever left by the infamous murderer.

Warren, on hearing this news, rushed to Goulston Street at around 5.00 a.m., before dawn had broken. The sensational murder of two women four hours earlier (one of these homicides being in territory under Warren's jurisdiction) had not proved sufficient bait to lure Sir Charles into the East End – the few chalked words were. Why?

This is the vital question. Why on earth should a few meaningless words chalked on a wall bring Sir Charles dashing into the East End when truly sensational events had been ignored?

After arriving in Goulston Street, and after examining the graffiti, Warren caused astonishment – and this astonishment has lasted up to the present day – by ordering that the message be washed away. His senior officers, presumably stunned by the stupidity of such an order, displayed more common sense. They realised that the writing, the only clue left to date by the man whom the whole of the London police force were hunting, could be valuable. Warren was advised against destroying it, but he was adamant – he insisted that the word 'Juwes' might spark off riots. Senior officers, clearly anxious to save so important a clue, suggested that the message be covered up for an hour or so until it was light enough to take photographs. Warren would not wait even an hour, and as for any covering, he insisted that that would be torn down. This surely would *not* have been the case. Although the police were generally hated throughout the East End they were also feared. Warren would only have had to put a few policemen on guard to prevent any covering being torn down, and this only for approximately an hour. Once dawn had broken the area could easily have been cleared for a short time, the covering removed and photographs taken.

The next suggestion which was made to Warren, one which any reasonable person might be expected to follow, was that the offending word, or even the top line, be washed out, leaving an entirely innocuous and totally meaningless phrase: '...the men that will not be blamed for nothing'. It was put to him that the remaining four lines of graffiti could then be photographed at leisure and the handwriting might yield valuable clues.

Warren rejected even this most sensible of solutions. He wanted the entire graffiti destroyed. He is said to have picked up a sponge and personally washed out the words - an extraordinary gesture when someone much less senior could have accomplished the task. There was condemnation of Warren's stupid action, and much criticism in the press.

As we have seen, Warren, in his long letter to the Home Office, insisted that Superintendent Arnold had also wanted to wash out the graffiti, but we have only Warren's word for that, and, as we shall see later, his statements were sometimes highly suspect. It is more likely that Arnold was amongst the officers who wanted only the offending word, or, at best, the top line obliterated.

Warren's supposed intent, to suppress the word 'Juwes', failed miserably. The graffiti became common knowledge although there was widespread confusion about the exact wording. In fact Warren's actions did more harm than good. The message had been seen and rumour spread quickly. The word 'Juwes', which makes no real sense, became commonly translated as the much more damaging 'Jews', but this would not have worried Warren. It is my belief that he was not concerned with protecting an innocent race. As we shall see, he had darker motives and these prompted his actions.

At Catharine Eddowes's inquest, PC Long gave evidence and spoke about his dramatic discoveries. Some newspapers reported that the graffiti had read:

'The Jews are the men who will not be blamed for nothing.'

Long claimed that the words chalked on the wall were, 'The Jews are not the men that will be blamed for nothing.' The City solicitor, Henry Crawford, clearly knew that Long's statement was incorrect. Crawford cross-examined the policeman, paying special attention to the spelling of the word 'Juwes'. Crawford thought that this central word had been spelt 'Juees'. As we now know, all of them were wrong. Warren's actions had already started to cause total confusion.

The flustered PC Long stumbled through his cross-examination in court. It was then discovered that he had been testifying from memory, which is strange, as Long had written down all the relevant facts in his notebook; once this was discovered Long was ordered to produce the notebook in court, yet even this did not produce results. The constable's notes were incorrect, which is astounding, as it was he who had discovered the graffiti and had initially stood guard over the message. One would have expected that he, of all people, would have written down such a startling discovery verbatim, but apparently not: in his notebook, the constable still had the word 'Juwes' written as 'Jews'.

We now know that there was absolutely no need for any of this confusion. Stephen Knight found, amongst the Metropolitan Police files of confidential letters, a covering note from Sir Charles Warren attached to a facsimile - an exact copy - of the Goulston Street graffiti. Mention of this facsimile is made by Warren himself in his report to the Home Office:

'...I considered it desirable to obliterate the writing at once, having taken a copy of which I enclose a duplicate.'

Why was this vital document not produced at the official inquest? That would have solved once and for all the farcical contradictions which were taking place in the court room. And furthermore, such vital evidence should have been automatically presented to the inquest. But this important facsimile was locked away in police files (not to be revealed for a century) when, by law it should have been produced in court.

Warren's actions appear to be totally mystifying, until they are unravelled. Then his behaviour makes perfect sense. His actions were meant to create confusion; and that is exactly what they did do - until now.

* * * * *

Several writers have repeated Warren's testimony, his assertion to the Home Office that the message was written 'on the jamb of the open archway or doorway, visible to anyone in the street.' That statement is simply not true. PC Long, at the inquest, clearly stated that the torn rag was lying in the passageway leading to the staircase, and that the chalked message was 'above it on the wall, written in chalk...'

Common sense dictates that the message, in the form in which it was written, would not easily fit on the narrow edge of a brick wall. The facsimile on police files is not cramped but spread out. It is my belief that Warren was lying and not just mistaken. He was trying to emphasise that the writing, and especially the sensitive word 'Juwes' was more visible to the general public than it actually was - which necessitated its instant removal. And, of course, any graffiti on the jamb of a doorway would be more difficult to cover up. So Warren was prepared to lie, even to the Home Secretary, in order to mask his true reason (which will shortly be revealed) for destroying the graffiti. The positioning of the message is illustrated overleaf.

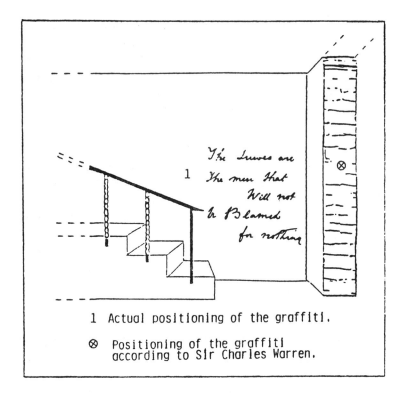

1 Actual positioning of the graffiti.

⊗ Positioning of the graffiti
   according to Sir Charles Warren.

But why did Warren produce the facsimile in the first place? The most likely explanation is that an officer had already made the drawing. Victorian police seem to have had a mania for making on-site sketches recording accurately details of the murders. There are police drawings of the corner in Mitre Square where the body was discovered. There are detailed, exact-copy, police sketches of the mutilations to Eddowes's body, etcetera. All of these details were later photographed. It is, therefore, highly likely that an officer waiting at the scene of the discoveries in Goulston Street would have routinely made an exact copy of the graffiti. And it would have appeared highly suspicious if Warren had destroyed both the original and the copy. Or perhaps the Home Office had heard of the copy and demanded to have it, along with an explanation for Warren's actions. Such an explanation was certainly given in the letter. To repeat: '...I considered it desirable to obliterate the writing at once, having taken a copy of which I enclose a duplicate...' The last phrase seems to infer that Warren made the copy personally, which seems unlikely. Surely the Metropolitan Commissioner would delegate such a tiresome task? And, as

I have said, I suspect that the copy had already been made by the time that Warren arrived at Goulston Street, some two hours after the original discovery. Whatever the reason for Warren's production of the facsimile it made little difference: to repeat - the copy was quickly placed on file at Scotland Yard and remained unseen for almost a century.

* * * * *

It is well-documented that serial killers frequently write to the police or newspapers and boast about their crimes. This is a common aberration, which, I have been told, represents a subconscious desire on the part of the killer to be apprehended, so preventing any further deaths. Serial killers are capable of the most extreme self-deception.

As an example of this, in 1913, in New York, a much-loved, conscientious parish priest, Father Hans Schmidt, secretly married a young servant girl. Shortly afterwards, overcome with remorse at breaking his sacred vows of chastity, the priest murdered his young bride. Over the next three days, in between conducting masses and other duties, all carried out with devotion and sincerity, Father Schmidt carved up his young bride's dead body and threw the limbs and torso into the river.

On days following several of the murders Montague Druitt played cricket. As we have seen, the human mind is capable of operating on different levels simultaneously.

It is my belief that James Stephen may well have been proud of what he was doing. To his warped way of thinking the murders would have been entirely justified, for he was saving the Monarchy in general and saving his close friend Prince Eddy in particular. He was also furthering his own fierce ambition.

I believe that Frederick George Abberline, that shadowy Ripper investigator, who, unlike most of his colleagues, wrote no book of memoirs, knew the reason behind the crimes. The following evidence will indicate that Abberline disapproved of the insane, exhibitionistic nature of the murders and must have remonstrated with J.K. Stephen. Abberline would have been powerless to stop the killings: a policeman, even today, could not interfere with even the most extreme actions of the Secret Service. State security is all-powerful and Stephen's work must have been placed in that category. However, my evidence points towards the fact that Abberline, although he was powerless to act, was unable to suppress his hatred and contempt for Stephen's insane actions - and the policeman must have said so, as I shall soon demonstrate. And J.K. Stephen reacted to that criticism in a typically unbalanced manner; a manner which, at that time, led him to take revenge on his partner-in-crime Montague Druitt. 'Now hate M.J. Druitt. He sent the woman to hell,' Stephen told Abberline, no doubt as an effort to justify his crimes. To which woman was J.K. referring? Probably Liz Stride, as she had been murdered by Druitt.

* * * * *

We have seen that the Ripper murders were particularly theatrical and exhibitionistic. This fits in with J.K. Stephen's character, as does the despatch of several letters to the police and newspaper offices. Letters were sent to the authorities in their thousands, mostly purporting to be from Jack the Ripper. Many were signed in red ink, some actually written in blood. It is my belief that amongst this deluge at least two messages were genuine. The Goulston Street writing certainly was - that was written by J.K. Stephen.

To summarise, the vital questions which must be asked - and answered - are:

1) Why did Warren fail to visit personally any murder site until he was told of the graffiti? Why did that message make him rush to the East End? (He visited Mitre Square later on.)

2) Why, when there was no reason, did Warren insist on totally destroying the chalked message against the advice of his senior officers?

3) Why did he allow endless arguments - even in a court of law - about the exact wording and form of the graffiti, when there was a facsimile of the message on file at Scotland Yard?

4) Why did he write a report to the Home Office which contained a clear lie about the positioning of the graffiti? Warren had stood on site discussing the fate of the message. He knew full well that the graffiti had been written on the wall at the base of the stairs, and not on his carefully described '...jamb of the open archway or doorway visible to anyone in the street.' There had to be good reason for such a senior officer - the Metropolitan Police Commissioner himself - to lie; to suppress evidence; to bend the law. What was the reason?

Once these questions are answered the identity of Jack the Ripper will be finally proved.

* * * * *

Let us start by examining the layout of the graffiti. On 30 September the

Ripper, after committing a double savage murder, paused to leave a message chalked on a wall. Jack, even given his steely character, must have been under considerable mental pressure. Any man bold enough to linger around an area teeming with policemen trying to catch him, who pauses to scribble a chalked message on a wall in a dark area, an area with easy access from the surrounding dwellings would hardly be likely to concern himself with presentation. Under immense pressure, the message which Jack clearly felt compelled to write should have been quickly sprawled in a few lines. Yet the format of the words shows a careful, and familiar style. This is a poet's layout.

If we look at Stephen's poems in *Lapsus Calami*, reproduced from his work published in *The Reflector* and various other sources, we see the distinctive layout frequently used in this type of work. Here is a reproduction from an 1896 edition of *Lapsus Calami*:

> O ye musical nine, who drink the Castalian waters,
> Seated on peaks of Olympus (or if ye prefer it ,
>   Olumpos,-
> Browning's a far better judge of the matter than
>   yours very truly-),

If we look at the graffiti there are also similar indentations.

And if we remove all the markings from around the 't' in the word 'not' in the graffiti we isolate an unusually shaped letter. If this is compared to the 't' in J.K. Stephen's signature there is a remarkable similarity. Admittedly the graffiti 't' is only a copy but there is no reason to suspect that the policeman who was making the facsimile would not have been totally accurate. This is only a small point, but the long 't' bar is most unusual; it is unlikely to have been duplicated by more than one person. This is why Sir Charles Warren was alarmed by the message – so alarmed that in his panic he was willing to lie, to suppress evidence, to break the law. We shall soon see what he was trying to hide.

* * * * *

Warren's highly suspicious behaviour led me to study the graffiti closely. There is nothing particularly alarming in the actual words, apart perhaps from 'Juwes', which, as we have seen, could easily have been erased. But what if the message had been written in code? It might then be essential to prevent the exact wording and lettering from becoming common knowledge. If only a few letters are out of place then any coded message is safe and Warren knew this. He did not care about the general context of the words – indeed it suited his purpose if people believed that his actions were to protect a race of people. No one would then question the possibility of there being a meaning behind the peculiar words. But this is exactly what I have done more than one century later.

I could see that the Goulston Street message was meaningless: it was the unseen message which counted – I became convinced that the strange spelling and wording did indeed form a code. This is the only reason which could account for Warren's apparently inexplicable behaviour. A coded message would explain why a few meaningless words aroused panic in the Commissioner.

I puzzled for several days, trying various cyphers from several code books without success. Then, whilst re-reading editions of *The Reflector*, I discovered that J.K. Stephen enjoyed playing word games. Here is an acrostic which he actually offered to readers of his magazine.

> The Mirror Of Mankind – though some folks quiz it,
> What the Reflector says it is – but is it?
> 1)   Our occupation – nay our whole existence,
> 2)   What we attain by talent with persistence,
> 3)   Fit audience for the wise; yet if not mended

4) It leads to this, and then the matter's ended.
5) Even to the far Gordan our rumour runs,
6) And where in Erie sinks colonial suns,
7) Who but the Daily News would care for numbers?
8) This is our Number - multitude encumbers,
9) Polished and true, the eye its image meets;
   It lures the birds to death and saves the fleet.

Various attempts by myself and several erudite friends failed to solve the above puzzle but this was only a brief and minor diversion. I had more pressing matters on which to spend my time. To try and discover a code in the graffiti was my main concern. It seemed significant to me that J.K. Stephen, as the above acrostic clearly shows, enjoyed word puzzles, as did many Victorians. This was the heyday of parlour games and simple pleasures. I began to wonder whether a simple anagram had been used?

The graffiti contains only 46 characters, and over one third of these are vowels. Out of the remaining 30 consonants several letters which are lowdown on the frequency table of normal usage (even in large texts) were used several times - in only 11 words. For instance, both B and W, which are in the last one third of normal frequency-usage, are each used twice, despite the low number of consonants available; 8 letters, including the normally high-usage C, are not used at all.

Out of any 46 letters, it is, of course, possible to find a list of assorted words or short garbled phrases, but I was convinced that amongst these selections there had to be a hidden message explaining the Metropolitan Police Commissioner's behaviour. As we shall see, there was indeed a hidden message.

I set to work, but one wrong word, stupidly inserted on my part, wasted a great deal of time. Warren's plan, which caused so much confusion amongst his contemporaries, still creates confusion even today. Just a few misplaced letters can cause havoc.

Once my mistake had been rectified I realised that from the restricted selection of 46 letters contained in the graffiti, two highly unusual names, along with their initials - F.G. Abberline, and M.J. Druitt - could be extracted. Both of these men are, of course, inextricably linked to the Ripper case. Frederick George Abberline, a police investigator, and Montague John Druitt, a leading suspect. Both of these names used up almost half of the available letters. The odds against two such unusual and connected names occurring randomly in so small a selection of characters are high; especially when, as we shall see, the remaining few letters can be used to form a perfectly coherent and relevant sentence. For the first time Warren's apparently stupid behaviour begins to make sense. By washing away the carefully arranged letters he was destroying a deadly but clever word game devised by the now insane J.K. Stephen. Endless numbers of Ripper researchers have tried to explain the graffiti's meaning without success. This is not surprising, as the original message has no sense. It is the hidden words which are so revealing.

The full anagram, which uses every letter of the graffiti, is as follows:

The Juwes are the men that	F.G. Abberline. Now hate M.J.
will not be blamed for	Druitt. He sent the woman to
nothing.	hell.

Each message contains:

E 7, T 6, H/N 4, A/L/O 3, W/R/M/I/B 2, J/U/S/D/F/G 1.

J.K. Stephen, in the familiar way of serial killers, was taunting the police by leaving them a mysterious message in anagram form, not on paper, but chalked on a wall for all to see, and, if possible, to puzzle out. Most dramatic of all - the message actually named one of the killers. It was clearly Warren's job to ensure that no anagram was either recognised or broken.

We now have a complete package of proof which explains the impossibly high odds of two unusual names and initials occurring randomly in only 46 letters. (I cannot anagram even one of the names and initials from my address book.) It also explains the extraordinary behaviour of Warren once he heard about the graffiti. It explains the layout of the graffiti which exactly matches the layout in many of James's poems, and finally, the highly individualistic 't' bar in both the graffiti and in James's signature is explained. Such a string of interlinked discoveries cannot be a coincidence.

It is not difficult to imagine Stephen, having been prickled by criticism from Abberline (and, by the malice of displaying Druitt's name, probably having quarrelled with his partner-in-crime) deciding to get revenge on both men in the most extreme manner. Stephen, the man who liked to set word puzzles for his readers, and who so gleefully mutilated the bodies of his victims, must have delighted in his own cleverness as he worked out an anagram which was a confession. The daring shown in this public confession aligns with the exhibitionism shown in other aspects of the Ripper crimes. (Interestingly, almost one century later, the serial killer nicknamed Zodiac, who terrorised America during the late 1970s, and who, like Jack, was never arrested, also wrote letters in cypher - to the newspapers.)

But now we are confronted with a new puzzle. Clearly Warren, by ignoring the previous murders yet hurrying into the East End for the graffiti, must have been expecting this dramatic gesture from Stephen. Warren must have been anticipating some kind of hidden message, even if the time, date and place remained a mystery. But clearly, from a quick glance at the graffiti, Warren could not have formed a solution to the anagram: it took me a considerable time to work out the exact wording, even with so few letters. It therefore becomes clear that Warren had been pre-warned. But when? And by whom?

* * * * *

J.K. Stephen, having been appointed Clerk of the Assizes for the South Wales Circuit by his father, was, during the summer of 1888, from time to time in that part of the country. Wales is separated from Liverpool by a narrow stretch of water - the River Dee - and the two places have always been within easy reach of each other. Interestingly, there were two puzzling letters, signed Jack the Ripper, which were posted in the Liverpool area.

* * * * *

J. Hall Richardson was a popular Fleet Street reporter who worked for the *Daily Telegraph*. His book, *From the City to Fleet Street*, describes celebrations for the opening of the *Telegraph's* offices in 1882. Richardson's memoirs, as I have recorded in Chapter 6, published the two Liverpool letters, both signed 'Jack the Ripper'. Puzzlingly, both these letters are lumped together: 'I quote one', Richardson says, then he quite clearly quotes two, the second letter undated. Traditionally this second letter was thought to have been dated - or posted - on 30 September, but I can find no confirmation for this assumption. Perhaps the letters, although both separately addressed, were posted together? A further puzzle in regard to these letters concerns the time lapse before their publication. Richardson's book was published in 1927, almost forty years after the murders had ended, and after the letters had been sent. Yet surprisingly, 1927 appears to be the first time that the Liverpool letters were published. Let us look at various dates:

'Dear Boss' letter. First use of name Jack the Ripper. Posted to the Central News Agency. Dated 25 September. Postmarked 27 September. Published in the newspapers 1 October.

First Liverpool letter. Dated 29 September, and signed 'Jack the Ripper'.

The puzzle inherent here is the fact that the writer of the first Liverpool letter knew the nickname before it had been published. Only the Central News Agency, who received the 'Dear Boss' letter, and the police (who were sent it) knew the pseudonym before it was published. Either the writer of all the above communications was the same man, or else he had access to official knowledge. I strongly suspect that Jack wrote only the Liverpool letters.

There has long been a mystery surrounding the Liverpool letters. At one time it was thought that they had been sent to the police and had been lost. Many previously recorded documents are now missing from the official Ripper files. However, it now appears that these letters were probably sent to the *Daily Telegraph*, which would account for their being published in Richardson's 1927 book. There is, as yet, no explanation for the fact that the letters do not appear to have been published by the newspaper at the time they were received. Admittedly thousands of crank messages were sent, but the first Liverpool letter was only the second time that the famous nickname had been used, and, to repeat, it was sent before the original had been published. That in itself should have given considerable interest to the documents. And as they are set out so carefully in Richardson's book he must have thought them important enough to copy exactly. He kept the copies for many years. Or maybe, as I suspect, Richardson kept the original documents.

From time to time, Ripper researchers have paid considerable attention to the contents of the Liverpool correspondence. The second letter gives an address, then says the police are fools because they cannot find the sender; this has aroused the particular interest of many researchers.

The fact that J.K. Stephen was within easy reach of Liverpool during the time the letters were sent, and that there was a general air of mystery surrounding the correspondence, alerted me. Then Andy Patterson from Oxford Films pointed out that the trial of Florence Maybrick took place in Liverpool in 1889. The presiding judge at this trial was Sir James Fitzjames Stephen, J.K.'s father. This means, of course, that Sir James, as a circuit judge, must have been in Liverpool regularly. It is therefore highly likely that his son could have visited him in the City. It has not been possible to establish exact dates before going to press, but research is continuing.

Could it be that reading these letters was the first time that Sir Charles Warren became aware of J.K. Stephen's sordid word games?

Let us consider the first Liverpool letter, which was sent around three weeks after Annie Chapman's death.

As we have seen, the Goulston Street graffiti contained only 46 letters. Obviously, with so few characters, the chances of cogent sentences being hidden are limited; but the first Liverpool letter, with 170 characters, provides a wide scope for various names and phrases to be extracted. Yet, with careful study, I discovered the astonishing fact that a long list of names central to the Ripper affair can be anagramed from the 170 letters, and even the projected date of Mary Kelly's death can be discovered. In fact, around half of the 170 characters contained in the first Liverpool letter can be turned into names and a date inextricably linked to the Ripper affair. Here is the list, with the names set out exactly as they are used:

Charles Warren. Annie Chapman. Bertie. A bitch Kelly. Montague Druitt. James Stephen. 9th November. HRH crown.

It cannot be coincidence that such a long list of names were randomly included in only 170 characters. And the whole message has a spectacular significance. Let me repeat the first Liverpool letter in its entirety:

Liverpool. 29th Inst. Beware, I shall be at work on the 1st and 2nd inst, in Minories at 12 midnight, and I give the authorities a good chance, but there is never a policeman near when I am at work. Yours, Jack the Ripper.

The extraordinary anagram of this letter reads:

To Charles Warren: 1) A Annie Chapman did not hold Bertie's 2 souvenirs. 2) I work at it - I lie in wait; i.e. the 9th November, Montague Druitt and I gag a bitch. I rip open Kelly. I save HRH crown on a 12th stroke. James Stephen.

The letter and the above anagram both contain:

201

E 19, I 17, T/A 15, N 14, R 12, O 11, H 10, S 8, L/D 5, W/M/C/P
4, B/V/K/G/U 3, Y/J 1. Numbers; 1 , 1, 2, 2, 2, 9.

Each statement in the decoded message fits the facts contained in the main
narrative of my book. The anagram of the Liverpool letter, sent after
Annie's murder, boldly states that Bertie's goods were being sought; but
Mary Kelly had stolen several items, and not, as I had originally worked
out, just one memento. Even the date of Kelly's planned death was accurately given, showing careful advance preparations. Was this date significant? 9 November was Bertie's birthday. And also the threat to 'rip open'
the unfortunate prostitute was meticulously carried out - although not on
Kelly personally.

Unstated facts are also of interest. There is a clear intent to murder
Kelly herself and not a substitute. So we can now assume that, up to that
date, Queen Victoria had not interfered. And the murder of Eddowes and
Stride are not mentioned - the link is from Chapman to Kelly. This fits in
with my thesis that Eddowes's death came only after she had alarmed the
Establishment by openly advertising her supposed knowledge of the
Ripper's identity. As we have seen, the unfortunate Liz Stride was in the
wrong place at the wrong time. The anagram must have been worked out
some time in advance, as the letter, dated 29 September, was posted on the
day before the double murder took place.

The second Liverpool letter, after decoding, is even more startling.

*   *   *   *   *

Sir Richard Holmes was the librarian at Windsor Castle from 1870 - 1906.
The castle was frequently used by Queen Victoria as it is by our present
Queen.

Clearly Sir Richard, with such a long period of employment at
Windsor, was ideally placed to write a book about the Royal Family; his
biography of Bertie, *Edward VII - His Life and Times*, was published in
1910 in two large, extensively illustrated volumes. The subject's life is
covered in considerable detail, enlivened by many anecdotes. Amongst
these anecdotes is a record of the Prince of Wales's well-known love of
fires: indeed, so great was Bertie's love of a good conflagration that he, and
a number of his close friends, actually rented a flat in Watling Street, near
to the local fire station. In this flat, 'above a butcher's shop' Sir Richard
informs us, the Prince and his friends kept their uniforms at the ready for
any alert. This extraordinary revelation illustrates the unconventional life-

style which Bertie maintained - and relished. The report of Bertie helping out at the granaries blaze, as recorded by a fireman, is published in Chapter 9 of this book. Sir Richard relates that the friends who shared the Watling Street premises with the Prince included the Duke of Sutherland (a gambler), Sir George Chetwynd, Lord Richard Grosvenor, and several other unnamed rakes.

Watling Street was (and is) in the East End, on the fringes of the City, and also on the fringes of streets solicited by Mary Kelly and many other prostitutes. It is not difficult to imagine what must have gone on in Watling Street once the cabal of rich, powerful, rampant rakes had escaped from the restrictions of high society. Although there is no doubt that Bertie, the Duke of Sutherland, and probably the other men did indeed enjoy dashing off to large fires, this hobby would also, conveniently, have provided an excellent cover for wilder, more intimate activities. High society would, no doubt, have shrugged off the fact that mature men acted like boys. Men have always done so - fathers still enjoy their sons' train sets more than the youngsters do. The flat would have provided a perfect cover for a relentless pursuit of sexual adventure.

No dates are given for the tenancy of the Watling Street flat, but there is no reason why this should not have been a long-term arrangement, the flat being passed on to others as the need arose. One of the men may well have owned the property. A flat in an area where the Prince would be neither expected nor recognised, and away from the prying eyes of Palace officials, would have been an ideal playground for Bertie, who would have been in his forties during the Ripper affair. The prince was renowned for his low boredom threshold; he required constant stimulation and amusement, and the Watling Street establishment would have provided this in the form which Bertie liked best of all - sexual pleasure.

* * * * *

The second Liverpool letter has proved a particular puzzle for Ripper researchers. The letter reads: 'Prince William St., L'pool. What fools the police are. I even give them the name of the street where I am living. Yours Jack the Ripper.'

Various suggestions to this puzzle have been presented. It has been suggested that the Ripper, in his reference to an address, was referring to his earlier letter, which mentions the Minories, an East End thoroughfare. There was great excitement when it was discovered that Druitt's cousin, Lionel Druitt, had possibly once maintained a surgery in the Minories. Another, more obvious, solution to the puzzle was that the Ripper was indicating that he actually lived at an address in Prince William Street, Liverpool. All of the previous solutions are incorrect. When an anagram of the second Liverpool letter is unravelled there is a staggering revelation. As we have seen, the Ripper says, '...I even give the name of the street where I am living...' and this is true, but it does not say that the name of that street is only given in code. And, amazingly, that street is Watling Street - Bertie's secret address.

* * * * *

The second letter contains 104 characters - considerably less than the first communication. Even so, there are a great many possible words from so wide a selection of vowels and consonants. However, the anagramed message is so potent and factual that, even lacking the extraordinary list of names given in the other two uncoded messages, there can be little room for doubt that this second letter was also written by J.K. Stephen - in his most sardonic mood. The uncoded message reads:

> I kill. Can the police trap me? I live in a Watling Street harem with people who love to fight fire. Come here. Yours, James Stephen. V.R.

Both messages contain:

E 17, I 10, T 9, L/R/O/H 7, A 6, P 5, S/M/N 4, W/V/C 3, F/G 2, K/U/Y/J 1.

This is the clearest of messages, and, once again, one which further endorses my thesis. We know from Sir Richard Holmes that Bertie did indeed stay in Watling Street; it is a certainty that the place would indeed have been 'a harem'; and the occupants of the flat certainly loved to fight fire. A further link to royalty is the sardonic V.R. (Victoria Reigns.) As we have seen, it is my belief that in his final *Reflector* editorial, J.K. points the finger of guilt at Bertie, obliquely naming him as the man who caused the murders. It is he, therefore, who had to assume responsiblity for the violence, a man as guilty as the actual killer himself. No doubt J.K. Stephen, in his twisted mind, firmly believed this to be the case. Therefore, when the Liverpool letter says, 'I even give the name of the street where I am living', it is trying to direct attention to Bertie as the real Jack the Ripper. A twisted message from the real (and insane) killer.

Common sense dictates that two highly unusual names extracted from only 46 letters is highly unlikely; an expert in statistics has informed me, however, that if that first anagram crosslinks with a second document then the odds become astronomical. A third link-up and the matter would stand in a court of law.

* * * * *

From the above coded message a jigsaw of facts has built up. We must now try to put them into some kind of order. What was the *modus operandi* of the killers on the night of the double murder? It is quite clear that the two Liverpool letters are carefully constructed anagrams which form a coherent and lucid message. This might even solve the problem of one of the letters stating on 29 September (inst) that a murder will take place a month earlier. J.K. needed a precise number of characters, and this wording fitted in perfectly with his needs. The fact that the message did not make complete sense only added to the enigma. More problems for a terrified populace, who, in the final analysis, did not see the original letters anyway. The *Daily Telegraph* did not, to the best of my knowledge, publish the texts. The letters were at least lucid, and made reasonable sense, unlike the Goulston Street graffiti; here, double negatives are confusing, and the word 'Juwes' appears to have been newly invented. Such sloppiness might indicate haste, a haste incompatible with the cogent anagrams of the Liverpool letters.

Let us try to work out a reasonable explanation. J.K. Stephen, in an insane rage, has decided on the date and manner in which he will kill Mary Kelly - apparently weeks before his plan is to be put into action. Overcome by his serial killer's urge to publicly advertise his crimes, the insane J.K. devises an unusual thrill for himself. He sets his plans down on paper, carefully coded (what can happen? - he is protected by the highest powers in the state). Delighted by his own cleverness, he shows the results to Montague Druitt. Druitt is not insane - he has been drawn into the scheme mainly by a desire for financial gain, and he is appalled by his confederate's sick game - especially as his own name is mentioned. Disturbed, he relates Stephen's actions to Inspector Frederick George Abberline. Abberline, powerless to prevent further homicide is, nevertheless, appalled, and communicates his feelings to J.K., who, in a childish rage, does not take kindly to such criticism. He also regards Druitt's behaviour as traitorous, and determines to take revenge on both men. He posts his Liverpool letter (or letters, together or separately - we cannot know) to the *Daily Telegraph*, possibly timed to coincide with the forthcoming murder of Eddowes, the linking of mail and death creating an even greater sensation. J.K. then travels immediately to London, no doubt delighted that a full if hidden confession will soon appear on many of the nation's breakfast tables. However, Abberline reports what is happening to his superior, Sir Charles Warren. There is no reason to suppose that Sir Charles might not have known J. Hall Richardson; Richardson, in his memoirs, reveals that he knew many important people, including the highest in the land, such as William Ewart Gladstone, whom he visited at home. It would not have been difficult to have the *Daily Telegraph* letters intercepted, which would explain the non-appearance of such dramatic material in the newspapers. But now Warren must have been on his guard.

* * * * *

As we have seen, during the course of the night's events on 30 September, it was necessary for Liz Stride to be attacked and killed in Berner Street. This was the first murder committed by Druitt, who, up to this point, had been a passive accomplice. Now Stephen sees his chance for revenge. Maybe he decided on his master stroke - the graffiti - at some time during the ride away from the murder site in Berner Street: maybe he even borrowed the chalk from Druitt at this point - it would not have been unusual to find a Victorian schoolteacher with chalk in one of his pockets. Possible anagrams could have been forming in J.K.'s twisted, vengeful mind, the Liverpool letters still delighting him as he and Druitt neared Mitre Square. Maybe he deliberately cut part of Eddowes's apron away as part of a sickening plan. Now that Druitt was totally enmeshed in the killings Abberline would be informed of the fact - in the most dramatic way possible.

It has long been suspected that Jack the Ripper lived, or at least had a safe house, somewhere in the East End. It is my belief that that safe place was the flat at Watling Street. There is no reason why Bertie's powerful friends, or even the Prince himself, should not have known what was going on. They all had their own reasons for wanting to help J.K. Stephen.

After dumping Eddowes's body in Mitre Square, the horse and cart either had to be stabled in new quarters - Dutfield's Yard was swarming with policemen - or had to be abandoned. Then both men, either together or separately, could have walked the short distance to Watling Street, and total safety.

* * * * *

We know that Eddowes was murdered at approximately 1.45 a.m.. We also know that at 2.20 a.m., PC Long, during his beat through Goulston Street, did not see the torn apron or the graffiti. Neither did any people coming in or out of the block of flats. (The East End was busy all through the night. The murder sites were soon crowded, despite the lateness of the hour.) These items appeared at some time before 3.00 a.m.. It is highly unlikely that the Ripper would have remained wandering the East End streets after his terrible double crime for an hour or more. He therefore obviously returned to Goulston Street at some later point to deposit the torn rag and to write his chalked message. This fits in with my argument that J.K. returned to the safe haven in Watling Street, which highborn rakes, committed to the future of the Crown, allowed him to use. Here, J.K. quickly devised a clumsy anagram, not at all like the polished messages in the Liverpool letters. He was even forced to invent a word - 'Juwes'. After about an hour, armed with Eddowes's fragment of apron, which would firmly link his message to the murders, he returned the short distance to the spot in Goulston Street where he had intended to deposit the body. Here he wrote the famous graffiti. His insane revenge was complete.

In the middle of the night, Warren is informed about the murders but does not think them important enough to oblige him to visit the East End. Then he is informed about the discovery of the graffiti, linked to the murders by the torn rag. Immediately Warren hurries to Goulston Street where, after a short brook-no-opposition discussion he personally washes the message from the wall.

Nobody before has ever satisfactorily explained this whole curious, and famous episode. But my thesis fits the known facts perfectly. There is, however, one further puzzle. Why was J.K. Stephen not eliminated? It must have become obvious to the Establishment that J.K.'s mind was unbalanced, to say the least. His knowledge was deadly and his insane actions were clearly a threat.

Again, we can only speculate, but there could have been several reasons which would explain the Ripper's survival for four years after the murders ended.

1) Recruiting an assassin to eliminate Stephen might have involved further, unnecessary risk for those in the highest echelons of society.

2) It is possible, and even likely, that after the final killing, J.K. Stephen's murderous fury abated. After all, his objective had been achieved, and there is nothing to indicate that he killed for fun - he killed for a purpose. That purpose achieved, he may even have appeared to have regained his mental stability.

3) J.K. Stephen might well have ensured that there was a hidden record outlining the secret of his encoded letters. Did J. Hall Richardson perhaps agree to hold on to the Liverpool documents without realising their full importance? As I have said - it is certainly strange that such dramatic documents were not published at the time they were received. Then, 39 years later, with many of the main players in the drama dead, Richardson maybe felt that it was safe to forget any promises made, and use the letters as piquant material for his book. Interestingly, Sir Charles Warren died in the year that Richardson's memoirs were published.

Whatever the reason, we know that J.K. Stephen survived for another four years after the murders, whereas Montague Druitt survived for only a few weeks. He died in mysterious circumstances. Did J.K. maybe once more demonstrate his loyalty and usefulness to the Establishment by murdering his former colleague and friend - perhaps on orders? The fewer people who knew the true Ripper story the better. Or might Druitt have initiated a blackmail scheme of his own? Was the cheque found on Druitt's body payment for silence or a final payment for services rendered? £2,250 (in today's money) was certainly a puzzlingly large cheque for Montague to be carrying around with him. Maybe J.K., in the drama of yet another murder, forgot to retrieve that payment?

There are many mysteries regarding the Ripper murders which can never be fully answered. Especially when we consider the destruction of so much valuable material. The private papers of King Edward the Seventh were all burned, as were, amazingly, all the private papers of his wife, Queen Alexandra. What could she possibly have had to hide? Eddy's papers were all burned, and there are no known surviving letters between him and his long-time friend and tutor J.K. Stephen, which is odd, because letters from Eddy to some of his other friends are still in existence. The papers of Sir William Gull, whose private diaries are said to have named the Ripper, were all burned. The private papers of Dr Thomas Stowell, the man who said that he had read Gull's diaries, were all burned. What could all these people have had to hide? There has been no explanation as to why so many valuable private papers, which would normally be held for future generations, or, in the case of royalty, for historical research, have all been destroyed. What secret was being hidden? I feel certain that we now know.

Select Bibliography

ABRAHAMSEN, DR DAVID. *Murder and Madness - The Secret Life of Jack the Ripper* (Donald I. Fine Inc., 1992).

ANONYMOUS. *The Prince of Wales* (Grant Richards, 1898).

BALL, T. FREDERICK. *Queen Victoria* (S.W. Partridge and Co., 1886).

BEGG, PAUL. *Jack the Ripper: The Uncensored Facts* (Robson Books, 1988).

BEGG, PAUL and MARTIN FIDO and KEITH SKINNER. *The Jack the Ripper A to Z* (Headline, 1991).

BENSON, ARTHUR CHRISTOPHER. *The Leaves Of The Tree* (Smith, Elder and Co., 1911).

BENSON, E.F. *King Edward VII* (Longmans Green and Co., 1933).

BROWNING, OSCAR. *Memories Of Later Years* (T. Unwin Fisher Ltd.).

COWLES, VIRGINIA. *Edward VII and His Circle* (Hamish Hamilton, 1956).

CULLEN, TOM. *Autumn Of Terror* (Bodley Head, 1965).

FIDO, MARTIN. (Also see above) *The Crimes and Detection of Jack the Ripper* (Weidenfeld and Nicolson, 1987).

HARRIS, FRANK. *His Life And Adventures* (Various editions from a privately published book, 1920).

HARRISON, MICHAEL. *The Life of H.R.H. The Duke Of Clarence and Avondale* (W.H. Allen, 1972).

HOLMES, SIR RICHARD. *Edward VII: His Life And Times* (The Amalgamated Press Ltd., 1910).

HOW, F.D. *Six Great Schoolmasters* (Methuen and Co., 1904).

HOWELLS, MARTIN and KEITH SKINNER. (Also see above) *The Ripper Legacy* (Sidgwick and Jackson, 1987).

KNIGHT, STEPHEN. *Jack the Ripper, The Final Solution* (George G. Harrap and Co. Ltd., 1976).

LANG, THEO. *My Darling Daisy* (Michael Joseph, 1966).

LEE, SIR SYDNEY. *King Edward VII* (Macmillan and Co. Ltd., 1925).

LONDON, JACK. *The People of the Abyss* (Nelson and Sons Ltd., 1902).

MARTIN, SIR THEODORE. *Life Of The Prince Consort* (Smith, Elder and Co.,1882).

MATTERS, LEONARD. *The Mystery of Jack the Ripper* (W.H. Allen, 1948).

MAYHEW, HENRY. *London Labour and The London Poor* (Various editions, first published in 1851).

ODELL, ROBIN and COLIN WILSON. *Jack the Ripper* (Bantam Press, 1986).

PEARSON, JOHN. *Edward The Rake* (Weidenfeld and Nicolson, 1975).

RICHARDSON, J. HALL. *From The City To Fleet Street* (Stanley Paul and Co. Ltd., 1927).

RUMBELOW, DONALD. *The Complete Jack the Ripper* (Penguin Books, 1988).

SMITH, SIR HENRY. *From Constable to Commissioner* (Chatto and Windus, 1910).

STEPHEN, J.K. *Lapsus Calami* (Macmillan and Bowes, 1896).

STOW, JOHN. *The Survey of London* (1598).

TROWBRIDGE. *W.R.H. Queen Alexandra* (T. Fisher Unwin Ltd., 1921).

VICTORIA QUEEN. *Letters, 1837-1861* in three volumes, edited by A.C. Benson (John Murray, 1908).

VINCENT, JAMES. *His Royal Highness the Duke of Clarence and Avondale. A memoir* (John Murray, 1893).

YOUNG, G.M. *Victorian England* (Oxford University Press, 1936).

Index

Crook, Alice, 109
Cross, Charles, 14, 15
Cullen, Tom, 69, 70, 75, 79, 123
Culpeper, Nicolas, 4
Cutbush, Thomas, 127

Davies, (Mary Kelly's husband), 58
Davis, John, 23, 27
Dalton, John Neale, 96, 97, 100, 105
Deacon, Richard, 140
Dew, Walter, 175
Diemschutz, Louis, 43, 44, 46, 176
Diplock, Dr Thomas, 129
Donovan, Timothy, 21
D'Orleans, Princess Hélène, 113
Druitt, Lionel, 203
Druitt, Montague John, 122, 123, 136, 137-142, 148, 153-156, 158-162, 166, 171-176, 178, 180-184, 186, 193, 194, 197, 198, 201, 205, 206, 208
Druitt, William, (snr.), 122, 123
Druitt, William, (jun.), 127, 129, 130-132, 136

Eagle, Morris, 41, 45
Eddowes, Catharine, 44-52, 56, 71, 73, 133, 135, 151, 165-170, 172, 174, 176-179, 181, 185, 187-190, 192, 202, 205, 206
Edward I, 1, 75
Ellis, William, 87
Evans, John, 22, 161

Fairclough, Melvyn, 66
Fido, Martin, 31, 76
Fitzgerald, Annie, 44
Fleming, Joseph, 59
Forster, W.E., 106
Foster, Alfred, 187

Gardner, (Mr), 40
George, H.R.H. Prince, 96-99, 110
Gibbs, Frederick Weymouth, 87, 88
Gladstone, William Ewart, 114, 115, 117, 206

Goldstein, Leon, 41
Gordon, Lord George, 112
Green, Emma, 18
Grosvenor, Lord Richard, 112, 203
Gull, Sir William, 108, 109, 165-167, 208

Hammond, (Coroner's officer), 76
Hardman, (Mrs), 27
Harris, Frank, 111
Harris, Harry, 49
Harrison, Michael, 145
Harvey, William, 104
Harvey, James, 17
Heckethorn, C.W., 124
Helson, Joseph, 31
Holland, Ellen, 13, 14, 156
Holmes, Sir Richard, 202-204
Horace, 122
Horwood, 4
Houghton, Baron, 106
How, F.D., 122
Howells, Martin, 74, 131
Humphrey, Dr Laurence, 145
Hutchinson, George, 62, 63, 80-82, 135, 181, 182, 185

Jacobs, (Mr), 42
Johnstone, Sir Frederick, 93
Jack the Ripper, 2-4, 9-11, 13, 14, 18, 22, 23, 25, 26, 28, 29, 31-34, 36-38, 43-45, 47, 48, 50-52, 54-57, 59-61, 63, 65-67, 69-71, 74, 75, 78, 80-85, 87, 95, 108, 109, 114, 119, 122, 126-129, 131-136, 137, 145, 147, 152, 154, 156, 161, 163-167, 170-172, 176-179, 185, 186, 187, 191, 193-195, 197-204, 206-209

Kelly, Henry, 80
Kelly, John, 46-48, 52, 156, 168, 169, 177
Kelly, Mary, 34, 48, 58-64, 66, 67, 69, 70, 75-82, 109-112, 118-121, 134, 135, 137, 138, 140-142, 145, 147-153, 155-158, 160, 161, 163-171,

212